WORDS ABOUT PICTURES

WORDS

ABOUT

PICTURES

■ ■ ■ ■ ■

The Narrative Art of Children's Picture Books

PERRY NODELMAN

The University of Georgia Press   Athens and London

© 1988 by the University of Georgia Press
Athens, Georgia 30602
All rights reserved
Designed by Mary Mendell
Set in Plantin
The paper in this book meets the guidelines for
permanence and durability of the Committee on
Production Guidelines for Book Longevity of the
Council on Library Resources.
Printed in the United States of America

00 99 98 97 96   P   6 5 4 3 2

Library of Congress Cataloging in Publication Data
Nodelman, Perry.
Words about pictures.
Bibliography: p.
Includes index.
1. Picture-books for children. 2. Book design.
3. Illustrated books, Children's. 4. Children's
literature—History and criticism. 5. Narration
(Rhetoric) 6. Narrative art (Visual arts) 7. Illus-
tration of books. I. Title.
Z1033.P52N63   1988   002   87-38084
ISBN 0-8203-1036-0 (alk. paper)
ISBN 0-8203-1271-1 (pbk.: alk. paper)
British Library Cataloging in Publication Data available

■ ■ ■ ■

CONTENTS

■ ■ ■ ■

P R E F A C E

───────

Picture books—books intended for young children which communicate information or tell stories through a series of many pictures combined with relatively slight texts or no texts at all—are unlike any other form of verbal or visual art. Both the pictures and the texts in these books are different from and communicate differently from pictures and texts in other circumstances.

We tend to assume that the main purpose of the paintings we see in art galleries is to provide visual stimulation or to excite our aesthetic sensibilities. But while the pictures in picture books may do those things, it is not their main purpose; they exist primarily so that they can assist in the telling of stories. Asserting that critics of illustrations of literature have too often "based their judgements on the same technical and aesthetic grounds that would apply to a print hanging on a wall," Edward Hodnett insists that "the criticism of the illustration of literature . . . cannot be separated from literature or carried on logically in conjunction with non-literary forms of illustration" (1–2). Attempts to use picture books to teach art appreciation are misguided for just this reason: as depictions of single, incomplete actions, moments of disruption and chaos, the individual pictures in picture books rarely possess the harmonious balance we believe ought to exist and seek out in other forms of visual art. The pictures in picture books are even unlike the so-called "narrative paintings" popular in the nineteenth century; rather than invite viewers to make imaginative guesses about the story it implies, a picture in a picture book confirms and makes more specific a story that is already implied by the context of previous and subsequent pictures and also at least partially told in an accompanying text. The pictures in picture books are literally "illustrations"—images that explain or clarify words and each other. But unlike other illustrations in, for instance, informational books for adults, which support a detailed text with relatively few pictures, the pictures in picture books take up most of the space and bear the burden of conveying most of the information.

For that reason, the texts these pictures accompany are also unique—unlike all other narrative texts. In word books or alphabet books, the texts may be only one word or one sentence. In picture books that tell stories, the texts are characteristically succinct and undetailed. They are always dependent upon the accompanying pictures for their specific meaning and import; they often sound more like plot summaries than like the actual words of a story.

Because the words and the pictures in picture books both define and amplify each other, neither is as open-ended as either would be on its own. And while the same paradoxical amplification and limitation of different means of communication by each other also occur in filmed or staged narratives, picture books also differ significantly from these; instead of providing different modes of communication simultaneously, they alternate between their two modes, and we cannot both read the words and peruse the pictures at the same time. (Young children who look at the picture while they listen to the words being read to them do experience both at once; but unlike the voices which emanate directly from the actors on stage or screen, the voice speaking a picture-book text remains separate from the visual information, a distinct stream of a noticeably different sort of information.)

As a result of these unusual features, picture books have unique rhythms, unique conventions of shape and structure, a unique body of narrative techniques. The object of this book is to explore those techniques—to discuss some of the ways in which the pictures in picture books engage with the words in order to communicate information and to tell stories in a unique way. My study sometimes deals with informational books, such as alphabet books and word books; but it concentrates on picture books that tell stories.

In "A Picture Equals How Many Words?: Narrative Theory and Picture Books for Children," Stephen Roxburgh says, "Narrative is the most vital element in literature for children, not only in the novel, but also in the modern picture book. Yet critical theory dealing with the narrative function of illustrations, as distinct from narrative elements in the text, is sadly lacking. It needs to be expanded if we, as adult readers of literature for children, want to understand the semantic structure of picture books" (20). It is unfortunately true that most discussion of children's picture books has either ignored their visual elements altogether or else treated the pictures as objects of a traditional sort of art appreciation that focus on matters like balance and composition rather than on narrative elements. In recent years, however, a number of commentators have begun to pay attention to the "semantic structure" Roxburgh refers to. In *Ways of the Illustrator*, Joseph Schwarcz offers pioneering discussions of some of the most peculiar aspects of picture books, and articles by Jane Doonan, Sonia Landes, Stephen Roxburgh, and William Moebius have suggested interesting avenues for further exploration. My own approach has much in common with those taken by these commentators; all of us seem to have arrived independently, and more or less at the same time, at the conclusion that picture books have distinct characteristics, that they organize visual information in a way different from what we usually expect of visual art, and that we might best understand them by considering them in the light of some form of semiotic theory.

The reason for that is clear: since the major task of the visual images in picture books is to communicate information, they make most sense in terms of an approach that focuses on the conditions under which meanings are communicated. Semiotics, which has roots in linguistics, is such an approach; its prime interest is in the codes and contexts on which the communication of meaning depends. It suggests the possibility of a system underlying visual communication that is something like a grammar—something like the system of relationships and contexts that makes verbal communication possible.

Nevertheless, the pages that follow are not exclusively semiotic in their focus. I came to picture books, as do most adults interested in children's books, from a background in literature; I began to educate myself in subjects like perception and art theory when I realized how inadequately my literary expertise accounted for the peculiar narrative techniques I was encountering. While works on psychology and on art helped me immensely in my understanding of picture books, and while my debt to E. H. Gombrich, Rudolf Arnheim, Norman Bryson, and others will be obvious to anyone who knows their work, there was still much in picture books they did not account for. But, as I began to realize, much of that could be explained by adaptations of the literary theory I already knew—not just the work of semioticians like Roland Barthes but also that of reader-response theorists like Wolfgang Iser. In their strange blending of the techniques of two different forms of artistic communication, picture books demand consideration by means of a number of different theoretical approaches at the same time. So, while it is primarily semiotic in orientation, this book represents such a blending of approaches; it constitutes an exploration of the nature of picture-book art that is shamelessly dependent on the work of others and shamelessly eclectic in its use of that work.

Most discussion of children's books, including picture books, dwells on their educational uses; my own approach focuses on qualities of pictures and texts rather than on pedagogical issues. I believe that a single-minded concern with pedagogy denies children's literature its rightful place in the canon of literature worthy of serious analysis and investigation. This is serious art, and it deserves the respect we give to other forms of serious art.

More significantly, a single-minded concern with pedagogy deprives children and other readers of the benefits, pedagogical and otherwise, that must inevitably result from more intense looking and deeper understanding. The more we are capable of understanding and finding words to describe our responses to works of art, the more we are able to enjoy them. Too many children and adults have too few words to say about picture books—only relatively crude generalizations that cause them to miss much of pleasure and value. That is unfortunate. My main purpose, therefore, is to offer a number of words that can interestingly and usefully be said about picture books. While I do not possess the educational expertise to offer a practical pedagogical guide to visual education, I write in the profound hope that educators will find my words worthwhile enough that they will want to develop means of sharing them with children.

After a first chapter in which I discuss the extent to which the narrative information in pictures depends upon a viewer's acquaintance with learned assumptions and codes of signification, I attempt to offer something like a taxonomic classification—a catalog of the many different ways in which pictures communicate information about their subjects. In chapters 2 through 6 I consider exclusively visual information, moving from the meaningful effects of books considered as a whole and then of pictures considered as a whole into an exploration of the effects of specific details within pictures; in chapter 6 I also explore the meaningful relationships of a series of pictures. In chapters 7, 8, and 9 I deal with aspects of the relationships between pictures and texts. Finally, in chapter 10 I suggest some implications that emerge from the book as a whole.

Such an attempt at taxonomic classification has its failings. It is bound to be incomplete, for the means by which pictures communicate, the codes they evoke and the contexts they imply, may well be infinite in number. Furthermore, these codes and contexts work simultaneously to create the effect of the whole; they never occur in the splendid isolation from each other that my catalog might seem to ascribe to them. That my focus on distinct specifics always misrepresents the pictures and picture books I describe is nowhere more obvious than in the fact that I must often return to the same or similar qualities of certain pictures in vastly different parts of my taxonomic structure.

Nevertheless, I can think of no better way of presenting the information I am attempting to convey. It would be impossible to express the surprising complexity of any one picture book clearly by trying to describe at once all the different modes of communication that do in fact occur in it at once; only by considering the implications of smaller, more easily graspable components in isolation from each other do we have some chance of appreciating the richness of a complete book. I hope my study as a whole allows readers to see beyond the misrepresentation of any one of its sections.

It would also be impossible to reproduce all the hundreds of pictures I discuss in the pages that follow; for that reason, I refer to the same well-known and easily available picture books whenever I can. Anyone acquainted with the following books should have little trouble in making sense of a large number of my descriptions of pictures: Nancy Ekholm Burkert's *Snow White and the Seven Dwarfs;* Virginia Lee Burton's *The Little House;* Pat Hutchins's *Rosie's Walk;* Trina Schart Hyman's *Snow White;* Gerald McDermott's *Arrow to the Sun;* Evaline Ness's *Sam, Bangs, and Moonshine;* Beatrix Potter's *The Tale of Peter Rabbit;* Maurice Sendak's *Mr. Rabbit and the Lovely Present, Where the Wild Things Are,* and *Outside Over There;* Peter Spier's *Noah's Ark;* William Steig's *The Amazing Bone;* Dr. Seuss's *Horton Hatches the Egg;* and Chris Van Allsburg's *The Garden of Abdul Gasazi.*

A grant from the University of Winnipeg helped pay the cost of permission fees for some of the illustrations used in this book.

I would like to acknowledge my debt to David Topper, who taught me about theories of the perception of art; to Walter Swayze and Kay Unruh-Des Roches, who taught me most of what I know about literature; and to Joshua, Asa, and Alice Nodelman, who taught me about childhood. And I would like to thank Billie Nodelman for her graceful and patient willingness to listen to me talk about all I had learned from the others, for what must have been far too many hours—and for helping me to understand it.

University of Winnipeg, May 1988

WORDS ABOUT PICTURES

■ ■ ■ ■

CHAPTER ONE

Pictures, Picture Books, and the Implied Viewer

Most picture books tell stories. They are fiction. Logically speaking, anyone who wants to understand them better needs only to understand more about fiction. But from the viewpoint of literary theory, the most perplexing aspect of picture books is that they exist at all—that there should even be a kind of fiction that depends so heavily on pictorial information. Not only do most narrative theories ignore the ways in which illustrations often have a part in the telling of stories, they also tend to focus on how narratives involve readers by *not* providing the kinds of information that illustrations offer. Someone analyzing a text's dependency upon its reader's familiarity with the codes of literary communication or with its intertextual connections with other writings, or looking for the sort of "gap" that Wolfgang Iser isolates as the basis for a reader's involvement with a text, will find the task complicated by pictures that make explicit the information unspoken by the text. Our heritage of many centuries of great unillustrated literature makes it clear that stories can be told adequately by words on their own. Why, then, add pictures to them? Or why even create series of pictures that tell stories on their own, without accompanying words? Why are there such picture books at all?

Most parents and educators would answer that question by referring to the qualities not of picture books but of their intended audience: young children, whom we believe respond more readily to pictures than to words. Yet there is no irrefutable psychological or pedagogical reason that young children should be told the vast majority of their stores through combinations of words and pictures. Indeed, there is evidence that the presence of pictures in books may be pedagogically counterproductive; in a study of young children beginning to learn to read, the psychologist S. Jay Samuels confirmed his hypothesis "that when pictures and words are presented together, the pictures would function as distracting stimuli and interfere with the acquisition of reading responses" (337)—and presumably, therefore, of the story information that texts convey. Given the opportunity, as were most children prior to the last century and as some modern children in developing countries still are, many young children find it possible to enjoy listening to or reading books without illustrations.

But history has determined that they should rarely have the opportunity. Even the earliest books intended for children were illustrated, simply because they were informational: the book most often cited as the first children's picture book, Comenius's *Orbis Pictus* (circa 1657) is an illustrated catalog using pictures to define the meanings of the accompanying words. Later, when noninformational children's books came into existence, they were illustrated also—presumably because most books were illustrated: in the early nineteenth century, George Cruikshank illustrated both Grimm, intended primarily for children, and Dickens, intended primarily for adults. The first noteworthy children's storybooks that have a similar balance between words and pictures as do contemporary picture books were books illustrated by Walter Crane, Kate Greenaway, and above all Randolph Caldecott in the last third of the nineteenth century, and then by Beatrix Potter in the early years of this century; they seem to have become the foundation of a whole genre of storytelling simply because they were so immensely popular that other writers and artists were led to produce similar books. Indeed, history seems to suggest that the connection between children and pictures that we so take for granted was purely fortuitous, a random combination of circumstances that has nothing to do with the actual characteristics of children.

But while it may indeed have nothing to do with those characteristics, it is not purely fortuitous; as always, our assumptions about such characteristics are more significant than the actual facts. The early use of pictures for their informational value obviously relates to the longstanding conviction that books for children should have a primarily educational purpose; and the mere fact that those early picture books were so popular suggests that Caldecott and the others merely filled a void created by popular ideas. Attitudes toward children that tended to promote their special relationship with pictures were already in existence; for instance, there is a fairly obvious connection between the pure sensual pleasure offered by brightly colored pictures and the tolerance for and delight in the innocent joys of childhood that developed in Europe and America during the course of the nineteenth century. Such attitudes still control our dealings with children today and explain the continuing existence of picture books.

But they do not, in fact, justify it. For, whatever the reasons for their invention, and whatever rationalizations we can imagine for them, picture books need no justification but the fact that they are a successful and interesting way of telling stories—that they can and do give pleasure to viewers and readers, both children and adults. Nevertheless, the rationalizations usually provided for picture books are instructive. An exploration of some of them should help to unveil some of the special characteristics of picture books and some of the special difficulties they create for viewers and readers.

Because the intended audience for these books is young and inexperienced, most adults tend to assume that the reason for their peculiar features is purely educational. Most accounts of their educational value derive from two contradictory ideas about the purpose of illustration, both of which are implied by the definition of the word "illustration" offered by *The American Heritage Dictionary:* "Visual matter used to clarify or to decorate a text." Because pictures can provide information that completes the meaning of the words, their purpose is clarification—as it was in *Orbis Pictus.* Alternately, because pictures attract attention to themselves, their purpose is understood to be merely decorative; they can be a source of immediate sensual pleasure in and for themselves, as were the books by Caldecott and Potter; indeed, even in *Orbis Pictus,* the author's preface suggests that the book will serve "*to entice witty children*" because "it is apparent that Children (even from their Infancy almost) are delighted with Pictures, & willing to please their eys with these sights."

Pictures do offer that sort of pleasure, simply because they are concentrated versions of aspects of physical reality—color and texture and line—that tend to provide pleasure in and for themselves, even in the world outside of pictorial depiction. But their potential to please is based on an even more basic quality of pictures. In "The Visual Image," E. H. Gombrich suggests that "the visual image is supreme in its capacity for arousal" (82)—the excitement of awareness and interest; if a picture is present, in a book or on a wall, it is hard to disregard. It is for that reason that pictures are found in most advertising. In relation to books for the young, the fact that illustrations inevitably arouse interest causes them to be understood as a means of manipulating children into paying attention to books and consequently to the words in them. As Sutherland, Monson, and Arbuthnot say, "Certainly the prevalence of illustration in books for children in the past and in the present reflects an adult decision that pictures will attract and hold children's interest or will help them to learn about a subject" (124).

Alternatively, as that last clause suggests, we believe that pictures themselves can teach—offer clarification. In regard to books for the young, this translates into the idea behind *Orbis Pictus:* pictures are a visual aid, a means of transmitting information to inexperienced listeners and readers that could not be conveyed by words alone. "This is a banana"—a very young child who has not heard the word "banana" before can learn what one is by viewing an accompanying image, and a more experienced child learning to read can get help in decoding the letters of the word from the image. The ability of pictures to clarify a text directly accounts for all the numerous illustrated alphabet books, counting books, word books, and easy-to-read stories available for children and is frequently offered as a basic explanation for *all* children's picture books.

Each of these common explanations of the purpose of pictures in picture books expresses part of the truth—pictures do clarify texts, especially texts designed to require their clarification, and they are indeed inherently interesting enough to attract attention and thus have the potential to offer pleasure; good ones can offer as much pleasure as do well-chosen words. But both explanations raise the same significant problem—albeit in slightly different ways. The implication of the idea that illustrations are primarily pleasant decorations is that they put no stress on the mind—that there is nothing in them that requires thought. Paradoxically, however, the idea that pictures can clarify also implies that they put no particular stress on the mind; it assumes that they can operate in that way simply because they are more easily and more directly understood than words—that pictures can communicate automatically and be understood effortlessly by even very young children.

It is certainly true that pictures communicate more universally and more readily than do words. The sounds we use to speak to each other and the symbols we use to represent those sounds in writing rarely have any significant connection with the objects, ideas, or emotions they refer to: they are literally what semioticians identify as *signs*, in that, like the red traffic lights that tell us to stop, their meaning is nothing more than a matter of agreement among those who use them. The sound of the word "cat" could as easily refer to a number as to an animal; in French a similar sound does refer to a number. And there is certainly no visual equivalent between the appearance of a cat and the appearance of the letters "CAT." Because the connections between signs and their meanings are arbitrary, one must be privy to illogical and, for an outsider, unguessable secrets in order to understand any utterance or piece of writing, and as literary theory has confirmed again and again in recent decades, what is true of language in general is especially true of literature, which communicates through many intersecting systems of signs and consequently assumes numerous special competences and reading strategies in those who will best understand and enjoy it. Whether they are structuralists or deconstructionists, Marxists or feminists, contemporary theorists all focus on the unspoken codes and assumptions of literature; we have discovered that verbal narratives demand so much specialized expertise that many critics rightly postulate the existence of an implied reader—a figure implied by the text who possesses the expertise it assumes.

But there is some question about whether visual representations similarly project an implied viewer. The connections between visual images and what they represent seem to be much less arbitrary—at least in those images that we are willing to label "realistic." In an important way, such images do actually look like—resemble—the objects they depict, and the process of understanding them does seem to be more a matter of recognition of their similarity to objects in the actual world than familiarity with an arbitrary code. An outline drawing of a tree shares its outline with that of an actual tree, a perspective drawing or a photograph shares not just its outline but its shape, the appearance of its texture, and perhaps even its color.

Furthermore, we do not seem to have to learn how to understand at least some of the information conveyed by pictures as we do need to learn to interpret the verbal and visual signs of words; even very young children are able to interpret visual images without ever having been specifically taught to do so. In a landmark experiment, the psychologists Julian Hochberg and Virginia Brooks deprived a child of pictorial representations for the first nineteen months of his life; when they then showed him outline drawings of familiar objects, he recognized and named them all—including some drawn in perspective, which is often assumed to be an artificial system existing only in visual depiction and not in the real world at all. They concluded that there must be some native human ability for pictorial recognition. John M. Kennedy's survey of research in this area in *A Psychology of Picture Perception* supports and broadens that conclusion; studies show that not only humans but also monkeys, pigeons, and possibly even spiders can derive information from line drawings, and Kennedy states that "it is now, beyond any tinge of doubt, simply wrong to assert that the recognition of pictures requires instruction in a convention of representation" (56). Apparently, then, pictures *can* clarify texts because they can indeed communicate effortlessly.

Nevertheless, anthropologists have frequently reported the curious difficulties in recognizing apparently realistic visual images—line drawings and even photographs and films—that have been experienced by those previously untouched by the culture shared by Europeans and their North American descendants, and by now, by most of the rest of humanity. Despite the increasing rarity of people untouched by this culture, these difficulties are worth exploring, for they make it clear that there are indeed many aspects of pictorial representation, and consequently of pictorial recognition, that are merely conventional and that therefore must be learned. Knowing that pictures do indeed project an implied viewer with specific skills—that pictorial recognition is to some extent a learned competence—should affect our understanding not only of the relationship between pictures and words but also of the consequent relationship between picture books and their intended audience, young children new to the culture that adults take for granted.

In *The Gutenberg Galaxy*, Marshall McLuhan describes a film designed to teach sanitary procedures to some Africans unfamiliar with our own contemporary culture; shown the film, the group it was made for noticed not the behavior of the man at the center of the screen but a chicken which appeared briefly in the corner of a few frames and which had not even been noticed by the filmmakers. These people did not understand a basic technique demanded not just by films but by all the pictures that we tend to consider realistic; according to McLuhan, "literacy gives people the power to focus a little way in front of an image so that we take in the whole image or picture at a glance. Non-literate people have no such acquired habit, and do not look at objects in our way. Rather they scan objects and images as we do the printed page, segment by segment. Thus they have no detached point of view" (37). Anyone who has watched young, preliterate children with little experience of books scan pictures in just this way, and consequently focus their attention on what are meant to be insignificant details, will appreciate the extent to which pictorial perception depends on this very basic learned competence; in *Research into Illustration*, Evelyn Goldsmith reports that research reveals "the tendency of young children to become obsessed by details in a picture at the expense of the whole" (358).

Cognitive psychologists assert that perception occurs in the brain rather than in the eye: we cannot understand the information our perceptual organs provide until we interpret them in the light of previous experience. According to Ulric Neisser, "Not only reading, but also listening, feeling, and looking are skillful activities that occur over time. All of them depend upon pre-existing structures . . . called *schemata*, which direct perceptual activity and are modified as it occurs" (14). All of our conceptions of meaning relate to such structures, so that to "see" objects is to match the actually meaningless images of them that our eyes provide with the categories we have already established. We could not look at a tree and know it as a tree (or as anything meaningful) unless we had the category "trees" with which to compare and explain our sense impression. Furthermore, we could not have the category "trees" without having a word for it, even a private one that we speak only silently to ourselves. All perception, therefore, including the perception of pictures, might actually be an act of verbalization—a linguistic skill rather than an automatic act.

In saying that, of course, I speak with the prejudice of a person steeped in language; I have simply assumed that all meaning is that which can be put into words and thus can be thought and spoken. To all intents and purposes, meaning is just that—at least if Jacques Derrida is correct in his description of what he calls "writing": "not only the physical gestures of literal pictographic or ideographic inscription, but also the totality of what makes it possible; and also, beyond the signifying face, the signified face itself. And thus we say 'writing' for all that gives rise to an inscription in general, whether it is literal or not and even if what it distributes in space is alien to the order of the voice: cinematography, choreography, of course, but also pictorial, musical, sculptural 'writing'" (9). For Derrida, the signified face, the one evoked by the word or picture that signifies it, is itself part of 'writing'; the experiences we have that elude the grasp of language and even of thought—such as, for instance, the actual immediate sensation of something that we then turn into language and identify as a face—are separate from and beyond both thought and language. They are what language always purports to speak of but never actually captures—the world prior to and outside of our thinking about it. Since that world does exist outside of our systems of meaning, it is literally meaningless; and while that does not prevent us from being conscious of it, it does prevent us from "perceiving" it, that is, seeing it in a meaningful way; what we actually perceive is a product of human thought and language.

As part of the system of meaning, then, perception is dependent upon prior experience. The first time we see a banana, it is not yet a "banana"— and if we lack contexts that draw our attention to it, it may not even be anything remarkable enough to notice as a separate object. Furthermore, a citizen of a far northern country who has been isolated from contemporary civilization might mark out a banana as a separate object but could not, on first sight, make much sense of it or, consequently, of a picture of a banana.

Less obviously, perhaps, even those Eskimos who are familiar with bananas as exotic fruits from a foreign clime must inevitably think of them differently from those who live where bananas grow. All objects are most significantly meaningful in the context of the network of connotations we attach to them, many of which we may not even be conscious of—not just personal associations and experience but also cultural assumptions: what they are usually used for, how they are usually used, and perhaps above all, what ideas and values they represent. As semiotic studies reveal, such contexts and connotations are everywhere; objects always signify more than their literal selves. In a footnote in *Mythologies*, Roland Barthes asks, "In a single day, how many non-signifying fields do we cross? Very few, sometimes none. Here I am, before the sea; it is true that it bears no message. But on the beach, what material for semiology! Flags, slogans, signals, sign-boards, clothes, suntan even, which are so many messages to me" (112). What Barthes forgets here is the extent to which even the sea itself bears messages, for those equipped with appropriate contexts— knowledge of meteorology, a career as a sailor, a consciousness of *The Odyssey*.

If actual objects speak so richly of cultural connotations, then so must the objects depicted in pictures. Discussing the "*immanently* social character" of paintings, Norman Bryson insists that "*all* the codes of recognition flow through the image just as they do throughout the social milieu; as part of the global structure of signifying practice they interact *at every point* with the economic and political domains" (139). While it is different, then, art is in no sense separate from the rest of our experience.

Consequently, the meanings of visual representations of objects are rarely if ever limited just to their literal evocation of actual objects. In *The Responsibility of Forms*, in fact, Barthes suggests that even the most apparently representational forms of depiction transcend the literal: "Thanks to its code of connotation, the reading of a photograph is therefore always historical; it depends on the reader's 'knowledge,' just as if this were a matter of a real language, intelligible only if one has learned its signs. . . . each of us, as the product of a real society, always possesses a knowledge higher than mere anthropological knowledge and perceives more than the literal" (16–17, 31).

The evidence Deregowski reports in "Illusion and Culture" is proof of that: East Africans, shown a picture which Western observers understood as a young woman sitting in front of and below a window, imagined the woman sitting outside rather than inside and assumed that the "window" was a tin she carried on her head (165). For Westerners, the idea of carrying a tin on one's head is odd enough to prevent us from interpreting the picture that way—just as odd as sitting inside beneath a window might be for East Africans, who apparently prefer to sit outdoors. Speaking of experiments in the pictorial perception of people with different cultural backgrounds in *A Psychology of Picture Perception*, Kennedy explains how we may misinterpret even pictures we seem to understand: "The fact is that in all the studies most subjects identified most of the depicted objects. What the depicted men and animals seem to be doing is another story; when subjects have to say where the objects are in relation to each other, and what the objects are doing to one another, cultural differences boil up" (79). If outsiders have such difficulties, then children obviously must know enough of their culture to understand the ways in which pictures represent it.

But it is not just differences in cultural experience that affect understanding of pictures; the nature of pictures themselves also creates problems. All pictures require some interpretation, simply because no picture contains as much visual information as the objects it depicts might actually convey. Artists cannot depict everything they see, for only so many strokes can be fitted onto a canvas or a sheet of paper, only so many of all the details of reality can be represented; and it is only logical that artists make their choices about what to depict in terms of preexisting codes and conventions that establish relative degrees of value for various aspects of the perceptible world and that come to represent the language of art as they understand it. In *Art and Illusion*, E. H. Gombrich persuasively shows how artists can represent objects visually only in terms of their previous knowledge not only of objects in the real world but also of other visual images; they inevitably begin with a schema, a model or pattern derived from already existing visual images, and then, if their intent is visual accuracy, they adjust the schema to make it more like the specific object they wish to depict. "Everything points to the conclusion that the phrase the 'language of art' is more than a loose metaphor, that even to describe the visible world in images we need a developed system of schemata" (87).

Such systems require surprising sorts of prior knowledge from viewers before they can understand pictures. For instance, one study of members of a different culture reports that "details of musculature in the drawings of a human torso were seen as incisions made by the witch doctor. Lines intended to indicate wrinkles were also seen as cuts in the face" (Duncan, Gourlay, and Hudson 9). For those who know the convention, the depiction of muscular swelling by means of lines do not conflict with the different use of lines to define edges; but the fact that others can interpret those lines differently suggests how conventional they are. It is not insignificant that many "simple" pictures intended for inexperienced children use almost the same crescent-shaped line to represent both the swelling of the nose and the incision of the mouth; children must learn the convention in order to understand the pictures—or, perhaps, learn the convention from such pictures.

Furthermore, the systems of meaning implied by art are not limited to just the basic schemata of visual representation. Clifford Geertz suggests that the formal attributes of works of art "materialize a way of experiencing; bring a particular cast of mind out into the world of objects, where men can look at it" (1478). In *The Responsibility of Forms,* Barthes identifies that "cast of mind," what we usually call the "style" of a work of art, as "a second meaning" (5) and suggests that art forms like drawings and paintings offer not just an *analogon* or literal depiction of reality but also a comment about reality that is implied by the artist's treatment of it. "In short, all these imitative 'arts' comprise two messages: a *denoted* message, which is the *analogon* itself, and a *connoted* message, which is the way the society represents, to a certain extent, what it thinks of the *analogon*" (6). In other words, it is not just the objects depicted in art that bear cultural meanings; the ways in which they are depicted do so also. Those unfamiliar with certain styles of art frequently express the inability to understand what they depict; they lack the grammar to comprehend a language.

How much recognition depends on convention becomes particularly clear in a consideration of those images that seem to represent reality most accurately. In separating out the "analogon" from other sorts of meanings, Barthes suggests that there is a level at which photographs in particular communicate automatically—those who know what the visual image is an analogy of should be able to name it. Indeed, focusing on the subject of photography in *Camera Lucida,* Barthes insists that the photograph is "an image without a code—even if, obviously, certain codes do inflect our reading of it" (88). Yet those codes are surprisingly significant. William M. Ivins discusses how those who first looked at photographs saw them differently from the way we do: "at first the public had talked a great deal about what it called photographic distortion—which only meant that the camera had not been taught, as human beings had been, to disregard perspective in most of its seeing. . . . It was not long before men began to think photographically, and thus to see for themselves things that previously it had taken the photograph to reveal to their astonished and protesting eyes" (138). In other words, our faith in the accuracy of photography depends on our acceptance of its version of reality—not on how it reproduces the reality our eyes see but on how it tells our eyes what to see of that reality.

Not surprisingly, then, anthropologists have frequently reported showing photographs to people of different cultures who could not figure out what they represent; Segall, Campbell, and Herskovits once suggested that "in a limited sense one can regard the photograph as we use it as an arbitrary linguistic convention not shared by all peoples" (33). "As we use it" is the significant phrase here. That a photographic image of a banana is not in fact a banana—that an actual banana may not even be present when we show a photograph of one—does not prevent us from saying of it, "This is a banana," which might well confuse someone unfamiliar with photography. As Kennedy says in *A Psychology of Picture Perception*, "Photographs are clearly special objects. Would not anyone meeting a photograph for the first time be puzzled, not know quite what to say, but certainly deny that it was, physically, the represented object?" (67)

This is not to say that photographs do not in some important sense represent accurate records of the visible world—*analogons*—only that recognition of their accuracy depends greatly on acquired attitudes not only about photographs but also about what in visual experience is worthy of attention. In regard to photographic convention, a more recent study by Jahoda and others using color photographs instead of the black-and-white ones common in earlier reports implies the extent to which comprehension of photographs depends on knowledge of their peculiar features. Natives who had seen few photographs of any sort nevertheless scored as well as their urban counterparts in recognizing the objects in colored ones. The implication is that those who had trouble recognizing pictures in earlier studies were thrown off not by the pictures themselves but by the convention that colorless images do accurately represent the colored world—a convention that those who conducted the studies so took for granted that they did not bother to consider it.

Furthermore, there is a conventional rhetoric of photographic imagery, an unspoken set of conditions for communicating visual reality persuasively; not everything a camera can capture on film is acceptable or even recognizable, even to those who take photographs for granted. Clever photographers sometimes try to stimulate our visual imagination by defying these normative conditions—showing objects in extreme close-up or from unusual angles that make them surprisingly unrecognizable. And we have all seen photographs of ourselves that do not, we say, look like us; while such pictures are accurate records of what the camera was pointed at, they show us in uncharacteristic moments that do not match our previous conceptions of our appearance—our schemata for our own self-images. Even taxidermists, who work with the actual skins of animals, must carefully select "realistic" poses for their work, that is, conventional ones that will allow viewers to recognize the animal in question because they match a previously established image of it.

Convention determines not just recognition but meaning: a stuffed tiger might seem either ferocious or asleep, depending on the conventional pose the taxidermist works to evoke—but only those familiar with conventional gestures signifying ferocity or sleep will properly interpret the finished work. In fact, pictures can communicate little to those who do not understand the particular conventions of the context in which they have been placed, for, as Gombrich says of the visual image in his article of that name, "Unaided it altogether lacks the possibility of matching the statement function of language" (82). A person utterly unfamiliar with photography would be less likely to recognize the subject of a photograph if it were shown without some explanation of its purpose. Similarly, without being told, we could not guess from a conventionalized image of a human figure with two legs that it signaled a washroom for men: the picture does not in fact visually depict the intended activity, and just as significantly it is only on washroom signs that only men wear pants and that all women wear skirts. Even the most representationally accurate image of, for instance, a banana does not say, "This is a banana," unless we put it into a conventional context, such as a children's picture dictionary, that will allow it to say that—to those who have learned the convention, either by being told it or from previous experience of similar books. The same picture removed from the dictionary and placed elsewhere might serve a different function and, consequently, communicate something different from its species. In a child's scrapbook for a project on the tropics, it might represent the entire range of tropical fruit. If it were hung on a wall, we might assume that its main purpose is sensual pleasure rather than information, and if the word "Smith" appeared on a plaque under it, those who understand the conventions of such plaques would realize that Smith is probably the name of the artist, not of the banana.

Clearly, then, our understanding of any given picture depends on our understanding of the purposes of pictures. Reporting on a study in which Africans who had little contact with Europeans preferred a split-type drawing of an elephant (showing it from above as if it had been split open, so that all four feet could be seen clearly), while Europeans preferred a top view that more "realistically" did not show the feet, Deregowski postulates that the difference in preference comes from a different understanding of what pictures are for: "split-representation drawings develop in cultures where the products of art serve as labels or marks of identification. In the cultures where drawings are intended to convey *what an object actually looks like,* this style is muted and the 'perspective' style is adopted" (187–88).

That comment itself reveals a cultural bias; Deregowski himself believes he knows "what an object actually looks like." In fact, an object might "actually" or more significantly "look like" a split-figure representation in a culture where objects as perceived by touch, or, perhaps, as understood by supernatural beings, were more significant than sights perceivable at a distance. But the visual community to which Deregowski and I and, I assume, most readers of this book belong finds most "real" those visual depictions that suggest the density, texture, and coloring of objects as our eyes see them from some distance away, so that the objects appear to exist in a three-dimensional space on the other side of the picture plane. Such pictures have become the norm only in the last four hundred years and only in the European tradition that precedes contemporary North American culture. While we are self-involved enough to see their development as an evolution in visual sophistication, it seems far more likely that earlier Europeans and those in other cultures did not develop this sort of art simply because they felt other aspects of reality were more central, more significantly real, and therefore more worthy of depiction.

It would be as ingenuous to assume that ancient Egyptians actually saw each other only in profile as it would be to assume that modern cartoonists believe that people have crescent-shaped mouths and perfectly round eyes. But according to Norman Bryson, "the reality experienced by human beings is always historically produced: there is no transcendent and natural given Reality," and therefore no image is automatically understandable: "the image must be understood instead as the milieu of the articulation of the reality known to a given visual community" (13). Because cultural and social biases determine what we consider to be significant about what we see, our manner of depicting the world inevitably mirrors our basic conceptions of reality: those profiles reveal something important about the world as the Egyptians understood it, and cartoons reveal something equally important about the world as understood by cartoonists and their audiences. All of the difficulties people of other cultures have with pictures that successfully represent reality for Europeans and Americans finally boil down to this key fact: while physiology tells us that our eyes all show us the same world in the same way, our culture and our history force us to interpret the eye's images in different ways and thus to see different worlds.

The pictures most of us would be willing to label as realistic are no less dependent upon cultural assumptions than any other—and certainly no more "real." Such pictures—perspective drawings, detailed oil paintings, photographs—depict the world as human beings never see it, divorced from the interpretive distortions of the subjective human mind. Indeed, Bryson suggests that not only do such images imply a way of seeing different from our usual one but that we believe them to be most "real" exactly because that way of seeing *is* so unlike our usual ones: in viewing the actual world we tend to glance at it from a series of different angles, to build up a picture out of a process of different perceptions that make us conscious of the ever-shifting process of the world and of our own place within it, but "the gaze of the painter arrests the flux of phenomena, contemplates the visual field from a vantage-point outside the mobility of duration, in an eternal moment of disclosed presence" (94). For Bryson, this disappearing of the process that we actually experience implies some disdain for the actual conditions of seeing and being, and interestingly, commenting in *Art and Visual Perception* on the strange devices artists once used to capture perspective on paper, Arnheim suggests, "it marks a scientifically oriented preference for mechanical reproduction and geometrical constructs in place of creative imagery" (284). It seems that our "scientific" orientation downplays or denies both the significance and the reality of numerous important aspects of existence.

The distance between what our eyes actually see and what photographs or realistic paintings show us makes it clear how much our conceptions of visual realism depend upon learned cultural assumptions. In fact, our conviction that such images do automatically communicate merely affirms how very much we equate their message of objective distance with truth. All visual images, even the most apparently representational ones, do imply a viewer, do require a knowledge of learned competencies and cultural assumptions before they can be rightly understood. John Ruskin once suggested that "the whole technical power of painting depends on our recovery of what may be called the *innocence of the eye;* that is to say, of a sort of childish perception of these flat stains of colour, merely as such, without consciousness of what they signify" (2). Ruskin assumed that good artists could see like children and therefore could see what was *really* there, below the crust of blindness that maturity imposes on our eyes. But considering the obvious presence of learned visual schemata in all art, Gombrich rightly concludes that artists do *not* see like children: "the innocent eye is a myth" (*Art and Illusion* 298).

And if, in fact, the innocent eye is a myth, then there is some question about whether even children see "childishly" in the way that Ruskin intended. MacCann and Richard claim that "actually, the child's eyes, more than the adult's, see the whole of the artist's statement. Untutored, unaware of fashion or fad, the child's eyes take in all that the page offers"

(23). But "all that the page offers" is a tremendous amount, including much that we simply take for granted, but that must, in fact, be learned consciously or unconsciously by each individual human being who experiences pictures and books that contain them. In fact, the "innocent" eye, the one without knowledge of contextual significations, is merely a rather ignorant one: it sees much less than the experienced one and nowhere near all the page has to offer. Some children may indeed see pictures in this way, but it is hardly desirable that they do so.

Furthermore, if comprehending all pictures depends upon learned competences, then the specific pictures that we find in picture books do so even more intensely. Many other sorts of pictures disguise their dependence on contextual meaning—they do indeed seem to offer, and seem to have the purpose of offering, immediately understandable sensual pleasure; but it is inherent in the nature and purpose of picture books that the pictures in them be specifically oriented toward meaningful elements. Those picture books that have practical purposes, such as alphabet books and word books, require their viewers to focus on the names of the objects their pictures convey; picture books that tell stories force viewers to search the pictures for information that might add to or change the meanings of the accompanying texts.

Consequently, the reception of information about words is a basic source of our pleasure in picture books. In a discussion of his young daughter's early dealings with picture books, David Pritchard tells of her fascination with the process of giving names to pictures: "Suddenly, picture books were to possess the world, to greet its improbable creatures, and especially to shriek out its marvelous names: 'Baby! Sock! Lion!' What it was about these pictures that urged her to such spontaneous naming, at a time when we felt lucky to get as much as a mommy or daddy ourselves, I'm at a loss to explain" (66–67). The origin of picture books suggests an explanation.

In a discussion of *Orbis Pictus*, Svetlana Alpers explores why Comenius came to invent the book that was the forerunner of, and shares the basic characteristics of, the modern picture book. According to Alpers, Comenius believed that, while a perfect God created the things of the world, it was a fallible mankind that was given the responsibility of naming them. As flawed human products rather than perfect divine ones, then, names are anything but direct manifestations of the divine truth, as earlier theories had suggested; so language as a whole is a conventional system without any inherent significance in itself, and too great an involvement with it is dangerous, a distraction from the reality of God's creation. As an educator with such a theory of language, Comenius wished to encourage children to use language as a device to allow concentration on what *is* real—the world God created. In *The Great Didactic*, he says that "we ought to exclude from our schools all authors whose works merely teach words and do not at the same time lead to a knowledge of useful objects" (87). Instead, as Alpers says, "one must learn the names given to things and engage in acts of pointing or reference rather than acts of expression or statement" (95). *Orbis Pictus* represents a way of accomplishing that; the pictures are intended as pointers that direct attention toward actual objects and teach the connections between those objects and the conventional verbal representations of them. Such pictures are certainly less interesting in and for themselves than they are as signifiers of the meanings of words. Their only real function is to allow us to "possess the world" by having mastery of the names of the objects within it.

No wonder, then, that children like David Pritchard's daughter still feel delight at the opportunities for naming—and thus possessing—that are afforded by similar books. The pictures in them are primarily sources of information about the meanings of the words they accompany and thus imply a focus on meaning and naming that neither actual objects nor other pictures afford.

Not all pictures in picture books have so straightforward and immediate a relationship with language. Unlike the crude line drawings in *Orbis Pictus,* the pictures in contemporary picture books are often intricate in detail and sophisticated in style, even when they accompany simple texts, or even single words; and they more often accompany complex stories that focus on elements different from the ones on which the pictures themselves focus. But it is in the nature of picture books that they always seem to require us to focus our attention on the meaning of the pictures they contain and on the language that conveys meanings. As I hope to show, illustrators who understand their craft use all aspects of visual imagery to convey meaning; and the meaning-conscious mindset required to appreciate such pictures fully is always conscious of, and in search of, possible meanings. As did David Pritchard's daughter, most of us tend to look at these pictures with the urge to find information in them and to put the information into words; my own experience both with children and with adult students is that a major source of pleasure in picture books is the joy of discovering a meaningful aspect of visual information—a visual joke, a symbol, insight into characters and situations implied by the setting. In any case, the elements in these pictures that move beyond the direct representation of the text rarely offer just a purely sensual pleasure. Indeed, it is the fact that all of their elements always do seem to signify, and in a way that is important to our comprehension of the stories they are helping to tell, that defines the pictures in picture books as a specific kind of visual art.

Given their saturation with meaning, it is clear that understanding the subtleties inherent in the pictures in picture books takes great skill and much knowledge. But most picture books contain words as well as pictures, and the presence of specific words controls and defines the words we might ourselves provide for a picture; the relationship between them is not always a simple matter of providing a name, a label for an image. Simply because they are two different modes of expression, the relationships of words and pictures are complex and demand much skill of viewers and readers. They depend not just on our understanding of visual competences and codes of signification, not even just on those codes and the equally complex codes of language and of narrative uses of language, but also on intersecting relationships of both with each other. A text may amplify, distort, and even reverse the meanings of the pictures it accompanies.

All things considered, then, the picture book is a subtle and complex form of communication. It is unusual as narrative in its supplementation of verbal information with visual and as visual art in its focus on the meaningful aspects of visual imagery. It is unique in its use of different forms of expression that convey different sorts of information to form a whole different from the component parts—but without those parts ever actually blending into one, as seems to happen in other mixed-media forms such as film and theater, so that someone reading a picture book must always be conscious of the differences of the different sorts of information. Given that complexity, it seems clear that neither pictures nor the books they appear in can communicate directly and automatically. They imply a viewer with a mastery of many skills and much knowledge.

Yet for the most part they also imply a viewer who is innocent, unsophisticated—childlike. Picture books are clearly recognizable as children's books simply because they do speak to us of childlike qualities, of youthful simplicity and youthful exuberance; yet paradoxically, they do so in terms that imply a vast sophistication in regard to both visual and verbal codes. Indeed, it is part of the charm of many of the most interesting picture books that they so strangely combine the childlike and the sophisticated—that the viewer they imply is both very learned and very ingenuous.

Nowhere is that paradox clearer than in a consideration of those books that are intended for the least sophisticated of readers: babies and very young children. Such books contain brightly colored, boldly outlined images and decidedly limited verbal information; yet investigation of them reveals that they require of these youngest of readers a surprising number of skills, involving both verbal and visual implications. The paragraphs that follow explore the paradoxical nature of the viewer implied by these books by considering a representative group of them, all purchased in the same bookstore at the same time: two picture dictionaries, *Baby's Things,* printed on what appears to be thick paper impregnated with plastic, and *A First Book Open and Say,* printed on cardboard; *How Do We Help?* a cardboard book about animals; two books about infants, Dayal Kaur Khalsa's *Welcome, Twins* and John Burningham's *The Baby;* and Rosemary Wells's cardboard book *Max's First Word.* Of this group, all but *The Baby* are clearly intended for young babies, and the audience for *The Baby* is most likely to be only a little past infancy.

■ ■ ■ ■

An infant's first task on handling a book for the first time is to figure out its unique function. This particular object, unlike all the others that adults willingly place in babies' hands, is not a toy and not food. Its significance is not its shape or its taste or its texture but, rather, the variations in tone and color on its surfaces. It is not to be chewed or ripped apart; it is meant to be looked at. Most books for babies are printed on cloth or on thick cardboard in the understanding that their intended audience has not yet learned this basic skill.

Unlike mobiles or other toys that are meant to give visual pleasure, furthermore, a book is not intended to be viewed indiscriminately from any angle one chooses. It must be held in a certain direction—it has an up and a down. Many children take some time to learn the skill of orienting a book so that its images mirror the orientation of objects in the physical world, and before they have learned it, they happily view and interpret pictures in books that they are holding the "wrong" way; that there is a right way is merely a convention of viewing, for we can certainly interpret images accurately when they are upside-down, even though most adults do not feel comfortable about doing so.

The baby must also learn that the book has a front and a back. In English, of course, the front is the surface with the spine on its left when the book is held with its images oriented to mirror those of objects in physical reality; but Hebrew babies must learn a different convention. There is also an order, a correct sequence in which the various pages of the book are to be viewed: from front to back and turning only one page at a time—and more subtly, as I will show later, we assume that in books in English temporal movement in visual imagery is from left to right, so that the picture on the left side of a two-page spread is assumed to represent an event before that depicted in the picture on the right.

In many baby books this is not a significant skill, for these books do not often tell stories and consist merely of unconnected images of objects sometimes accompanied by labels, images that are meant to be interesting without any consideration of their sequence. Even so, many books of this sort do imply a sequence, for readers who have learned to expect one. In Dayal Kaur Khalsa's *Welcome, Twins,* for instance, what might be a disconnected series of pictures of typical events in the lives of twin babies actually seems to have a logical order: even though the variations in skin color in this explicitly nonprejudicial book—in some pictures brown, in some pink, in some even blue—suggest that each picture depicts a different set of twins, in succeeding pictures the twins eat, play, get dressed in warmer clothing, go out for a ride in a carriage, and get ready for bed. In other baby books the order is alphabetical, a sequence that can hardly interest infants and thus reveals the extent to which even these apparently simple books express and imply knowledge of conventions.

That some baby books require attention to the sequencing of pictures and some do not suggests that one must learn to discriminate between the two possibilities—yet another skill. Furthermore, some books confuse matters by oddly combining the two possibilities. In John Burningham's *The Baby,* each two-page spread seems to be, like those in *Welcome, Twins,* a depiction of a separate event. The text of the first spread, "There is a baby in the house," is followed on the next spread by "The baby makes a mess with its food," and a reader can easily assume that the book is merely a catalog of typical moments in the relationship between an older child and a new baby; even though the pronoun "it" in the text of the third spread, "We take it for rides in the pram," demands an antecedent, the first text has provided one, and the second and third texts might just as easily have been in the reverse order. A loose pattern of disconnected moments has been established. Later in the book, however, two successive texts say, "Sometimes I like the baby" and "Sometimes I don't"; the second of these would make no sense without a reader's prior knowledge of the first. Suddenly the sequence becomes more important than it first seemed to be, and in fact the two texts that follow bring what has now become a sort of story to a logical conclusion: *after* thinking about the baby, as has been depicted throughout the earlier part of the book, the child *then* says, "I hope the baby grows up soon." The comment seems to be a conclusion based on the events preceding it.

Even more dependent on knowledge of sequence is Rosemary Wells's *Max's First Word,* which uses sequential events to tell a simple story; in doing so it reveals the basic relationship between narrative and the ways in which we have learned to handle books. If we move as intended from front to back, we learn how Max's sister, Ruby, tries to make him say various words, without success. But when she encourages him to say "Yum," Max finally speaks: "Delicious! said Max." Appreciating this slight joke—as, I understand, many very young children do—depends not just on the ability to read the book in the right direction but also on knowledge of what a story is: the understanding that events in sequence may form a complete and developing plot, that is, relate to each other in such a way that later ones change and thus explain the significance of earlier ones. At the start we can understand but we do not know why it should matter to us that "Max's one word was BANG!" If we know the basic conventions of narrative, however, we quickly come to understand the significance of this fact as the reason for Ruby's attempt to make Max say other words, and then this first bit of information is amplified and thus made more meaningful by each repetition of the phrase "BANG, said Max." At the end the fact that the opening statement has finally become inaccurate is the significant change that makes this simple sequence of events into a satisfying whole— a story. But to appreciate it as a story requires not just the ability to turn the pages in the proper sequence but also the complex skill of both trying to interpret each event as one learns of it and being flexible enough to always be changing the interpretation in the light of later information until the story is actually over.

This is only one of the many skills of narrative strategy required to make sense of even the simplest of stories—skills young children must and often do soon learn merely from their experience of stories read by parents and heard on television. In doing so, however, they are performing a complex task, for if narrative theorists are correct in their assumptions, narrative is a unique form of communication requiring interpretive strategies different from those required by the rest of our experience. To begin with it requires an acceptance of the peculiar fact that "fiction" is an allowable lie—that one can with enjoyment pretend to believe in things that one knows never actually happened to people who one knows never actually existed. And even the very simplest of stories demands strategies of understanding not often required outside of narrative. We tend to assume that perception of irony is a sophisticated skill, but *Max's First Word* can be funny only to those who perceive the irony of Max's saying "Delicious" when his sister expected only "Yum." Indeed, *Max's First Word* satisfies M. M. Bakhtin's description of novelistic narrative as dialogic—an intersecting confrontation of different ways of speaking. It is literally about the contrast between Max's and Ruby's different languages, and given the presumed literary inexperience of the intended audience and the bland matter-of-fact voice of the narration, it might even be an example of what Wallace Martin calls "the most significant kinds of 'heteroglossia,'" or mixtures of differing languages—ones that "involve the potentially different discourses used by author and narrator, as compared to those of the characters presented and the audience to which the work is addressed" (52). For Bakhtin, the object of such narratives is to be antirepressive—to defamiliarize reality; the defamiliarizations of books like *Max's First Word* cannot be easy for those who yet have little familiarity with the actual world.

In much of *Max's First Word* each side of each two-page spread seems to represent a different event; consequently each spread depicts two events, which babies must learn to read from left to right in order to understand the story. The separation between two pictures that we see simultaneously and that are in fact physically contiguous to each other is a common convention of children's books, and infants must learn it even to appreciate the fact that in an exceedingly simple book like *Baby's Things*, which consists of unrelated photographs of common objects, the yarn shown on the left side of one spread had nothing to do with the chair on the right side; otherwise the differences in scale between the two objects might make the skein of yarn seem to be immense or the chair very small.

In other books each picture occupies a complete spread: we must *not* separate the two sides from each other. Once again, the possibility of such differences requires that young viewers learn to make discriminations and adjust for different circumstances in different books; and again, the task is complicated by subtle variations within books. Even though the two pages of the first spread of *Max's First Word* have different colored backgrounds—solid orange on the left, solid mauve on the right—the one on the left shows only Max, the one on the right only Ruby, and Ruby is turned toward Max and seems to be looking at him across the spine. In other words, this might accurately be read as one complete picture. But throughout the rest of the book, there are figures of both Max and Ruby on each side of each two-page spread. It takes some skill to readjust after the first spread and not assume that there are suddenly two Maxes and two Rubys in this story.

In terms of most of the skills mentioned so far, a baby has been coping with the special characteristics of books as physical objects whose various purposes demand knowledge of how they are meant to be handled. But in order to understand them, the baby must also learn much about how to interpret the pictures these physical objects contain. What R. L. Gregory says of photographs in *The Intelligent Eye* is true of all pictures: they are "flat objects seen as flat, and at the same time as quite different three-dimensional objects in a different space" (51). We must learn to look at the two-dimensional object and expect to "see" three-dimensional objects in a different space; and there are important differences between them. The objects in pictures have only one surface. They are very small, usually smaller than the real objects they represent. They tend to lack the gradations and subtleties of the color and texture of objects in reality, so that a whole lawn of grass may be the same shade of green and all of a shirt the same shade of yellow. Furthermore, the objects depicted in most baby books exist in a world without shadows; in *A First Book Open and Say*, in fact, the insides of a pair of green shoes are white, not the black we might expect. Unlike real objects, furthermore, those in these pictures often have thick black lines around them. They are often not complete: legs of high chairs or tops of heads do not actually exist, for they are cut off by the edges of the picture. Or alternatively, the objects in many baby books are completely surrounded by empty backgrounds and seem to float in space. In either case, the environments these objects are found in come to an end a short distance away from them in all directions, to be replaced by a frame of white void or merely the edge of the page. And perhaps above all, they never move. Paradoxically such images are easily recognizable, even to very young children—but only to those who understand and unconsciously bring into play the conventions of pictures, for as Gombrich says in *Art and Illusion,* "The likeness which art creates exists in our imagination only" (191).

The pictures in some baby books are realistic photographs, in others cartoons, in others stylized depictions of stereotyped houses and stick figures. Each of these is indeed "like" reality in that each successfully conveys a different quality of actual objects: photographs successfully express details of surface and texture, and cartoons a sense of objects in motion, while stereotypes operate somewhat like dictionary definitions of objects— they express the essence of the type of object represented rather than the specific nature of any given one such subject. But in order to appreciate these likenesses we must have learned to distinguish which aspects of reality each of these modes of representation best evokes. We must not expect stereotypes or photographs to convey motion, cartoons to convey ideas.

According to Patricia Cianciolo, "the younger the child, the more representational the art style should be" (*Illustrations in Children's Books* 30); but according to Muriel Beadle, "Until children are well into the school years their attention is caught by objects or scenes that are strong and simple—big bold strokes, bright clear colors, sharp contrasts, and similar overstatements. They need more clues to what they're seeing, hearing, tasting, or touching than adults do" (Sutherland, Monson, and Arbuthnot 98). Two similar books for babies represent the styles recommended in these two contradictory comments: while both *Baby's Things* and *A First Book Open and Say* are collections of labeled pictures of objects, the first contains representational photographs and the second, strong and simple stereotypes. The question is, can either of these two vastly different modes of representation more automatically or more easily convey reality to beginners, as Cianciolo and Beadle suggest?

Because most "primitive" art shows typical views of objects rather than representational ones, it seems logical to assume that the recognition of such stereotypes is a more primitive skill than the recognition of photographs. But such images are not in fact simpler: they merely represent a different attitude toward visual reality. Stereotypical images like those in *A First Book Open and Say* are less representations of the appearance of surfaces than they are unrelated collections of intellectually defined attributes. Thus, we look at the complex coloring of an actual object such as a puppy, label it as brown, and convey the idea of brownness by depicting one solid mass of color; and we look at the puppy's eye, categorize its shape as round and convey the idea of roundness by drawing it as a perfect circle. Consequently, interpreting typical drawings like the one of a puppy in *A First Book Open and Say* is actually an act of *verbal* dexterity: developing a list of attributes and slotting in the appropriate specific information that the image provides.

The distance of this operation from the information the eye actually presents is made clear by the fact that in *A First Book Open and Say,* the depicted objects float on solidly colored backgrounds, so that there are no size cues and no sense of relative proportion; one spread depicts both a toy top and a house as about the same size, and the lack of visual cues makes it hard to determine whether it is meant to be a toy house or a real one. Furthermore, while none of the pictures depicts shadows and most are head-on views with no sense of depth, those of the top and of shoes imply a different angle of vision that suggests the depth of perspective drawing—but only suggests it, so that one must not only understand the basic assumption of representational art about the significance of one's angle of vision in perception in order to interpret these pictures but also understand that perception can appear as merely another intellectualized attribute—just another item on the list of attributes that make up the picture.

Also, obviously, one must know when to look for it and when to ignore it. Because we never actually do see objects so totally head-on that their sides completely disappear, as do those of the house in *A First Book Open and Say*, such images would be nearly incomprehensible if interpreted as perspective drawings. But the pictures in baby books often simultaneously depict aspects of different modes of representation, presumably because illustrators so take their repertoire of techniques for granted that they are not conscious of the potential for confusion. For instance, the cartoons in John Burningham's *The Baby* sometimes depict the characters against representational backgrounds and sometimes show them floating against white space in the manner of stereotypes; in some pictures objects in the background are colored, in others only their outlines are depicted. More subtly, in *Welcome, Twins* depth cues such as foreshadowing and overlapping of objects contradict the heavy outlining and shadeless coloring of stereotypes, and it takes some skill to decipher all the differing simplified shapes—circles, triangles, rectangles—that represent human hands and feet as seen from differing points of view.

Since stereotypes require so much intellectual activity, we might assume that the photographs in *Baby's Things* would be easier for a baby to understand. They might be, given the baby's acquaintance with the basic cultural assumption that photographs do show something of significance about the visually perceivable world—for they are traces of objects that did once actually exist. But the pictures in *Baby's Things* also subtly confuse differing representational modes by depicting photographically accurate objects against solidly colored backgrounds, one per page, so that they evoke the characteristics of stereotypes. But despite their empty backgrounds that seem to be meant only to disappear, these pictures do show shadows, which have the disconcerting effect of turning the backgrounds into something like actual surfaces, thus making these pictures seem most peculiar: under what circumstances would three eggs appear alone against a totally yellow background? There are also constant demands for adjustment from picture to picture, for the shadow of an apple is to its left, that of a brush and comb on the other side of the same two-page spread to the right.

Furthermore, understanding pictures like these requires the skill of determining the angle of vision they imply; the pictures in *Baby's Things* all imply different angles, and some of them are surprisingly odd ones, chosen, presumably, so that the pictures can serve the purpose of typical representations. We see a brush from above so that its bristles seem very short, but some daisies are viewed from below, and a chair is seen as a standing, full-grown adult might see it. Not only do the differences require constant adjustments, but the odd angles demand interpretation; for instance, an apple is seen from above, but its stem is at the top of image, which makes sense only if the apple is, strangely, lying on its side—why does it not roll away? And the three eggs seen from a similar angle might easily be floating in space—despite shadows, the picture offers no sense of their distance from the yellow background.

Babies with any access to books at all are likely to encounter pictures both like those in *Baby's Things* and like those in *A First Book Open and Say;* and they will certainly also experience cartoon images like those in *Max's First Word.* Obviously, many quickly learn the skills required to understand and distinguish between these three modes of representation and perhaps even others that are sometimes found in books intended for very young children, including impressionism and even abstraction.

But even after babies can make some general sense of these pictures, they still have more to learn. Illustrators make use of a whole repertoire of strategies and techniques to convey both images and ideas; viewers of cartoons must learn that black lines can represent light, as in the rays of the sun, or fuzzy areas such as smoke; viewers of all pictures must learn the conventional meanings of various layouts or shapes or colors or even styles—that we tend to assume that cartoons will express a humorous response to the situation or that the same objects may be depicted in different sizes in different pictures or that certain patterns of lines or shapes are meant to focus a viewer's attention on specific objects. In terms of the latter, for instance, infants must learn to look for specific, significant objects rather than do what seems to be more natural for prelinguistic beings and give equal attention to the entire picture plane; otherwise, in *The Baby* they will be more interested in the plant in the background of the picture accompanying "There is a baby in our house" than they will be in the baby in the foreground.

Theoretically, of course, hearing an adult speak those words might cause a child to search out the named object, a baby, in the picture; but knowing that we should use the information offered by words to understand what matters about the pictures that accompany them is also a learned skill. Indeed, since the words in a picture book are themselves visual symbols, a child who cannot read must learn that these specific marks on the surface of a page are to be distinguished from all the other marks: that the marks "EGGS" are not part of the visual representation of eggs and that they are to be disregarded in visually interpreting it.

Beyond that most basic of skills, the relationships between words and pictures are varied enough to require a variety of strategies of interpretation. There are important differences between a picture simply labeled "Baby" and one accompanied by the words "There is a baby in our house"; the first merely offers a label, and one must understand that the specific baby depicted is not significant: it merely represents all the varying objects that might be labeled "baby"—indeed, making that not necessarily logical and quite sophisticated move toward generalization and coming to understand that the images in picture books frequently represent categories rather than particularities is the most basic skill required for the appreciation of baby books. Quite differently, on the other hand, "There is a baby in our house" requires us to pay attention to the distinct individuality of this particular baby and its specific circumstances.

Furthermore, the words "There is a baby in our house" imply a specific narrator—somebody who lives with the baby. But it takes some skill to figure out exactly who it is. First, one must understand the peculiar convention of picture books that the same character can both appear in a picture as seen by an objective outsider and speak from the viewpoint of subjectivity—that instead of seeing the scene as from the speaker's eyes, we see the speaker in the picture. In *The Baby*, it turns out to be the child depicted in the accompanying picture who is speaking the words of the text. But to complicate matters further, we could not possibly understand that until we reach the fourth two-page spread. The previous pictures show either the baby alone or accompanied by both the child and the older woman, and not until the text of the fourth spread does the grammar make it clear that it is not the woman who is talking: "Sometimes I help Mummy bath the baby."

We might, perhaps, assume that young readers would have already identified the speaker as the child because children are "egocentric" and "identify" with characters like themselves; but if that is the case (and I suspect, in fact, that such identification is also a learned skill), they would then have problems with books like *Max's First Word,* in which the narrator is not Max at all, but an objective outsider who can tell us, "Max's one word was BANG!" The fact that children do not have such problems suggests how quickly they learn to distinguish between various kinds of narrators. As usual, furthermore, the texts of these books mix various conventions in potentially confusing ways that require both knowledge of conventions and strategies of interpretation. The title of a book called *How Do We Help?* implies that the narrators will be the characters. An egocentric child might be surprised to discover that the "we" it refers to are not children but realistic-looking farm animals, but the texts accompanying the pictures switch tactics and seem to be narrated by a detached observer: "The Goat gives us milk to make cheese" and "The Hen lays eggs." The task of interpretation is further complicated by the fact that the pictures do not show the hen laying eggs or the goat giving milk—and the picture for "The Pig gives us meat and ham" does not show a slaughterhouse but merely a pig in a meadow.

Nor is this just a matter of ineptitude or reticence on the part of an illustrator: many pictures in admirable picture books evoke situations different from those that their words imply. For instance, the picture in Burningham's *The Baby* that accompanies the words "I hope the baby grows up soon" merely shows the baby lying on the floor in front of a fireplace. It depicts neither the speaker nor any evidence of growth or the lack of it, so that its function has little or nothing to do with clarification of the text. And in *Max's First Word*, the pictures actually tell a story entirely different from that told by the text on its own: the text is mostly dialogue, and it is the pictures that show us who Max and Ruby are, where the words are being spoken, and what the occasion and result of those words are. One must learn to relate the two different sets of information to each other in order to develop an accurate sense of the entire situation.

Beyond all these assumptions and strategies concerning the specific qualities of books, pictures, and pictures in relation to words, babies confronted by these books face an even more basic difficulty: they must be acquainted with the objects words describe and pictures show before they can accurately interpret the words and the pictures. And in order to have that acquaintance with objects in reality, they must have learned the most basic skill of perception: the ability to define separate, distinct objects in the visual field—to distinguish figure from ground. As I suggested before, that ability is to some extent a linguistic one and is certainly a process that involves thought: having a name or even, prior to speech, a category in which to place an object is the factor that allows us to distinguish it from what then becomes its ground and thus to identify it as a separate figure. An infant with no prior experience of apples either in life or in pictures, and consequently no category in which to place and name the red shape on the page that depicts an apple in *Baby's Things*, might not consider that shape to be significantly separate from its red-and-white background.

Yet even the simplest of baby books depict objects that might well be unfamiliar to infants: *Baby's Things* includes daisies, eggs, and yarn, and *A First Book Open and Say* depicts decidedly old-fashioned toys like a top, a toy soldier dressed in a busby, and a train engine. To some extent, the oddity of these toys may be accounted for by the fact that the publisher of this book is British; and of course even books for infants inevitably assume and take for granted their culture, so that an American child hearing the words "We take it for rides in the pram" from *The Baby* would need an explanation not just for "pram" but also for "it" as a pronoun for a young human.

But even the baby books of one's own culture are likely to cause such difficulties—for, in fact, objects like tops and toy trains appear again and again in children's books despite their absence from the lives of most contemporary children. The Transformers and Cabbage Patch dolls that children actually own rarely appear in books other than commercial tie-ins, perhaps because of problems of copyright.

In fact, the world as typically depicted in books for young children is quite unlike the world as young children experience it. These baby books tend to depict bright, colorful objects in full light, objects that are clean and undamaged; the shoes in both *Baby's Things* and *A First Book Open and Say* are unscuffed, the apples and flowers and toys undamaged and perfect. Even in *Max's First Word*, the shadowless cartoons depict no food stains on Max's high chair, no confusion of toys on the floor; and the colors are all vibrant—colors we associate with happiness. The sanitized atmosphere these images convey represents an idealized vision of the pure innocence and joy of childhood, a vision that is inevitably at odds with the realities of the lives of most infants, who do get food on their high chairs and make messes with toys. Although these books purport only to provide labels for objects, they also work to convey the message that order and brightness and cleanliness are desirable qualities—that they are *attractive* and therefore especially worthy of our visual attention—and I suspect that a parent's expectation that a child will find this specific sort of image enjoyable acts as a form of moral education. In other words, the conventional implications of these images act to teach a child an image of childlikeness that most children would not otherwise know.

Similarly, comparatively few contemporary children have actually seen a living farm animal, except perhaps in zoos, but *How Do We Help?* echoes book after book in depicting such animals in rural environments and assuming that children are familiar with them. A child who cannot recognize such objects from experience in reality must learn them from images—from the experience of pictures. And because images so uncommon in reality are so common in picture books and indeed in all children's literature, learning them is a significant part of a child's early visual education.

Words like "cow" or "duck" are often among the first ones spoken by young children; that they can recognize and name such images long before they know the names of significant objects in their actual environment speaks of how successfully they can learn the conventions of picture books. So does the presence in book after book of a sort of creature who not only does not appear in the children's environment but does not actually exist anywhere at all outside of books. The characters in *Max's First Word* are cartoon creatures who look unlike anything in the real world, although they vaguely resemble rabbits. But even then, they are rabbits who wear human clothes and use human furniture and who apparently can speak like humans. It is a cliché that such pictures are so common in books for young children because children "like" animals; it is certainly possible that children learn an interest in such humanized animals from their frequent appearances in books. Later I discuss the significance of the animals in picture books in greater detail.

■ ■ ■ ■

This catalog of the codes, conventions, assumptions, and interpretative strategies implied by baby books is hardly exhaustive. Considering the extent to which we take these matters for granted once we have learned them, I know I am bound to have missed some obvious ones; and furthermore, the more subtle narrative aspects of picture books that I discuss in the following chapters all come into play in one or another of these books for very young children. While the world they depict seems childlike and the information they import seems brutally obvious, these books do indeed imply a surprisingly sophisticated reader and viewer.

They do not necessarily do so because the children in their intended audience are sophisticated; obviously we assume just the opposite. I suspect that the peculiarities of these books are accounted for less by the actual abilities of the intended audience than by their producers' acquaintance with already existing baby's books and their thoughtless acceptance of the conventions such books have developed and operate by. In merely accepting and duplicating modes of depiction and communication that have become conventional, these writers and illustrators take far too much for granted. There is a real need for baby books that understand the dependence of all books on learned assumptions and strategies and work to develop this knowledge in their audience in a thoughtful and organized way.

Despite the obvious inadequacy of many of these books, however, children do learn from them—and not just the simple information about what objects the words "apple" or "house" refer to that the books explicitly try to teach but, more subtly, all the skills required to interpret a picture and its relationship to an accompanying text before one can even begin to understand about the apple or the house and also all the cultural values that the pictures and words imply. Much of this visual learning occurs without obvious teaching. David Pritchard tells of the ease with which his daughter came to associate images with objects: "The bewilderment I'd been expecting to see, the slow dawning as image and object fused in her mind, was nowhere visible. . . . This apparently unquestioning acceptance of representation in all its guises—from photographs in magazines to the wildest exaggerations or most stylized simplifications in picture books— was to be a continual source of amazement to me in the months to come" (66). That such amazing learning does indeed take place has important implications.

For one thing, it means that children have learned much that they are not conscious of learning. Words, pictures, and picture books are merely parts of a vast and complex system of significance that defines our reality for us, and as Clifford Geertz says, "it is out of participation in the general system of symbolic forms we call culture that participation in the particular we call art, which is in fact but a sector of it, is possible" (1488). Recognizing the "reality" and the import of a specific kind of visual image and knowing how to understand its relationship to the words in a picture book is primarily a matter of immersion in our own specific culture; the mere experience of living in an environment where there are pictures and books automatically provides most children with that immersion.

Nevertheless, the immersion is itself an act of learning—and a highly complex one, even though its very nature means that we tend to take it for granted. My own experience in discussing books with many different young children is that they are often amazed and delighted to discover what they know already—that they did in fact know how to see a three-dimensional object in the markings on a two-dimensional plane, or that they knew a book would be funny before they heard the words because the pictures were cartoons. One purpose of this study is to bring such invisible knowledge to the surface so that we may better appreciate the amazing learning capacities of children—and so that we can allow children themselves to appreciate it also.

If they have learned so much already, furthermore, it seems likely that even very young children can learn much more and can develop strategies that would allow them to enjoy all the subtle and varied means of communication through combinations of pictures and words that I discuss throughout this book. My own experience with children confirms that many of them can learn to develop a rich and subtle consciousness of the special characteristics of picture-book narrative—and can immensely enjoy doing so.

But such knowledge cannot be learned if it is not taught. In "Learning from Illustrations," Evelyn Goldsmith refers to psychological research which supports the conclusion "that what is often called 'visual literacy' cannot be taken for granted, even in twelve-year-olds" (111); yet, commenting on the vast amount of information that comes to us visually, John Warren Stewig rightly asks in *Children and Literature*, "where, in the curriculum do children learn to 'read' such visual input—to examine it carefully part by part, extracting meaning and interacting with what is extracted? Such processes are central to the reading program, but few children learn to read pictures effectively" (79).

They do not do so, I suspect, partially because we assume that the reading of pictures requires no training but primarily because of pedagogical attitudes that focus more on what children already know than on what we might teach them. Guides for teachers about using books with children most frequently suggest that those books should be chosen on the basis of a child's previous familiarity with their subject and style. For example, three different commentators suggest that young children could not appreciate Charles Keeping's *Through the Window,* a picture book in which a young boy views a dog being run over by a brewery wagon. In *Children and Literature,* John Warren Stewig says, "The complexity of the dark, heavily patterned illustrations indicate the book is best for older children" (116). In *Introduction to Children's Literature,* Glazer and Williams say that the illustrations in Keeping's book are "too sophisticated for most children below the fourth or fifth grade" (58). And in *Illustrations in Children's Books,* Patricia Cianciolo suggests that, while "the reader of primary school age would very likely recognize the tragedy that occurs when runaway horses kill Old Soap's dog in *Through the Window* . . . he would probably be a few years older before he would recognize the symbolism" (14).

In fact, *no one* of any age could understand the symbolism of *Through the Window* without first learning not just that there is such a thing as visual symbolism and how to look for it but also what any specific visual symbol means; and there is no reason why even young children cannot learn those things. To deprive children of the pleasures of books like *Through the Window* because we are unwilling to provide the information they need to appreciate such books suggests a surprisingly limited idea of pedagogical possibilities; for as Kenneth Marantz rightly says in defense of the vast and often untapped capabilities of children, "To deny youngsters Hyman's *Snow White* or Baskin's *Hosie's Alphabet* is to cut off for some children two potentially profound art experiences. Would Disney's cardboard heroine be more suitable for 'young' eyes?" (155).

Many adults do believe that figures like Walt Disney's cardboard heroine *are* more suitable. Years of familiarity have persuaded them to identify such colorful and relatively simple images with the tastes and interests of children. I suspect, therefore, that it is not actually the symbolism or the complexity of books like *Through the Window* or Hyman's *Snow White* that make them seem unsuitable for young children but rather that they look unlike the vast majority of picture books: their pictures are not in a style that we have conventionally come to identify as childlike.

Yet, in his *History of Book Illustration,* David Bland makes it clear that "suitable" pictures—the kind of simple, colorful pictures we usually offer young children—have appeared in children's books on this continent only in the last fifty or so years; this style, brought to North America by Russian expatriates like Boris Artzybasheff and Feodor Rojankovsky, was an invention of Russian and Polish artists in the early years of this century (398). If this style is inherently childlike, we have to wonder at the delight of children in previous centuries at different kinds of art, and as Bland says, "if these lithographic books do not seem original to us that is only because we have been imitating them so closely ever since they were introduced to us" (424).

Interestingly, a study by John Warren Stewig seems to suggest that more *older* children from *more* educated backgrounds preferred flatter pictures with less detail than did younger children from less educated backgrounds ("Assessing Visual Elements"); on the other hand a recent British study, in which children were shown pictures in a variety of styles, revealed a clear preference for traditional realism (see Glazer and Williams 91). Although apparently contradictory, both studies can be interpreted as revealing the extent to which children are capable of learning from experience: the children in Stewig's study seem to have responded to the "childlike" art of the conventional books provided in most elementary classrooms by coming to prefer it, while the older children in the British study may have been influenced by a different set of assumptions and, having moved on to the more "realistic" books we tend to offer older children, may have learned to accept socially conventional ideas about realism. Indeed, Ciaràn Benson suggests that educational practices, especially the teaching of reading, create this preference by using pictures only for their ability to represent the objects signified by accompanying words; this creates a "narrative expectancy" (128), an exclusive focus on the descriptive aspects of pictures that might well lead to a preference for traditional realistic styles.

In any case, the children in both studies seem to have been victims of self-fulfilling prophecies about their tastes and abilities; they might have learned to understand and appreciate more had the adults with responsibility for their education believed them capable of it and worked to achieve it. This "more" is the subject of the following chapters.

■ ■ ■ ■

CHAPTER TWO

——

Format, Design, Predominating Visual Features: The Meaningful
Implications of Overall Qualities of Books and Pictures

Most often, the texts of picture books exist before the pictures. Editors
commonly commission illustrations and consider the design of a book only
after having accepted a text. Consequently, it is impossible to talk sensibly
about the meaning of the pictures and the implications of book design in
isolation from the words that evoked their creation in the first place. Although I focus specifically on aspects of book design and of illustration in
the pages that follow, I inevitably interpret those qualities in the light of
narrative information I have learned from their accompanying texts.

Nevertheless, it is essential that the meaningful aspects of books and
pictures be considered, to begin with, without specific reference to texts,
simply because these varying sources of information convey quite different
kinds of meanings—all of which have narrative import. Texts do not so
much provide illustrations with their narrative content as they inform us
about how to interpret that narrative content—and vice versa. What Roland Barthes says of captioned press photographs is also true of picture
books:

> The totality of information is . . . supported by two different struc-
> tures (of which one is linguistic); these two structures are concurrent,
> but since their units are heterogenous, they cannot mingle; here (in
> the text) the message's substance is constituted by words; there (in
> the photograph) by lines, surfaces, shadings. Further, the two struc-

tures of the message occupy separate if contiguous spaces which are not "homogenized." . . . Therefore, though a press photograph is never without written commentary, analysis must first of all deal with each separate structure; it is only once we have exhausted the study of each structure that we will be able to understand the ways in which they complement each other. (*Responsibility of Forms* 4)

What follows in this and the next four chapters is a study of the meaningful implications of picture-book design and picture-book illustrations considered without specific reference to the complementary nature of their texts. It becomes possible to explore the unique nature of that complementarity only after considering the narrative content of the books as objects and the pictures by themselves.

■ ■ ■ ■

As we all know, the same words said differently can convey different meanings. Said sadly, the sentence "The boy fell down the stairs" demands our concern; said with a giggle, it might evoke laughter. We call this quality of language "tone," as in tone of voice; it changes the meaning of an utterance and the attitude we take toward it even though no part of what is said is changed.

While there is no word equivalent to "tone" that applies to visual images, they can certainly create similar effects. A cartoon of a boy falling down stairs demands a different response from a broodingly dark representational depiction of the same subject, yet we probably could not identify any particular area or object in the picture as the source of our different attitude toward it. The nontextual elements that create mood or atmosphere in picture books are not really separable parts or components. They are not objects within an individual picture but, rather, predominating qualities of a book as a whole—matters like the size or shape of pictures (or even of the book the pictures are found in), the artist's choice of medium and style, the density of texture, and the qualities of colors. Aspects of books and pictures such as these focus our expectations even before we explore the pictures closely enough to notice the relationships between their details; they imply an overall mood or atmosphere that controls our understanding of the scenes depicted.

That they can do so explains one of the most basic characteristics of picture books. The texts in them tend to be so simple as to be without tone—like the sentence "The boy fell down the stairs." The virtually toneless texts of books like Pat Hutchins's *Rosie's Walk* and Maurice Sendak's *Where the Wild Things Are* relate events with almost no mention of the emotional reactions of those who participate in them, beyond the occasional "he was happy" or "he was sad," and even then with no attempt to evoke what it might feel like to be happy or sad. Characteristically, then, picture-book texts merely assert; we learn only that Rosie went for a walk or that Max made mischief. The emotional quality of what is asserted must be conveyed by the pictures, which then inform those who look at them about the tone of voice in which to read the words—the attitude to take toward them.

As with most of the other information pictures communicate, they imply attitudes only through systems of signification that work to create specific expectations in viewers; and like other aspects of pictorial significance, these systems depend upon a viewer's prior acquaintance with a variety of forms of experience. Our expectations of a book with glossy, four-color pictures differ from those we have of a fat leather-bound volume with small print and no pictures at all only because of our previous knowledge of a number of different kinds of books. Meanwhile, however, more obvious and basic aspects of experienced reality may lead us to associate bright colors like red and yellow and orange with warmth and sunlight and thus to expect a book in which those colors predominate to be a cheerful one. Furthermore, some of the codes that control attitudes, such as our conventional association of smaller books with younger children, seem to be arbitrary; while others, such as the focus on the significance of setting that occurs in wider books, seem to emerge logically from practical considerations. In all these cases, however, our expectations define our attitudes to the stories books contain; and picture-book artists can therefore use conventional expectations to give the tone and imply the attitude they desire to the words they illustrate. In this chapter I discuss the ways in which varying formats of books and varying uses of predominating color, line, and shape influence our attitude toward the events a book describes. Because the relationships between individual visual styles and conventional codes of signification are both particularly problematic and particularly relevant in the communication of narrative information, the implications of style are the subject of a more detailed discussion in the next chapter.

Before I begin to discuss the signifying qualities of various aspects of books and pictures, I must point out that I have drawn most of my examples from a group of highly respected and, I believe, highly successful picture books. The illustrators and designers of these books clearly have a firm grasp of the significance of all aspects of format and illustration, and my discussions of them may seem to imply that all aspects of all pictures always convey appropriate meanings. As the existence of many poorly conceived books asserts, that is clearly not the case. Anyone who wishes to find examples of picture books that send confused messages through an apparent lack of consciousness of the signifying implications of some of their own attributes does not have to look very far. Interestingly, one need not even seek out specific examples of misused signifiers—one need only choose a book which seems inferior in terms of overall style and subject, and it is bound to contain example after example of uncontrolled details.

Meanwhile, the admirable books I focus on here seem complete even before investigation of their details—and remarkably, the various systems of signification they evoke all seem to support and amplify the same central effect. Because they do, the meaningful aspects of these books often seem invisible—they disappear from view in the very act of creating the effect that prevents us from easily noticing them; and it is for that reason that they need the sort of attention I am about to pay them.

As my earlier discussion of books for babies suggested, our understanding of the story a book contains depends first of all on our understanding of what a book is for; and that depends on our earlier experience of books. For those who have not enjoyed their previous encounters with books, any new one will seem a dreadful object, and their reading of the story it contains will be colored by that dread. The actual physical appearance of individual books is just as obvious an example of how prior expectations control our responses to stories: it influences our attitude to the stories the books contain before we even begin to read them. We expect more distinctive literature from hardcover books with textured, one-color covers and more conventionally popular material from books with luridly colored plastic coatings. We tend to think differently about paper-covered books and ones with hard covers, and as a result we respond differently to the same story in different formats; what might seem forbidding and respectable in hardcover often seems disposable and unthreatening in soft.

The size of a book also influences our response to it. We tend to expect rambunctious, energetic stories like the ones by Dr. Seuss from large books and more fragile, delicate stories like those by Beatrix Potter from smaller ones. In fact, larger books do allow larger effects, while smaller ones demand restraint from an illustrator, lest they appear overly fussy; but these differences are as much a matter of convention as of technical limitations. We tend to read smaller books expecting charm and delicacy—and to find it even if it is not there—and to read large books expecting energetic rambunctiousness—and to find it even if it is not there. For instance, commentators tend to find Mercer Mayer's very small books about a boy, a dog, and a frog charmingly delicate and to celebrate the vitality of Mayer's larger books; yet Mayer's style is consistent (and consistently heavyhanded) throughout his work, despite these variations in format.

We associate both very small and very large books with the youngest of readers. Presumably, the very small ones can be held by very small hands, while the very large pictures in the very large ones can be interpreted by inexperienced eyes. Consequently, the very largest and very smallest of picture books tend to be the simplest in content and in style, and we approach their stories with expectations of simplicity—childlikeness—as soon as we see them. Books of middle size—for instance, Trina Schart Hyman's *Snow White*—are often subtler and more complex, and we unconsciously accept this greater degree of subtlety simply because it suits our expectations for books of this size. Meanwhile, larger books, like Nancy Eckholm Burkert's *Snow White,* or smaller ones, like the series of wordless books by John Goodall, that look painterly and are filled with subtle details, often strike adults as overly sophisticated for young readers. Again, the difference is less in the books themselves than in our general expectations.

Nevertheless, our attitudes toward different sizes of books do have some ground in actual technical limitations; the deficiencies of pictures intended for a smaller format that have been reprinted in a larger one make that distressingly clear. Unlike much of Maurice Sendak's work, the pictures in the four books in his Nutshell Library are simple cartoons, and for good reason; subtleties of line would not be noticeable in such a small space and might well create a crowded effect. As rereleased separately in a larger format and enlarged, however, these same drawings seem overstated, the lines too thick, the areas of unshaded color uncharacteristically large and harsh. Although depicted through the exact same pictures and words, the actions of the boy Pierre, who doesn't care, seem delightfully irrepressible in the smaller format but insufferably self-indulgent in the larger one. Similarly, one of Richard Scarry's characteristic animals, isolated from a pageful of similar animals in a large book and enlarged to fill a page by itself in a smaller book like *Early Words,* comes to seem peculiarly unenergetic. The rabbits in *Early Words* pose stiffly, and their faces never do anything but smile; yet the same figures, smaller and surrounded by many other similar figures involved in many different activities, convey an impression of intense activity. They can do so not just because the variety of different poses creates interesting tensions in the group as a whole that are not present in any one of its components but also because these smaller images do not arouse our expectation that faces seen close up will convey emotional information; we look at the same image differently when it is a different size and rightly find ourselves having a different response to it.

The shape of a book influences our response to the story it contains as much as its size—but not, except in the case of oddities like books in the shape of their subjects, because of any conventional attitudes we might have to certain shapes: after all, most books are similarly rectangular. But different sorts of rectangles do impose different restrictions on artists and, consequently, accommodate different sorts of pictures that do in fact require different sorts of responses.

While most picture books are wider than they are high, most people are higher than they are wide, and so are most of the animal heroes of picture books. The extra width of wider books allows illustrators to fill in the extra space around the people they draw with information about the places they occupy—their setting; and if we operate, as illustrators almost always do, on the assumption that such external appearances reveal internal characteristics, we learn much of character in such pictures through the details of background. Thus, we come to understand much about the fastidious bachelorhood of Burkert's dwarfs and the more mysterious strangeness of Hyman's dwarfs through these illustrators' differing depictions of the dwarfs' homes and possessions, as seen in relatively wide pictures behind the characters: Burkert's dwarfs live in a bright, tidy house in which the furniture is servicably plain, Hyman's in a dark womblike one in which all the furniture is carved with mysterious icons. Books like these tend to focus on relationships between characters and their environment; they ask us to take an attitude of detachment, to stand back objectively and interpret characters in terms of details of their settings—and we will do so exactly to the extent that our experience of books has provided us with the expectation to do so.

But in narrower books, or in those books in which illustrators have chosen to place pictures only on one side of the two-page spread, there is less opportunity for depicting setting and, as a result, greater concentration on and closer empathy with the characters depicted. Not all illustrators take that opportunity; although Chris Van Allsburg's pictures for *The Garden of Abdul Gasazi* take up only one side of each spread, they are still wider than they are high, and wide enough to emphasize the smallness of the hero, Alan, in relation to his settings. But Beatrix Potter frequently lets her characters fill the narrower pictures of her small books, especially at moments when they are experiencing strong emotion; and many picture books illustrated with cartoons are narrow also and focus on action and facial expression rather than on environment. For instance, Dr. Seuss's *Horton Hatches the Egg* is a relatively narrow book, and the pictures frequently occupy only one side of a spread; they rarely show much of the settings, and we learn about the elephant Horton through the cartoonist's techniques of gestural exaggeration rather than through Horton's relationships to the world around him.

Interestingly, Horton's dispute here is with himself, internal: should he sit on Mayzie's egg or not? Frog and Toad of Arnold Lobel's series of cartoonlike books are also usually involved in internal emotional conflicts rather than physical ones or even disputes with each other, and they too appear in narrow pictures that emphasize gesture and expression rather than wide ones that emphasize setting and physical relationships with others. To be sure, Max's equally intense internal conflict in Sendak's *Where the Wild Things Are* occurs, at least in part, in wider pictures in which complex settings are the main focus of our attention; but these wider pictures cleverly express Max's feelings in terms of his relationship with his environment, which functions as a concrete expression of his mental state. Significantly, the title of this book refers to a place, as do the titles of Sendak's other books that focus on setting and express internal conflict in terms of imaginary but nevertheless external places: *In the Night Kitchen* and *Outside Over There.*

The choice of paper stocks is another physical aspect of books that influences our attitude toward the events depicted in the pictures printed on them. Glossy paper gives colors a glistening clarity, but it is distancing, partially because the light shines equally through all the colors and creates an overall sheen that attracts attention to the surface of a picture and therefore makes it more difficult for us to focus on specific objects depicted. This shiny surface acts somewhat as Arnheim suggests varnish did in evening out the colors of traditional oil paintings: "A color composition based on nothing but such a common denominator could describe only a world of absolute peace, devoid of action, static in mood. It would represent that state of deadly serenity at which, to borrow the physicist's language, entropy approaches an absolute maximum" (*Art and Visual Perception* 348). It is interesting how often picture books on shiny stock do imply a sort of serenity, or at least stillness; but in books like Sendak's *Outside Over There* and Hyman's *Snow White* it is not by any means a deadly serenity, for the complex tensions, contrasting colors, and imbalances of the pictures form a paradoxical relationship with the serene evenness of the surface. In fact, these books evoke a believably magical atmosphere by exactly this sort of paradoxical tension—a tension that is pushed to its two extremes in Van Allsburg's *Wreck of the Zephyr*, in which the startling impossibility of a boat sailing through the sky is counterpointed not only by the evenness of the shiny surface but by the serenely unstartling effect of a highly limited palette of colors that creates an effect something like that of varnish. Meanwhile, more decorative books with less (and less unsettling) pictorial narrative information, such as McDermott's *Arrow to the Sun*, use glossy stock merely to enliven already highly vibrant colors; there is little stillness here because the contrasts of the bright colors disturb the evenness of the surface.

More roughly textured paper seems to invite our touch and in that way supports an atmosphere of involvement and intimacy, even sometimes of claustrophobia; that is certainly the effect of Van Allsburg's books in black and white on roughly textured paper—*Jumanji* and *The Garden of Abdul Gasazi*—as opposed to the more open and less unsettling world Van Allsburg creates in colored pictures on glossy stock, as in *Wreck of the Zephyr* and *The Polar Express*. Also, rougher stock can be more easily worked into various levels of light and darkness, so that illustrators who wish to focus on specific objects in their pictures can do so more easily on more roughly textured paper; the exaggerated perspective and resultant sense of separation and isolation of objects in Van Allsburg's black-and-white books is again a good example.

Clearly, then, we have begun to establish our attitudes toward stories even before we have actually looked at the pictures or read any of the words in the books that contain them. When we do begin to look more closely at the pictures, we do so in the light of the information we have already accumulated—not just from our assumptions about books in general but also from our basic understanding of what pictures themselves are. We take it for granted that, unlike wallpaper or the sky, a picture is particularly worth looking at—that it is likely to contain something of special interest or particular meaning to us simply because an artist has chosen to offer us this specific visual information and must have had some good reason for doing so. We also take it for granted that we are free to look at the objects in pictures, indeed, that the mere existence of the picture means that we have been invited to do so and that we can do so guiltlessly. Furthermore, any picture that has been offered to our attention, especially one found in the context of a picture book, implies that the image it depicts is significantly meaningful, worthy of our consideration. Illustrated stories could not exist if we did not take it for granted that differences in place and time influence both the characters of people and the meaning of events; that surface appearances therefore help to make people and events what they are by creating differences that matter; that such differences are noteworthy enough to be recorded; that they are noteworthy not just because surface appearances themselves create feelings and attitudes but because they *mirror* interior feelings and attitudes; and therefore that the way things look is highly evocative of what they mean. In their very existence, then, picture books express our assumption of the metaphorical relationships between appearance and meaning.

Because they do, we can and do tell books by their covers; we use the visual information we find there as the foundation for our response to the rest of a book. Illustrators often try to create appropriate expectations by pictures on covers or dust jackets that appear nowhere else in a book and that sum up the essential nature of the story. The precise impersonality of Burkert's version of *Snow White* is summed up in the tidily framed, meticulously precise, and highly impersonal portrait of the heroine on the cover. The anarchic ebullience of Spier's *Noah's Ark* is conveyed by the appearance together on the cover of all the creatures depicted in different pictures later in the book. The decorative lethargy of Errol Le Cain's *Twelve Danc-*

ing Princesses is expressed by a cover that turns the princesses into a symmetrical border for the words of the title. The cover of *Where the Wild Things Are* suggests how much the book expresses the internal by means of the external in showing not Max himself but his boat and a sleeping Wild Thing—the objects Max imagines. That this cover should thus give away the imaginative surprise that the plot of this book builds toward suggests how little Sendak is interested in suspense and how much he wants to establish a dreamlike atmosphere. All these covers help establish the mood that the rest of each book conveys.

On other covers we see William Steig's Pearl enjoying the forest, blissfully unaware of the sneaky fox about to accost her in a picture that sums up the focus of *The Amazing Bone* on the dangers of trusting appearances; we see Alan chasing his dog through a group of scary topiary figures of animals in an otherwise unseen part of Gasazi's garden that sums up the focus of *The Garden of Abdul Gasazi* on tensions between the real and the magical; we see Burton's Little House inside a symbolic circle that sums up the focus of *The Little House* on cyclical patterns and on wholeness. Unlike these books, many picture books have covers which merely contain duplicates of pictures also found inside; but those pictures still often seem to have been chosen to convey the essence of the story inside and thus to set up appropriate expectations for it.

After the cover, we might begin to notice more specific qualities of pictures as a whole. To begin with, a frame around a picture makes it seem tidier, less energetic. Cartoons in picture books usually focus on physical action and rarely have frames, unless they are in a strip format that requires different pictures on the same page to be separated from each other. Furthermore, looking at events through strictly defined boundaries implies detachment and objectivity, for the world we see through a frame is separate from our own world, marked off for us to look at. It is interesting that many picture books depict objects that act as frames on their title pages, like doorways inviting viewers into another, different world. There is the gate of Gasazi's garden. Hyman gives us the title of her *Sleeping Beauty* inside an arch, and Burkert, the title of her *Snow White* inside the actual frame of a mirror.

Books which take an objective, unemotional view of the events they describe often have frames around all their pictures—sometimes, even, around the words of their texts. In Errol Le Cain's *Twelve Dancing Princesses*, the sumptuous frames around the words of the text balance the two-page spreads by giving some visual weight to otherwise white pages; as a result, the two sides of each spread, one mostly white space and the other richly illustrated, seem more equal to each other. That symmetry not only creates a sense of tidy order, it also increases the decorative atmosphere of the book as a whole. The focus here is less on what is happening or whom it is happening to than on how pretty it all looks, how sumptuously ornamental; we are to indulge our senses rather than care for the characters. Not surprisingly, both the pictures and the borders around the text have heavy black frame lines around them and are surrounded by narrow borders of white space. In *The Garden of Abdul Gasazi*, another book in which each two-page spread consists of one mostly white page of text and one page of illustration, there are also borders around the words of the text, and these also create balance. But the white space that frames the pictures in this book has a different effect, simply because the pictures themselves are different. They depict intense activity that seems mysteriously inactive; the tidiness of the frames adds to their paradoxical nature and emphasizes the mystery. Not surprisingly, books that focus more centrally on action and emotion rarely have frames of white space; for instance, Trina Schart Hyman's melodramatic pictures for *Snow White* extend to the edge of the page.

As Hyman's work suggests, however, a frame around a picture has a different effect from that of a frame within a picture. While she rarely frames her pictures, she often uses framing devices within the pictures—the open windows that Snow White's mother stands out against, the trees that frame Snow White, the various arches of trees and windows and such that appear on every page of *Sleeping Beauty*. Rather than add objectivity or detachment, these heighten the dramatic focus; they force us to pay attention to specific parts of the pictures.

Framing is usually consistent throughout a picture book: the pictures have frames or they do not have frames. In *Where the Wild Things Are* and *Outside Over There*, however, Sendak sometimes frames the pictures in white space and sometimes does not, apparently depending on the mood he wishes to convey. According to William Moebius, "Framed, the illustration provides a limited glimpse 'into' a world. Unframed, the illustration constitutes a total experience, the view from 'within'" (150); *Wild Things* provides examples of both, as first we gaze at Max making mischief in framed pictures that demand our separation from him and later experience a joy we can share in the unframed pictures of his rumpus with the Wild Things. In fact, and as many commentators have pointed out, *Where the Wild Things Are* has a more carefully orchestrated use of framing than any other picture book. The presence of white space around the pictures of Max as he makes mischief seems to constrain him, hold him in. The pictures gradually become bigger and thus the borders smaller as Max is sent to his room, until the pictures fill the right side of the two-page spread; the constraint seems to lessen. Then, as Max embarks on his journey to where the Wild Things are, the pictures creep onto the left side. When he arrives, the picture fills the top of both pages; when words cease in the frenzy of the rumpus, the pictures fill the page. Then, after the rumpus, the process reverses itself, until the book ends on a totally white spread that contains no picture and only four words. Watching a set of slides of this book flash quickly past on a screen is a startling revelation of the relationships possible between visual and emotional constriction—between framing and meaning.

More mysteriously, the pictures in *Outside Over There* usually fill the page, except for a white bottom edge on which words appear—but not the four pictures in which Ida hugs the changeling left in place of her sister, then realizes it is a changeling, and then puts on her Mama's rain cloak. There seems to be no obvious reason why these particular pictures should have a frame of white space all around them, except, perhaps, that they represent the one point in the book in which Ida is not able to believe that she is in control of the situation. Here, as in *Wild Things*, Sendak may be using white space around pictures to suggest a character's sense of being restricted.

But while white space around a picture can act as a frame, create a sense of constraint, and demand detachment, it can also do just the opposite; it can provide a focus that demands our involvement. That happens when a picture ends at the edges of the objects it depicts; isolating characters against a white space the shape of their own bodies forces attention upon them. In the first picture for *Peter Rabbit*, Beatrix Potter shows us rabbits as animals, wearing no clothes, seen with the detachment of observation within a landscape framed by a white border; but in the second picture the rabbits have been humanized by clothing and stand against a white space that now has the irregular shape of their bodies. We have no choice but to be more involved with these characters, just as we must be intensely involved with Peter later in the book at those moments of intense distress when Potter depicts him against a white background.

The relationship between pictures and white space tends to control where the words of a text can be placed; often, therefore, the physical relationship of text to picture is less significant than that of white space to picture. Nevertheless, book designers can work to affect our attitude by choosing where within the white space available they place a text. Even though the words of text communicate differently and require kinds of responses different from pictures, written language is like pictures in one important way; both are things to be seen. When we open a picture book, both words and pictures confront our eyes, and consequently they have literal relationships as well as symbolic ones. The words of a text are not just symbols of spoken sounds but part of the visual pattern on the page, without reference to their actual meaning.

As such, they communicate information beyond their specific meanings. Most obviously, the size of type conveys information about the intended audience; it is a convention that books for younger readers contain larger type sizes. In "Learning from Illustration," Evelyn Goldsmith says, "As far as I know, six-year olds do not normally lack visual acuity, so I suppose it has come about because the passages of text tend to be short, and if they were printed any smaller they might appear insignificant" (114). Whether there is a practical reason or not, the convention influences our understanding of books that use it.

The relative placement of words and pictures also does much to influence our reading of a page as a whole and of a book as a whole. One way in which it does so is to create or disturb the visual balance of each spread of a book. In *The Garden of Abdul Gasazi*, the words on each left-hand page balance the images on each right-hand page not just because of the borders surrounding them but because they are hefty and regular blocks of print. But while many of the two-page spreads in *Where the Wild Things Are* also consist of one page of words and one containing a picture, the words almost always occupy very little space and thus leave most of the pages they appear on empty. That adds to the dramatic tension of the story. The asymmetrical imbalance between a page full of color and another with nothing but a few black marks on it gradually disappears as Max finds an imaginative way to purge his own tension and as the pictures grow to fill the space. The only pages with both words and pictures on them that seem relatively balanced are the ones directly before and after the wild rumpus, which have equal blocks of words under the picture on both sides of the spread. In this way as well as in every other, this book builds toward and then away from that central sequence.

Obviously, then, there can be narrative significance in the relative placement of words and pictures. In "Learning from Illustrations," Evelyn Goldsmith suggests there is evidence to support the idea that "the placing of a picture to left or right, above or below the text, can affect the amount of time spent reading the text itself" (116). Consequently, when the text has usually appeared below the pictures and suddenly appears above one, the rhythm of our response to the events we are learning about changes. In Steig's *The Amazing Bone*, for instance, the words usually appear under the pictures, so that we would logically view the pictures and then read the words. But in moments of intense action there are two pictures on each page, with words either above them or below them or both; and in moments of intense emotion, when Pearl is in serious danger or, at the end, when she returns happily home, the words tend to appear *above* the pictures. We usually look at a page from the top down, and because of their inherently attractive nature, we tend to look at pictures first, then read words. When Steig puts the words above the pictures, therefore, he puts us in an ambivalent state: should we read first or look first? This ambivalence adds tension to the tense moments of his book. Chapter 9 of this book deals with other effects of our movement between pictures and text as we read a picture book, particularly those which use either of the two most common arrangements of text and picture: the text on the left side of a two-page spread with the picture on the right, or the picture on the top and the text on the bottom.

But more unusual arrangements are possible—and as with most disruptions of conventional design, they create strong narrative effects. In Burkert's *Snow White*, for instance, the pictures and words are separate from each other, on alternating two-page spreads; while each of the pictures appears at exactly the right point in the story, the pictures and text are separate enough that they seem like two parallel but isolated experiences rather than one integrated one; and the moments Burkert chooses to illustrate emphasize this gulf by being ones that are surprisingly insignificant to the plot of the story. As a result, these strong pictures do not so much illustrate the story of Snow White as they become a different story on their own.

On the first page of Burton's *The Little House*, however, the words and pictures are so closely integrated that the visual markings for language actually become part of the depicted scene. The words fill in the white space between two rows of flowers that stands for the walk leading up to the house and thus represent the stones of the walk as well as the verbal signs that communicate the story. In an interesting discussion in *Ways of the Illustrator*, Joseph Schwarcz speaks of how illustrators place letters within their pictures as part of the visual image; he sees it as a playful game, part of humanity's fascination with the system of communication it has invented (65). In fact, pictures which introduce letters as characters or as part of the landscape are something like puns; verbal puns insist on the importance of accidental similarities between the sounds of words, and these visual puns connect the visual appearance of letters and words, which are in fact inherently meaningless in themselves, with the meanings they signify. A good example is found in *In the Night Kitchen*, where Mickey's "QUIET DOWN THERE!" fills a space as large as the space depicting Mickey himself in his bedroom; here, as often in picture books, the relative size of the lettering represents varying degrees of loudness. In a different use of the visual patterns of words, the words seen as a whole on each page of *The Little House* form shapes on the page that duplicate the spiraling curves in the pictures that accompany them, an effect that supports and amplifies the general atmosphere of the book as a whole.

Words can also act as visual objects that create relationships *within* the image; for instance, the speech balloons in *In the Night Kitchen* appear behind the bakers when those bakers are riotously involved in singing a song, but when one of them is perplexed by Mickey's eruption from the oven, he is partially occluded by the speech balloon containing words in front of him. The words in *Arrow to the Sun*, printed directly on top of the pictures with no white space around them, are even more integrated into the pictures: they provide visual weight, so that if they were not present, the pictures would have a different organization.

According to David Bland, illustrations in perspective make book design difficult: "The problem . . . is to reconcile the flatness of the text with the depth of the picture" (*History* 65). The picture in *The Little House* in which the words form the walk up to the house is visually ambivalent for just that reason: if the words are understood as words, they imply no depth; but since the space they occupy gets wider toward the bottom, they do imply the walk in perspective. The words as words stand in front of the picture, but as a representation of the walk they are within the depth the picture implies.

That is not particularly annoying in *The Little House*, because the pictures are so cartoonlike that perspective in them is more an idea than an actual effect. But in other books there is indeed a problem in relating the depthless space that words occupy to the implied depth of pictures. In fact, the more representational pictures become, the more they need to be separated from the rest of the page by a frame or border. That is another positive effect of the borders around the pictures in *The Garden of Abdul Gasazi;* we have the sense that we are looking through the border into the world beyond it, so that the flatness of the page on which the words are printed does in fact make sense as being a flat surface positioned in front of the scene depicted.

But in a few interesting instances, illustrators create curious ambiguities by framing the words with the pictures. In Hyman's *Snow White* the words are either on a white piece of paper that seems to be pasted on top of the pictures, or they are in what seems to be a hole cut through the pictures and behind them. The result in either case is a dissipation of some of the realistic feeling of the pictures. This is clearly a flat surface we are looking at; we cannot forget that the pictures possess only the *illusion* of depth. In this highly emotional book, that has the effect of counterpointing and relieving some of the intensity.

In *Outside Over There,* Sendak makes a different use of the same technique. Sendak places words inside label-like insets in the middle of an illustrated page only at the beginning and end of the book—before and after Ida's adventure—and in the very middle, when Ida hears her father's song. The words within these labels all refer to Ida's parents and separate them and the pages they appear on from the rest of the book, in which Ida is on her own, free to indulge in her own fantasy. In reminding us of the illusory depth of the picture and thus stressing the illusory nature of the reality we see before us, the labeled pages subtly require us to realize the differences between our own reality and the illusions of fantasy—both Ida's fantasy about the goblins and Sendak's fantasy about Ida.

At the end of *Outside Over There* there is no label; we see Ida playing with her sister as the words float in the air above her. Are the words in front of the pictures or behind them? It is hard to tell; in fact, the same white space that implies background for the figures is merely blank white space around words at the same time. That sort of arrangement is surprisingly common in picture books—and, once one becomes conscious of it, rather unsettling. The ambiguity is unresolved—and contrary to David Bland, who finds such ambiguities a quality of bad design, I believe that they often add to the interest and tension of picture books. In the case of *Outside Over There*, for instance, the visual ambiguity of the page tends to qualify the apparently happy ending; after all, Papa is not home yet, and Momma still looks depressed. The pictures in *The Little House* move around the text in a way that creates this sort of ambiguity in perspective *only* in the unhappy sections of the story. At the beginning and end, the words and the pictures are separated on opposite pages, or else the pictures on the page with the words are just disconnected visual symbols that create no perspective demands; but in the middle of the book the words appear in what the pictures imply is sky, and even ground, and the effect is tense rather than contenting. As often in picture books, the qualities of balance and regularity that theoretically contribute to good design are absent. The result is not bad art but good storytelling.

But such deliberate divergences from the principles of good design require clever planning by illustrators before the tensions they create can speak of more than just ineptitude. As a further example of that, the blocks of white space that contain the text and dilute the depth illusion in the pictures in Hyman's *Snow White* also demand other narrative strategies. These blocks of white space sometimes seem annoyingly obtrusive to the many viewers who suspect there are interesting things to look at behind them, and Hyman must work hard to focus visual attention away from or around the white space. She does so most often by framing it with a part of the scene that is in shadow or with figures whose heads or limbs point toward a central focus on the other side of the spread; but on one occasion she cleverly uses it to divide and thus cleverly counterpoint the image of the solitary queen preparing a poisoned apple on the full page of illustration to the left and the image of Snow White surrounded by loving dwarfs that appears in the Queen's mirror to the right of the text. Here the Queen's evil behavior is signified by a silhouetted black cat that takes up a position behind her similar to her own, so that it appears to be her shadow, while across the divide of the block of text, Snow White also inclines at a similar angle but in the opposite direction; and while the image of Snow White contains a hand that clearly echoes the Queen's tensely positioned hand on the worktable on the other side of the spread, this hand on Snow White's arm also continues the counterpoint, for it belongs to a dwarf in the process of comforting Snow White. Hyman thus gives these difficult white blocks narrative import by cleverly focusing attention away from and around them.

But Charles Mikolaycak does the exact opposite in his brooding pictures for Zilpha Keatley Snyder's *The Changing Maze*. The mysterious garden maze of this story comes to seem even more mysterious when the composition of the pictures forces our attention toward significant and interesting objects within it that are in fact hidden behind the white block on which the text appears—various statues, parts of the protagonist's body, and, at the climax of the story, the chest of gold that the plot centers on. Both Mikolaycak and Hyman have turned an apparently unfortunate choice of layout that ought to have been a liability into a useful source of narrative information.

The Changing Maze also seems mysterious because the events are depicted in a muted palette of somber greens and browns and sickly yellows and grays that evoke an eerily mysterious mood. The perception of color has a direct sensuous appeal; Julia Kristeva goes so far as to suggest that the color in visual art speaks not only of conventional meanings—blue suggesting the blue of the sky, for instance—but also to the unconscious, that aspect of being which resides outside of the boundaries of the world we can name with language and thus think about, and, "as a result, color . . . escapes censorship; and the unconscious irrupts into a culturally coded pictorial distribution" (220). Presumably, therefore, all pictures in color both evoke a code of signification and speak either satisfyingly or disturbingly of matters beyond meaning or intention. But the paradoxical result of this simultaneous communication is that specific colors come to evoke specific emotions and attitudes and thus can work to convey mood more exactly than any other aspect of pictures. A nonnarrative effect thus develops profound narrative implications.

The conventional meanings of colors are of two sorts: those, like the red of a stoplight, that are merely arbitrary and culture-specific and those that relate specific colors to specific emotions. As I will show later, the culture-specific codes tend to be more significant in terms of their ability to give weight and meaning to the objects within pictures, but it is the emotional connotations that most influence the mood of picture books—the connections between blue and melancholy, yellow and happiness, red and warmth, which appear to derive fairly directly from our basic perceptions of water and sunlight and fire. Since such associations do exist, artists can evoke particular moods by using the appropriate colors—even, sometimes, at the expense of consistency: Max's room in *Where the Wild Things Are* is blue when he is first sent to it, a much more cheerful yellow after his visit to the Wild Things; and his bed changes from moody bluish purple to cheerful pink.

The emotional implications of colors are particularly clear in those picture books in which one color predominates. The association of blue with melancholy is so much a part of our cultural tradition that the predominance of blues in Evaline Ness's melancholy *Sam, Bangs, and Moonshine* affirms the mood of the story, and the predominant blue of Steig's *Amos and Boris* seems to express two common associations—both melancholy and serenity. Indeed, Kristeva suggests that, because we seem to perceive blue with the rods of the retina's periphery, "the perception of blue entails not identifying the object; that blue is, precisely, on this side of or beyond the object's fixed form; thus it is the zone where phenomenal identity vanishes" (225). That may account for the passive and peaceful serenity that blue often evokes; not surprisingly, cultural codes identify blue with the serene Virgin Mary.

The red of fire conventionally implies both intensity and warmth. Consequently, although red is the only color in Dr. Seuss's *How the Grinch Stole Christmas*, the red of the Grinch's eyes clearly implies anger, while the red of the sky as the villagers sing happy Christmas songs implies warmth and love. Yellow, the conventional color of cheerfulness, dominates in many cheerful children's books and is also found in combination with other colors in picture books that specify the particular sort of cheerfulness intended. With the warm oranges and reds in *Rosie's Walk*, yellow provides a balance for what might be a frightening story in a different color scheme. The cheerful yellow combined with serene blue in Kurt Wiese's pictures for *The Story about Ping* and in Steig's *Amos and Boris* is quieter—cheery in a more calming way.

Green, traditionally the color of growth and fertility, predominates in the vibrant pastoral world of Sendak's pictures for *Mr. Rabbit and the Lovely Present*. The monochromatic warm brown of McCloskey's *Make Way for Ducklings* amplifies the story's warmth. In combination, green and brown, the colors of earth and of foliage, often create an atmosphere of organic richness. They predominate in the dank but undeniably fertile world of Raymond Briggs's *Fungus the Bogeyman* and in less intense hues in Lobel's Frog and Toad books, where they imply the same reptilian earthiness in a less intense and less unsettling form. They appear again, and again less intensely, in *Anno's Journey* and make the imaginary Europe of that book a fertile but distinctly unthreatening place. These three books also form a spectrum in terms of the yellowness of their greens and browns—the most disgusting, *Fungus*, is yellowest; the most pleasant, *Anno's Journey*, the least yellow. Similarly, the yellow-greens and browns that appear in the caverns of the wicked Onis in Blair Lent's pictures for Mosel's *The Funny Little Woman* make them seem repulsive, while the deliciously springlike world the woman escapes into at the end of the book is a purer green; and the more muted but still yellowish greens and browns of Mikolaycak's pictures for *The Changing Maze* more broodingly imply a similar kind of mysterious dank danger as that of the Oni's cave.

Gray, the color we attach to characterless people, often suggests bleakness, lack of intensity, a cool detachment. The oppressively predominating gray of the stone walls surrounding Snow White's mother in Burkert's picture of her demands our detachment from her but also contrasts with the vibrantly colored patterns we see surrounding her as we look through her window into her room; perhaps as a foreshadowing of her daughter's fate, she is a small spot of lively beauty in an otherwise bleak and forbidding world. In *Intercity,* the wordless story of a train trip, Charles Keeping creates a similar relationship between what can be seen around a window and what can be seen through it. The feeling of boring detachment in the predominantly brownish gray pictures of passengers on a train contrasts with the vibrant colors of the world outside the train's windows, which the passengers ignore. The contrast between the monochrome of the passenger pictures and the rich colors of the window pictures supports the central theme of the book: we see the passengers as they themselves see the world, and we see the richness of the world they miss because they do not bother to look at it.

As Keeping does here, many illustrators vary the predominating color in different pictures of the same book in order to convey the different moods of different parts of stories. In Adrienne Adams's pictures for *Cabbage Moon,* for instance, the monochromatic backgrounds change to suit the events that take place in front of them rather than the literal situation: the villainous Squink steals the moon against a melancholy blue sky and makes salad out of it in a sickly yellow-green room, which turns into an angry red when the angry dog bursts into it; later, a princess and prince declare their love against a more romantic pinkish red.

In Susan Jeffers's *Wild Robin* the pictures of Robin's boring everyday life are mainly browns and greens, whereas the mystical land the fairies take him to are suffused with violet, a color often associated in picture books with fantasy. The pictures for Van Allsburg's *Wreck of the Zephyr,* a fantasy about a flying boat, are predominantly purple. The forest that grows in Max's room in *Wild Things* is a combination of purplish blues and purplish pinks; the goblins of *Outside Over There* wear purple cloaks and reside in a purple-toned cave. In Raymond Briggs's *The Snowman,* the pink bedspread and curtains of the boy's room become purple in the night light in which he awakes to find his snowman come to life; his pinkish robe turns purple too. As dawn comes and the snowman becomes unmoving again, the robe and the curtains and the spread turn pink. A psychological study by Lois Wexner suggests that most people associate purple with stateliness and dignity, I suspect because of its cultural connections with royalty; but in picture books, it is usually associated with the effects of moonlight, darkness, and mystery.

If a picture in which one color predominates strongly suggests a particular mood, then so does a picture that leaves out one particular color. The pictures in *Rosie's Walk* seem so peaceful and unthreatening not just because of their style but also because they contain yellow and red and even green, but no blue at all. Whether or not we associate the absent blue with sadness, these pictures do establish a definite mood, a mood different from the much calmer and more serene mood of Kurt Wiese's pictures for *The Story about Ping*, which emphasize blues and yellows and downplay red.

In the experiment by Lois Wexner I mentioned earlier, "no mention of color names was made by the experimenter. This was in order to avoid associations to color stereotypes" (432). Nevertheless, Wexner's conclusions suggest strong associations between particular colors and particular emotions, many of them confirming the suggestions I made above: blue is calm and serene, red both exciting and hostile, yellow is cheerful. Perhaps more interestingly, however, Wexner also discovered that different colors might be associated with the same emotion by different subjects. For instance, her studies show that many people associate cheerfulness with yellow, a smaller number red, an even smaller number orange and green. On the basis of this study, then, we might expect a particularly cheerful book to be predominantly yellow, with a lot of red and some orange and green; and that is exactly the color scheme of *Rosie's Walk*.

Other picture books also seem to share the schemes implied by the various responses of Wexner's subjects. They selected red, orange, and black almost equally to suggest defiance and hostility; these are the predominant colors of the assertive story of hostility *Arrow to the Sun*, and an orangey red and black are the only colors in H. A. Rey's story of a defiant monkey, *Curious George*. Many selected blue, and almost as many green, to represent calmness and serenity, with a smaller number choosing yellow; green predominates in Sendak's serene pictures for *Mr. Rabbit and the Lovely Present,* blue and yellow in Steig's *Amos and Boris,* which describes tempestuous events but still has a surprisingly calming effect. Security is associated with blue by most, with brown and green by some others; interestingly, blue, brown, and green are the predominant colors of the land of the Wild Things, a theoretically frightening but undeniably safe place for Max. Most of Wexner's subjects associated tenderness with blue, some with green; those two colors form most of the backgrounds of Briggs's wonderfully tender *The Snowman.* Red and brown are almost equally associated with protectiveness; they predominate in Burkert's picture of Snow White in the dwarfs' house, along with blue, which with brown implies security. It seems that picture-book illustrators often take advantage of associations with color combinations of which they themselves may not even be aware.

Other qualities of colors can also convey the emotional content of pictures. Consider the two pictures of Max in his bedroom in *Where the Wild Things Are.* Not only do the colors of the wall and the bed change, but their doing so changes the effect of the pictures as a whole. In the first picture the pink of the bedspread is different from the purple of the bed, and both jar with the greenish yellow carpet; in the other picture everything is suffused with a warming yellow that brings the room together; the bed matches its spread and a bowl on the table. The unified calm of this picture contrasts mightily with the discordancies of the first one. Artists frequently use related colors to imply calm and discordant ones to suggest jarring energy or excitement.

The predominant color of *Mr. Rabbit and the Lovely Present* is green, a peaceful green of a growing, abundant world. But the green is slightly different in each picture; and closer inspection reveals that, as Mr. Rabbit and the girl discuss different colors, the green of the landscape around them is suffused with light of the color they discuss. As they discuss red the woods behind them contain red foliage, the ground beneath them pink splotches, presumably flowers; but as they discuss yellow the woods are lit with yellow-orange, and they walk toward a brownish yellow road. None of these pictures seems to be using colors symbolically; the yellowish green is not necessarily more cheerful than the pinkish green one. They all imply the same calm serenity; and they do so, I think, because of the unified concord created by their suffusion with tones of one secondary color.

In *Rosie's Walk*, on the other hand, there are large areas of pure color, all different from each other. The effect is slightly jarring but cheerfully exuberant. Books as different as Clement Hurd's/Leo and Diane Dillon's *Goodnight Moon* and *Why Mosquitoes Buzz in People's Ears*, which also use unrelated colors in shocking combinations, all share a quality of energy and excitement, whereas even pictures as vibrantly colorful as the scenes through the window in Keeping's *Intercity* express bucolic serenity as least partly because of their careful blendings of different shades. Barbara Bader speaks of "the loose casual liveliness that comes of letting contours and colors overlap" (*American Picturebooks* 337); there is certainly a different mood in the casual pictures by artists like Roger Duvoisin from that created by the precisely outlined colors of artists like Sendak or Peter Spier or Leo and Diane Dillon.

In fact, pictures that use many different colors are not necessarily lively. Spier's pictures for *Noah's Ark* seem calm, even those depicting the storm, certainly in comparison to the wonderfully alive contrasts of *Why Mosquitoes Buzz in People's Ears*. Part of the reason for that is the almost total absence of red in Spier's pictures; but part also is the relative saturation of the colors used. We distinguish colors in a number of ways—by hue, that is, classifications like red or blue that refer to different segments of the spectrum; by shade, the degree of relative darkness or brightness, as when we speak of light red or dark red; and by saturation, the relative intensity of colors, as when we speak of bright red and pale red. The colors in *Why Mosquitoes Buzz in People's Ears* are more saturated and therefore more intense than the colors in *Noah's Ark;* the less saturated colors of *Noah's Ark* seem more gentle, less assertive.

On the other hand, differences of shade suggest not the differences in levels of energy implied by the word "intensity" but the symbolic differences we usually read into darkness and light, shade and sunshine. Pictures that use dark shades seem both more somber and more cozy than lighter pictures; consider the difference between the jazzy opening pages and the comforting closing ones of Clement Hurd's *Goodnight Moon,* in which the gradually darkening room is evoked by a gradual darkening in the shades of the colors. The always light pictures in *Rosie's Walk* are neither threatening nor comforting; they create an atmosphere of unseriousness that prevents us from either being threatened by the fox or overly joyful about Rosie's ignorance of him. The darker tones of *Where the Wild Things Are* imply both threat and coziness; the darkness can both frighten and allow the contrasting coziness of lighter spaces. For that reason, I think, we expect dramatic emotion from the high contrasts between areas of light and shadow in books like *Wild Things* or Hyman's *Snow White* and greater detachment from more evenly toned pictures like either the light-filled pictures of *Mr. Rabbit and the Lovely Present* or the generally brooding dark-toned pictures of Van Allsburg's *Wreck of the Zephyr.*

But the psychologists Benjamin Wright and Lee Rainwater suggest that it is neither hue nor shade which most meaningfully communicates emotional connotations; "it is saturation which manifests itself most powerfully in the analysis of the relations between connotations and perceptions" (98). Their study reveals that an atmosphere of happiness depends on lightness and saturation more than on hue; that showiness depends almost exclusively on saturation; that forcefulness depends on color darkness; that elegance depends on both saturation and hue, blue being particularly elegant; and that calmness depends on darkness in association with blueness. Of the qualities they explored, only warmth seems to depend exclusively on hue, redness in particular.

The truth of these findings may be confirmed by a quick second look at the books I discussed earlier in terms of hue alone. The cheerful *Rosie's Walk* is light in shade throughout, the brooding and forcefully emotional *Snow White* by Hyman almost always dark. *Arrow to the Sun* is intense and definitely showy, while the stylishly elegant pictures for *Sam, Bangs, and Moonshine* are both predominantly blue and highly saturated.

Furthermore, it is possible to identify picture books that express interesting combinations of the qualities Wright and Rainwater discuss. *Why*

Mosquitoes Buzz in People's Ears is showy (highly saturated color), forceful (the shades tend to be dark reds and greens and oranges), and elegant (intensely black backgrounds). *Peter Rabbit* is happy (light), not very showy (unsaturated colors), not very forceful (lighter shades), and at times elegantly tasteful (especially in the predominating use of blues and browns). *Where the Wild Things Are* is not particularly happy (quite dark), not showy (the colors are muted), forceful (the shades are dark ones), at times warm (particularly under a pink sunrise), elegant (many of the colors in the book have a blue cast to them), and, perhaps most interestingly in terms of the frenzied action depicted, very calm (dark and blue).

If the uses of color I have cataloged help to create atmosphere, then so, obviously, does the absence of color. In picture books, as in movies, color is the norm; currently, black and white seems to be reserved for movies that ask for special responses from their audience—for those that deliberately evoke nostalgia about the way movies once were or for those that work to announce themselves as serious and different, as important as documentaries. While some picture books are in black and white for economic reasons, serious picture-book artists who choose to avoid color in a medium noted for its use of color often have similar special points to make.

The obvious example is the work of Chris Van Allsburg. The black-and-white pictures in both *The Garden of Abdul Gasazi* and *Jumanji* evoke the feeling of black-and-white still photographs that have been slightly overdeveloped to emphasize their contrasts. They are uncompromisingly objective and detached—unlike the world we see subjectively with our own eyes simply because they *are* so much like photographs. Paradoxically, we commonly associate black and white with uncompromising truth, utter absence of subjective coloring: documentary. Van Allsburg's pictures have the quality of documentary, of detached observation that shows exactly what there is to see without the frivolous intrusion of color, and they are unsettling simply because what we see so uncompromisingly is often magic and impossible.

Furthermore, the heavy contrasts of these pictures emphasize the patterns created by the various shapes and so do the black lines that outline each shape, so that the relationships of those shapes on the flat surface of the page are as significant as the relationships of the figures the shapes represent in the three-dimensional picture space. As a result, and as happens in photographs with high contrast, the often intense action the pictures depict is slowed down, held by the patterns; like still pictures of people caught in moments of fast action, the pictures are astonishingly still, as if the people and animals and trees had been turned to stone. The magic of these pictures depends to a great extent on these paradoxical relationships between what is depicted and the photographic techniques used to depict it—between our expectations of documentary truth and our perception of magic, between activity and stopped time.

The documentary quality of certain sorts of black-and-white depiction—our faith that they show us the real, unvarnished truth—is used to advantage by David Macaulay in his black-and-white picture books about the construction of various buildings, particularly *Unbuilding*. This book shows in documentary detail an event that has not yet happened, the dismantling of the Empire State Building. The ink drawings are precise and careful, close enough to the working diagrams of engineers and architects to evoke conviction. In color, the unbuilding of the Empire State Building would be a charmingly whimsical fantasy—as perhaps, are the colored drawings by architects of buildings they have not yet built. In black and white, it achieves the tongue-in-cheek pseudoconviction of fairy tales, that characteristically matter-of-fact reporting of utterly nonfactual events.

Van Allsburg and Macaulay both achieve a sense of reality by imitating and thus evoking our conventional expectations of conventionally realistic depictions, photographs, or architect's sketches; but in other circumstances, black-and-white drawing is not necessarily a good medium for the representational depiction of the way the world looks. It shows us less of the visual world than our eyes do—shades, but no hues—and forces us to fill in what is not actually shown. Perhaps that explains why black-and-white documentary seems so truthful and serious—it demands our mental activity, so that we cannot just sit back and soak it in. But since black-and-white pictures are, in fact, less complete than those in color, they actually reveal less of surfaces, of physical objects and facial characteristics.

Furthermore, color, placed in between the lines that represent objects, fills in shapes and gives the objects solidity; so without color, the lines become more obvious, and without the solidifying qualities of weightiness and bulk they can more forcefully depict motion. Generally speaking, and unlike the work of Van Allsburg and Macaulay, most of the black-and-white drawing in picture books is cartooning or caricature, and most of it emphasizes action over appearance—not how objects look but what they do.

That focus also explains why black-and-white illustrations seem so much more appropriate in longer books than in picture books. Picture books emphasize showing as much as telling, and their pictures often fill in the details of emotion and of setting that their words leave out and that color seems most suited to convey. But in longer books, words can convey at least some of those details, and pictures in color seem superfluous when they merely duplicate information the text itself communicates. On the other hand, good black-and-white pictures that emphasize line over shape can add energy to long books in which details of emotion and of setting might otherwise retard the action. While they are not in picture books, three widely admired sets of illustrations of children's novels—Tenniel's for Carroll's *Alice* books, Ernest Shepherd's for Milne's *Pooh* books, and Garth Williams's for E. B. White's *Charlotte's Web*—are worth considering here, partially because they reveal something about the use of black and white in comparison with color and partially because they suggest important differences between picture-book illustration and other children's book illustration.

All three emphasize line over shape. No area is ever completely black in any of these pictures; even the blackest of spaces retains evidence of crosshatching in small bits of un-inked white, so that even the insides of fireplaces and such lack solidity. Furthermore, even the pictures that depict inactivity—the sleeping king in *Through the Looking Glass*, Eeyore looking at himself in a stream in *Winnie the Pooh,* the supersatisfied Templeton after his rich feast at the fair in *Charlotte's Web*—have numerous complexities of line that either imply activity in the environment or else force the eye into activity in its act of perception.

Not surprisingly, however, most of the pictures in these books focus on actual movement. Tenniel's pictures for *Through the Looking Glass* depict numerous moments of shaking and pulling. His generally less energetic pictures for *Alice in Wonderland* show moments either just before or just after strenuous action and create tension by implying action: we see Alice about to open the door in the wall, about to drink, about to grab hold of the rabbit, and so on. Both books contain sets of pictures showing physical transformations, such as a disappearance of the Cheshire Cat, and both reach a climax in pictures depicting frenzied activity: the cards flying into the air in *Wonderland* and the candles growing toward the ceiling in *Through the Looking Glass.* These active pictures balance Carroll's often slow-moving text, which dwells delightfully but not always excitingly on verbal games-playing and theoretical discussions.

Shepherd's drawings are more cartoonlike than Tenniel's and more energetic. He uses action lines to show Pooh falling from a tree, footprints to show where the animals have been, pictures in series that look almost like comic strips to show Pooh practicing jumps or Eeyore admiring his tail. The pictures often have no background at all, yet the faces of the animals often seem emotionless, so we must concentrate on what they do. Considering the quietness of Milne's stories, these drawings are surprisingly energetic; like Tenniel's, they provide a necessary balance to the text.

While Williams's line is heavier than Shepherd's, he makes up for it by using complexities of crosshatching and shadow-texturing more often and by concentrating on depictions of intense activity. He shows just about every occasion in *Charlotte's Web* when people or animals are swept off their feet—Lurvy toppling over Wilbur, Wilbur in midair as he tries to spin a web, Avery turning a handstand at the fair. Even in less frenetic moments, Williams implies muscular tension in the bodies of his characters, particular their hands. In the calm of the doctor's office, Mrs. Arable clutches nervously at her purse; in the calm of the barn, Fern's hands always seem to imply a hyperactive clutching or grasping—the high-spirited energy of youth. *Charlotte's Web* is a surprisingly inactive novel—in fact, it is about how violent action is prevented, and it is filled with poetic descriptions that retard the action. So the energetic line of the drawings balances the often dreamy music of the text.

These three sets of pictures show what illustrations at their best can accomplish in longer books; if there are few equally distinguished picture books that use the techniques of black-and-white cartooning, I suspect that is because the balance between words and pictures in picture books is crucially different from that in longer stories. In picture books, the words usually stick to telling us about what happens, and we expect the pictures to add something the words do not tell; and black-and-white cartoons do best what the words of a good picture-book text have already done.

These differences become clear in a comparison of the black-and white work of illustrators with their picture-book work in color. Charles Keeping's use of parallel and concentric lines to create texture is his most characteristic gesture. But even the intense activity of the horses' mad rush in *Through the Window* does not disrupt the heavy, foreboding, and mysteriously dead solemnity of that book; the dark shades of these pictures hold down the energy of their lines. Surprisingly, something similar happens in the different light-filled pictures of *Intercity,* in part because washes of color restrain the energetic line, in part because the rhythmically repeating parallel lines create an overall sense of pattern that focuses our attention on the surface organization of each picture as much as on its subject; and that is as it should be, since Keeping intends us to look at these scenes framed by a train window as we would look at paintings in a gallery, more significantly objects of aesthetic pleasure than representational depictions. But when Keeping uses the same repeating parallel lines in black-and-white pictures, like those in Garfield and Blishen's *The God beneath the Sea* and *The Golden Shadow,* the effect is startlingly energetic—even in spite of the gray wash in many pictures. With no color to hold them down, the lines become more significant than the shapes they make; and Keeping takes advantage of that by using different repeating patterns of lines in the same picture, so that the surfaces are filled with contradictory and energetic sets of radiating and parallel lines and splotches. In these pictures, as always seems to happen when line becomes predominant over shape, energy and activity predominate over solidity and pattern.

That is not to say that all artists in black and white focus on the energies of line. Some, like Wanda Gag, use black-and-white's potential for heavy contrast to create more restfully decorative effects. Even though there is much use of line to create shadow in Gag's *Millions of Cats*, the heavy contrasts between light areas and dark ones orient the pictures toward pattern rather than toward action. In techniques like block printing, in which the ink is not laid down on the paper by the line of a pen, the blocks of black and white tend to operate more like colors, creating solid shapes rather than energetic lines. Furthermore, such a technique associates these pictures with the static conventions of folk art, which tends to be more oriented to pattern than to action. Not surprisingly, Gag's story also focuses more on pattern than on movement, on repetition rather than on forward movement. While a lot happens in *Millions of Cats*, the story tends to offer more pleasure to those who have heard it before than to those who are hearing it for the first time. It is comfortingly predictable rather than threatening or even very exciting.

But if *Millions of Cats* is comfortingly secure, it is not just because it emphasizes shape over line, pattern over energy; it is also because the shapes happen to be primarily rounded and curved ones—the sort of shapes we associate with softness and yielding. Such associations have an obvious effect on our attitudes to pictures. The sad story of urban blight that Burton tells in *The Little House* never seems particularly sad, simply because the spiraling curves of the original country landscape continue throughout, and because almost nothing in the book is actually angular or sharp-edged. The house itself has gently curved walls, as do even some of the skyscrapers that eventually surround it in later pictures; and those skyscrapers that do have straight lines are nestled among curved roads and against curved clouds. Compared with these unthreatening curves, Keeping's bristling depictions of whiskers, feathers, and bloodstains in *The God beneath the Sea* are unsettling; our eyes respond to all these sharp points the way our bodies might if we sat on them. Meanwhile, the numerous small squares and triangles that cover parts of the surface of many of the pictures in books by Brian Wildsmith—the picture of lions on the title page of *The Circus* is a good example—create a sense of dead lassitude that forces us to admire these pictures as pleasantly decorative compositions, if we admire them at all.

Most picture books contain no clearly predominating shapes; and as I will show later, the various shapes in them imply different relationships between objects. But at least one book has not one but two predominating shapes: almost everything in *Arrow to the Sun* is either angular or curved. The boy is angular, so is the arrow he becomes, so is the pueblo; the women are curved, as are the pots and the earth and a snake with a tale in its mouth. The fact that everything is either one definite shape or another creates an interesting tension in pictures that otherwise might seem decorative and unenergetic.

Similar shapes in groups create patterns; as *Arrow to the Sun* makes clear, a predominating pattern or set of patterns also influences our attitude to pictures. The many tidy rows of leaves and feathers and pears that fill many of the objects of *Rosie's Walk* hold down the areas of the pictures that they occupy and thus force attention on the more energetic unpatterned areas of randomly splashing water or randomly flying hay. But they also create an overall effect of unified calm. On the other hand, conflicting sets of differing patterns, like those in Keeping's work, create tensions with each other that are active and disruptive.

Paradoxically, perhaps, both intensely patterned and intensely disrupted visual surfaces convey relatively less narrative information; if books like *Millions of Cats* and *Rosie's Walk* sometimes verge on the merely decorative, the intensely energetic work of an artist like Beverly Brodsky moves toward the depiction of highly wrought emotions that are strangely detached from specific visual objects, so that they convey an attitude but nothing specific to take the attitude toward. Indeed, Brodsky takes clever advantage of just this aspect of her work when she manages in her *Story of Job* to convey the wrath and power of God himself through intersecting patterns of wildly swirling lines and disrupted splashes of color; her pictures do not so much work to convey narrative information as they operate as an emotional counterpoint to the narrative of the text—a sort of evocative background music.

Eventually, both excessive pattern and excessive lack of pattern approach and then pass over the boundary between representation and abstraction. A totally repetitive image cannot tell a story, for nothing is disturbed, and there can be no conflict, no plot; a totally unrepetitive, unpatterned image cannot evoke enough order to focus our attention on the areas of disorder that convey narrative tensions. Consequently, narrative art is always a combination of pattern and randomness, order and disorder—one might even say, of abstraction and representation, for narrative art always offers both an image of a depicted object and purposeful distortions of that image that evoke codes of signification and thus convey information about the object.

One final overall quality of pictures is often isolated as a significant creator of mood: the various media in which illustrators work. Commentators on picture books often suggest that the characteristics of differing media limit the range of subjects each medium can convey or impose certain moods upon pictures made in them. For instance, Glazer and Williams say, "It would be difficult to illustrate a story about a fog with sharp-edged woodcuts" (87) and suggest that in Feodor Rojankovsky's *Frog Went A-Courtin'*, "the medium gives a slightly grainy aura to the pictures, as if a child had helped make them. The crayon, supplemented with pen and ink, pleasantly matches a child's simple song" (65). Indeed, the differences between black-and-white pictures and ones in color that I discussed earlier do depend in part on differences in media, and so do the differences between line drawings and block prints. As E. H. Gombrich says in "Standards of Truth," "The image cannot give us more information than the medium can carry" (248). Black lines on white paper cannot reveal the color of objects in the real world, and block prints reveal texture only with difficulty; collage inhibits the creation of depth, and watercolor in its translucency creates the impression of light more readily than tempera.

But while it might be difficult to illustrate a story of a fog with sharp-edged woodcuts, it is not necessarily impossible: the pictures in Lionni's *Swimmy* successfully use techniques of block printing to convey a feeling of undersea fluidity. As for the childlike quality of crayon, consider *The Snowman,* in which Raymond Briggs uses a crayonlike graininess to achieve a subtle luminosity more suggestive of impressionist painting than of childlike art. While the characteristics of media certainly influence the way they are used, they do not necessarily limit artists to particular effects.

Artists do, certainly, choose media in terms of the effects they wish to create; but it is their *conviction* that certain media are best suited for certain effects that let them create those effects, not the media themselves. An artist who believes that woodcuts ideally convey boldness and power will choose to make woodcuts to express boldness and power; an artist who believes that woodcuts convey simplicity and folksy charm will choose woodcuts to convey simplicity and folksy charm. Furthermore, viewers are not likely to confuse bold power with charming folksiness; if we look well, we will see in these two sets of woodcuts what their artists made them convey. In *Prints and Visual Communication,* William Ivins shows how conventional attitudes grew around various media, so that people who believed that "a wood-engraving should look like a wood-engraving and be all neat and tidy with its net of lines" (105) attacked William Blake for making nonengravinglike engravings. Ivins concludes, rightly, that "what makes a medium artistically important is not any quality of the medium itself but the qualities of mind and hand that its users bring to it" (114).

That is not to say that our conventional expectations of media do not influence our attitudes to various pictures. Sometimes such attitudes do actually result from limitations inherent in a medium—when an artist conscientiously exploits such limitations, as does Van Allsburg in his use of the limited hue but wonderful shading possibilities of pencil on white paper in *The Garden of Abdul Gasazi.* But more often, a choice of medium conveys an attitude toward the subject of a picture because the artist has exploited our conventional expectations for pictures in that medium. As the comments by Glazer and Williams suggest, our association of crayons with children might well lead us to expect childlike qualities in crayon work; sharing such associations, an artist like Rojankovsky might well choose such a medium in order to create childlike drawings. Similarly, many artists make gentle watercolors and starkly "primitive" woodcuts.

In *Ways of Seeing,* John Berger suggests that the richness of detailed information about the physical surfaces of objects possible in oil paintings made oils an ideal medium to convey power; from the Renaissance on, vast numbers of oil paintings were commissioned to show the expensive possessions—the houses and jewels and furnishings—that rich men could afford to buy. In picture books, this tradition of richly detailed environments is found mainly in pictures that illustrate fantasies, particularly fairy tales. It begins in the sumptuous work of artists like Arthur Rackham and Kay Nielsen and Edmund Dulac, who made pictures for expensive gift-book editions of fairy tales in the early years of this century, and it continues in the work of artists like Burkert and Hyman and Le Cain. All these artists create a sense of the reality and the wonder of the fantasy lands they depict by filling them with objects and details and textures and wonderfully decorated surfaces. The more these pictures look like traditional oil paintings, the more solidly real seem the fantasy places and objects they depict and the more strongly they relate to our conventional association of wonder with richness and with owning things.

But interestingly, these artists do not always work in oils: their pictures, usually watercolors, simply have the look, the density and detail and dwelling on rich surface textures, that we expect of traditional oils. In evoking the characteristic effects of one medium through the use of others, these artists reveal how very much our expectations of media depend on convention. In fact, the medium itself is not the message. The medium is never the message. Having chosen a medium to help them achieve the attitude they want to communicate toward their subject, artists must then use their knowledge of the various techniques of dynamics and atmospherics that I describe in this book in order to make the medium evoke that attitude.

■ ■ ■ ■

CHAPTER THREE

───────

Style as Meaning

Unlike such qualities as format and color, discussed in the last chapter, style is not a separable entity. It is the name we give to the effect of *all* the aspects of a work of art considered together. In *Art and Illusion*, E. H. Gombrich suggests a similarity between style and the different accents with which different people speak the same language (364). In *Ways of Worldmaking*, Nelson Goodman offers a similar metaphor: "a style is a complex characteristic that serves somewhat as an individual or group signature—that bespeaks Resnais or Whistler or Borodin, that distinguishes early from later Corot, Baroque from Rococo, Baoulé from Pahouin" (34). And in *Ideology and the Image*, Bill Nichols uses the metaphor of the moiré pattern: "the appearance of a new pattern created from the combination of two others"; Nichols speaks of "a distinctive coalescence of codes (in the manner of an ideolect) whose interference with and reinforcement of one another set up a *moiré* pattern known as the textual system or style" (48). "Style," then, refers to that which is distinct about a work of art—that which transcends the implications of its specific codes and marks it out as different from other works.

Accent or signature or moiré pattern, style involves all actions or gestures about which there can be a choice—matters of content as well as of form. In picture books, then, style emerges from characteristic patterns of structure or attitude and also from choices of subject; in order to express Beatrix Potter's style a book must both use her characteristic medium and characteristic range of colors and also depict small animals involved in human activities.

Style asserts identity: an illustrator who depicts small animals in soft watercolors rather than weird creatures in exuberant cartoons reveals significant information about her personality. Indeed, the conventional assumption is that the styles of visual artists most importantly represent an assertion of individuality. André Malraux describes how artists struggle to escape stylistic conventions, so that developing a personal style of one's own is a triumph over the personal style of one's teachers or the public style of one's time: "whether an artist begins to paint, write, or compose early or late in life, and however effective his first works may be, always behind them lies the studio, the cathedral, the museum, the library or the concert hall" (315). Illustrators also must struggle to find their styles; the style of Maurice Sendak's early books is close to the commonplace conventions of most cartoons, and it seems that Mercer Mayer's career as a picture-book artist would have been different if Sendak had never invented his Wild Things. And we do, certainly, tend to admire Sendak more for his original work in *Where the Wild Things Are* than for his more derivative work in earlier books and more in general than we do the generally derivative work of Mayer.

But the value conventionally assigned to style as a triumphant expression of individuality may be misplaced and is particularly inappropriate in relation to picture books. A work of art that exclusively expressed the personality of its artist would surely be meaningless to anyone else—and if that work of art were a picture in a picture book, it would not be serving its function as part of a meaningful narrative.

In fact, as Malraux says, "styles are significations, they impose a meaning on visual experience" (324). However individual a style may be, then, it always expresses more than just individuality, and because styles do convey meanings, illustrators must make the choices that create style in picture books deliberately in the context of their conception of the narrative effect they intend, rather than unconsciously in the context of their experience or merely in terms of their personal preferences. Beatrix Potter's style may express her personality, but more significantly it also exactly communicates a specific interpretation of the stories she illustrates.

Furthermore, the very essence of the work of illustrators demands that they most often work to communicate the styles of people other than themselves—the distinct qualities of the authors of the texts they illustrate as expressed in those texts. Illustrators are subsidiary artists, their work a parasite on work that already exists. Even wordless picture books illustrate a story the artist conceived before he drew the pictures that imply it. To be sure, the most successful picture books are often those like Potter's, which are written and illustrated by the same person; but in "Picture Book Genesis," Maurice Sendak tells how he completed the text of *Outside Over There* before he even began work on the pictures: "my own texts have to be very good as far as I'm concerned before I illustrate them" (31).

The few picture-book texts written in response to preexisting pictures reinforce the extent to which illustration is an art that demands the prior existence of another art. Ivan Chermayeff's brightly colored images of geometric shapes in *Sun Moon Star* do not so much demand the words Kurt Vonnegut provided for them as much as it allows them; like Rorschach inkblots, indeed like most pictures without specific words attached to them or contexts to clarify them, they are open to many different interpretations, and inventive storytellers could find many different stories in them. That Vonnegut finds the story of the birth of Jesus in these abstract shapes is persuasive, but just as impressively ingenious is that it is a clever way of rendering actually meaningless images meaningful.

In its very nature as an attempt to evoke a preexisting meaning and style, illustration is not personal. Consequently, the struggles of picture-book artists to escape the styles of others and find a unique idiom are particularly complicated. While a picture-book artist may have a distinctive style, no good one has *only* that. In *The Openhearted Audience*, Maurice Sendak says, "Style, to me, is purely a means to an end, and the more styles you have the better. . . . Each book obviously demands an individual stylistic approach" (41).

But Sendak's different styles in different books can evoke different meanings for the paradoxical reason that style does imply the identity of the person or civilization that produced it or the ambience of the usual circumstances of its use; thus, a style used in different circumstances will evoke informative associations with its original circumstances. For this reason, the comic-strip-like quality of Sendak's pictures in *In the Night Kitchen* imply a focus on comic possibilities for anyone who knows comic strips; and his dreamily romantic pictures for *Mr. Rabbit and the Lovely Present* subvert the possibilities of comedy in an inherently comic situation.

Nevertheless, the particular style of an illustration does still transcend the other styles it evokes. Sendak's work in *In the Night Kitchen* is different enough from the comic strips it derives from to be able to express the unique tone of its story; his work in *Mr. Rabbit* combines dreamy romanticism with cartooning in a way that carefully specifies the meaning of this particular text as he understands it. The peculiarities of picture-book style are best explained by the paradoxical combination in good picture books of the narrative informativeness of preexisting styles with a more specific signature or accent—a moiré pattern exclusive to each book that combines aspects of format, color, shape, and content in a way that conveys specific information.

It might be argued that there is still a purely *personal* element in the styles of some picture-book artists—a triumphant expression of individuality; and admittedly, Sendak's pictures all have a recognizably Sendakian flavor no matter what material he illustrates or what other styles he borrows. But since this is a narrative art, the style of a picture-book illustration is less significantly personal than informative; and I would argue that even that which is quirky in Sendak—the large feet of all his children, the peculiar combination of seriousness and comedy in almost all his work—functions primarily as a source of information, a way of specifying the particular tone and flavor of stories as he wishes us to understand them.

Consequently, my focus in the discussion that follows is not on how personal picture-book style is; and because the moiré patterns of style result from combinations of other codes that I discuss throughout this book,

I do not even say much about that which is distinct in the styles of individual picture books. What I focus on here is the unique way picture-book artists express the styles of texts by using a repertoire of preexisting styles to convey information about the stories they illustrate.

■ ■ ■ ■

As a medium which requires collaboration between people with different skills rather than the unqualified expression of one person's unique vision, picture books are much like theater. There too the style of a specific production emerges from a number of different individual contributions, and there too style is less significantly an expression of individual personality than a source of meaning. Actors "illustrate" the characters they play on stage both by expressing specific lifestyles and by referring to specific preexisting styles of acting; but the illustrator's work is more specifically like the work of a stage designer—as Beni Montresor's *Cinderella* makes clear.

Based on Rossini's opera, this version of the story has an elaborate proscenium arch on its title page—a variation on the many doorways and windows that appear on the title pages of many picture books and that afford us symbolic entry into the different world of the story to follow. While the arch cannot actually be seen on the pages that follow, the characters always stand on what look like boards, whether the action takes place inside or out; and they take positions designed to make carefully organized stage pictures. In effect, Montresor has designed a production of the opera; he has provided costumes for the actors he has drawn and sets for them to stand in.

Only a little less obviously, however, Errol Le Cain and Marcia Brown have done something similar for their different versions of *Cinderella,* and so have Jack Kent and Nancy Ekholm Burkert in their different versions of *Snow White.* The texts demand that Sendak's Wild Things need some sort of forest and Van Allsburg's Abdul Gasazi some sort of garden; Sendak's Max and Van Allsburg's Alan could not appear before us naked without seriously changing the impact of their stories. It is not surprising that

Sendak has turned in recent years to designing sets for operas, for his career as a picture-book artist gave him the experience he needed.

Both designers and illustrators start with a text, a work of art created by somebody else. Both must assume that their purpose is to provide visual information that supports the verbal information of the text; and both provide settings and clothing that are not merely historically or sociologically accurate but that are also almost always symbolic of atmosphere or character. In order to make their work speak in this way, both stage designers and illustrators must especially make use of their knowledge of style—both of the conventions of period style and the stylistic conventions of visual imagery.

Thus, Marcia Brown and Le Cain both use the stylistic conventions of specific times and places in their versions of *Cinderella*, not only for the sake of historical accuracy—Le Cain's text even refers to the gophered cuffs he depicts—but also to evoke the moods or attitudes that we inevitably associate with specific periods. The narrow-waisted, puff-sleeved, wide-skirted dresses that both depict have conventional associations with the glamour and richness of "the past" as a whole—the world of "once upon a time." But more exactly, Brown's elegant costumes place the story squarely in Charles Perrault's elegant late-seventeenth-century court, while Le Cain's express the opulence and exuberance of the court of Elizabeth I of England. As in stage productions of Shakespeare set in differing times, these choices imply an interpretation of the material: our knowledge of the characteristics of the places and periods these styles evoke allows Brown to establish a delicately charming atmosphere, Le Cain a riper air of decadence.

In these two versions of *Cinderella*, furthermore, differences in period style are supported by differences in execution—differences that evoke the varying significations of different visual styles. Brown's muted but energetic cartoons communicate both the charm of the story and the humor of some of the characters; she makes their evil seem more silly than dangerous. Le Cain's richer and heavier pictures seem somber, even a little brooding. Their ornate borders, heavily patterned surfaces, and sharp lines evoke a decadent atmosphere which implies that this is a story about people besotted with adornment.

In *Looking at Picture Books*, Brian Alderson claims that Le Cain's pictures are "too splendid and too clever to suit Perrault's simple tale" (38), but an investigation of Perrault's text quickly reveals that both interpretations are possible. Perrault's tongue-in-cheek attitude makes it clear that he himself was sophisticated enough to find the story of Cinderella a little silly, but many popular versions of the story simply disregard Perrault's tone and focus on the cheerful optimism of the events themselves. Thus, while Le Cain and Brown have reconstructed the world implied by the text in different ways, both have responded to elements of the text that allow their reconstruction to be convincing. That reveals the extent to which the illustrations in picture books, like the settings and costumes of a play, are merely one solution to a problem—one out of many potentially convincing ways of filling a gap. Not all picture-book texts are as open to a variety of readings as is a fairy tale like "Cinderella," a story which can be told in a number of different ways even without illustrations, but since they are incomplete by definition, picture-book texts can always be realized and completed in different ways, and made into different stories, by different kinds of pictures.

While Brown's cartoons express a unique identity that makes them seem unlike other cartoons, Le Cain's pictures are more recognizably reminiscent of another particular style: the art nouveau illustrations of the late nineteenth century. His characters all look like slimmer or fatter versions of Oscar Wilde as drawn by Aubrey Beardsley. While Le Cain comes close to plagiarism here, his act is less a crime than it is evidence of his understanding of the art of illustration; because styles do act as signifiers that express the values of those who first produced them, an illustrator can use a particular preexisting style to evoke and thus illustrate a particular set of values. Consequently, mimicking the characteristics of the styles of other artists, even of other times or cultures, is a characteristic habit of picture-book artists. The most significant fact about the variety of styles Sendak uses is that none of them is exclusively his own; some evoke nineteenth-century engravings, some are strongly reminiscent of Mickey Mouse cartoons. Barbara Bader says that Sendak "is a frank and enthusiastic scavenger, a bent that Ardizzone identifies with the born illustrator" (*American Picturebooks* 498).

As scavenged and recycled by Le Cain, Beardsley's style is a convenient way of implying the values we associate with Beardsley and his milieu: decadence and opulence. Nevertheless, Le Cain evokes Beardsley in the un-Beardsley-like context of illustrations for a children's fairy tale produced at a different point in history, and the different context automatically changes the meaning of the style; Le Cain's pictures make reference to Beardsley's characteristics at one remove rather than merely being expressive of them. In fact, the scavenging of styles for narrative purposes is never an act of plagiarism, for their meanings are always changed by their new contexts; as Malraux says, "Valéry cannot be like Racine; he can but equal or echo him. There is no 'dubbing' a style" (410).

Because we see the various styles of art through the filter of history, we interpret them in terms of our own current understanding of their times and their makers. Malraux says, "Van Gogh utilized Japanese flat color; the Fauves utilized Byzantine or primitive forms; Picasso employs those of fetishes. But all alike are far from being dominated by these forms, and farther still from the world these forms meant to their inventors" (270). It is less our accurate perception of the original meanings of styles than our current understanding of them that gives them narrative value.

The art in picture books makes that abundantly clear. Barbara Bader quotes Blair Lent's comment on his pictures for *Tikki Tikki Tembo:* "Although the old man in the book has been suggested by Chinese water colors, I have in no way attempted to imitate Chinese painting. These illustrations are interpretations by a Westerner of a fabled land" (*American Picturebooks* 458). The painters of the signboards of English inns were not in the business of consciously evoking the simplicity of folk art; they were trying to show what mattered to them about the things they depicted as well as they could. But when Gail E. Haley borrows that signboard style for the pictures in *The Green Man*, she does so to convey that quality of folk-art simplicity in her story. Similarly, the Greeks probably developed their distinctive style of statuary and vase painting as their way of expressing their fascination with the ideal, particularly the idealized human form as they conceived it; but when Barbara Cooney borrows that style in her pictures for the Greek legend *Demeter and Persephone*, it speaks to us less directly of the ideal as such than it does of ancient Greece itself. It evokes that people different from ourselves and that time distant from our own rather than expressing their values; it expresses their values only in quotation marks—not the ideal as we might understand it ourselves but the Greek version of the ideal.

A particularly revealing example of how picture-book artists "quote" styles rather than merely duplicate them is Anno's use of some of the mannerisms of medieval art in his *Anno's Medieval World*. These pictures are only vaguely medieval in feeling; while they have the decorated borders of illuminations, and while some of the trees look like those in medieval tapestries, they are otherwise expressive of Anno's usual charming blend of the American primitive and the Japanese traditional, of Hokusai and Grandma Moses. But these pictures evoke the great gulf between ourselves and the people of the Middle Ages because Anno has drawn the marks of aged paper into his pictures: trompe d'oeil creases, yellowing, and water stains. For people who lived in the Middle Ages, medieval art was contemporary art; and illuminations certainly were not drawn on paper that looked hundreds of years old. Anno evokes the atmosphere he wants by creating the feeling of medieval illuminations as we see them today. As in all illustrations that evoke the styles of other times and other cultures, the meaning of those styles for us has more signifying potential than what they meant for those who first saw them, and for whom, presumably, they so expressed the values of their own culture that their stylistic characteristics were not remarkable or even noticeable.

Because styles speak so strongly of the values of those who originated them, illustrators who borrow them may even evoke ideas and attitudes of which they are not themselves consciously aware. While illustrating "Snow White," neither Nancy Ekholm Burkert nor Trina Schart Hyman could have been conscious of the interpretation of the differences between traditional Dutch and Italian painting that Svetlana Alpers proposed many years after their work was finished; yet Hyman's work, vaguely Italianate in style, certainly seems to express the values Alpers finds in the art of the Italian Renaissance, and Burkert's pictures, more than vaguely similar to paintings in the Dutch style, are likely to evoke from sensitive viewers the same interpretations as those Alpers gives to Dutch art. Presumably, Hyman and Burkert consciously or unconsciously knew and wished to express what these styles signified, even if they would not have put it in the terms that Alpers's insightful analysis provides.

Alpers speaks of "two differing modes of picturing the world: on the one hand the picture considered as an object in the world, a framed window to which we bring our eyes, on the other hand the picture taking the place of an eye within the frame and our location thus left undefined" (45). The first, Italian sort of picturing implies a clearly positioned viewer that makes the self and its perceptions central, and thus focuses attention on the significance of human emotions and actions, just as do Hyman's carefully framed, richly histrionic pictures. The second, Dutch sort of picturing causes us to interpret paintings primarily as objective information about "the world seen" rather than as interpretations of the world understood. Burkert's pictures share not only the cool objectivity but also many of the qualities that Alpers claims create it in Dutch art: the absence of a clearly defined viewpoint and of internal framing devices, great contrasts of scale (as in the picture of the large objects on the Queen's workbench in relation to the much smaller figure of the Queen in the background), and a firm sense of the pictures as surface.

As does Burkert in her *Snow White* and Le Cain in his *Cinderella*, illustrators of fairy tales frequently choose styles that evoke periods of history not particularly related to the tales but that they perceive to share the values they find in the tales. In her version of Andersen's "The Nightingale," Burkert carries the process one step further; in *Looking at Picture Books* Brian Alderson suggests that her pictures here combine *two* styles, chinoiserie and art nouveau, in order to express the curiously oversophisticated and European feeling of this pseudo-Chinese tale (39).

Ed Young's pictures for Jane Yolen's *The Girl Who Loved the Wind* represent an extension of this principle to the illustration of nontraditional material. Invented by a contemporary American, the story has no real connection with the Persian art Young implies in his pictures. Yolen places her story only vaguely "in a country far to the east" that could be anywhere from Scotland to Vietnam; and the only named character has a name that is culturally unspecific and sounds mysteriously eclectic: Danina. Furthermore, the words of the story by themselves sound more like the sort of literary fairy tale that is based on the European tales of the Grimms and Perrault than it does like stories based on Persian sources—more like Hans Christian Andersen than like Omar Khayyám or the *Arabian Nights*.

But Young's pictures so successfully evoke the mood of Persian miniatures that that mood permeates the story. It comes to seem Persian in feeling not just because we see that the characters wear Persian clothing and occupy Persian interiors but also because the style in which these objects are depicted is so characteristically neat and ornate at the same time, so richly detailed in such a carefully organized way. In itself, the story captures the matter-of-fact tonelessness common in European fairy tales, but it also manages to express a serious moral earnestness on a subject highly suited to the time of its publication: one's right to freedom from repression. Accompanied by Young's pictures, the same words come to express both the rigid repressiveness and the rich sensuality of the culture the pictures evoke—a culture unlike either our own or the one that produced European fairy tales. The pictures change the implications of the words, but, interestingly, they express through the visual conventions of another culture values surprisingly equivalent to the ones implied by the story.

Just as interestingly, they imply the conventions of another culture by means of techniques unknown to it but common in our own culture. In *The Story of Art,* E. H. Gombrich says that the figures in a Persian miniature so stand out that they seem to have been cut out of colored paper (104). Young's pictures actually contain elements of collage; they *are* cut out of colored paper.

A style borrowed from one particular painter can be as evocative of attitude as the borrowed style of a whole culture. In his various books of magical illusions, Anno calls upon the techniques of Escher; in *Stevie*, John Steptoe uses the bright colors and heavy black lines of Roualt to create a mood of brutally forceful emotions, and Sendak's reminiscences range from Dürer to the illustrator of the comic strip *Little Nemo*.

At first, the dark and vaguely pointillist shading in Arnold Lobel's pictures for Jack Prelutsky's *Circus* seems like a mere affectation. There is no reason why these poems about the energetic activity of circus acts should be accompanied by pictures whose shading and patterning evoke the calm translucency and lack of movement of a Seurat painting. But Seurat himself painted a picture called *The Circus;* and given the mathematical precision of his pointillist style and his concentration on pattern over content, Seurat's picture communicates the same surprising sense of stopped movement and calm repose that Lobel's illustrations imply. Seurat found a restful formal pattern amid the high energy of a circus; and in fact, Prelutsky's poems so emphasize pattern and regularity over subject that they have the same effect. These are actually poems about the interesting patterns of organized sounds, not about the circus at all. Lobel may or may not have deliberately imitated Seurat's style here, but he does reproduce it, and in duplicating the curious lack of energy in Seurat's style, Lobel matches the actual tone of Prelutsky's poems.

Perhaps more surprisingly, the basic styles of representation can suggest attitudes toward their subjects just as much as can national styles and individual styles. As I have suggested, so-called realistic art inevitably implies an attitude of scientific objectivity. We assume that folk art is pleasant and harmless and so respond to the theoretical danger of *Rosie's Walk* as pleasant and harmless. We assume that surrealism is imaginative and mysterious because the surrealist style has traditionally been used in relationship to mysterious, imaginative subjects, and the pictures in *The Garden of Abdul Gasazi* imply a mysterious, imaginary world where impossible things have a distressingly possible actuality.

We similarly assume that impressionism is intent on capturing the beauty of the ever-changing physical world. For the original impressionists, the impressionist style implied a concern with transient appearances that tends to downplay the narrative significance of pictures; Barbara Bader suggests that this style may be the least "illustrational" of all styles of art (*American Picturebooks* 499). The impressionists were interested in depicting the green light cast on a face by the momentary shade of a tree, not the personality of the person the green light fell on. Their pictures said merely, Here is the beautiful way things look, not The way things look here can give us insight into this person or this place.

But as Meyer Schapiro suggests in his discussion of style, "The observer is often indifferent to the original meanings of works" (87). A hundred years later, impressionism can evoke a mood that has narrative potential. Simply because we did learn from the impressionists to find beautiful the transient appearances they tried to capture, we find pictures that we recognize as impressionist evocative not just of natural beauty but also of the peaceful comfort we associate with our appreciation of such beauty. Furthermore, the once commonplace world of trees and of vibrant light that Renoir and Monet depicted is not so commonplace for most of us; pictures in the impressionist style of tree-filled glades and shining waters evoke for most of us less a sense of things as they are than a nostalgia for the way they once were. For us, the impressionist style represents a quieter, more peaceful time, and it is less shocking than restfully numbing.

Maurice Sendak's choice of the impressionist style for Charlotte Zolotow's *Mr. Rabbit and the Lovely Present* at first seems absurdly inappropriate, but he uses that sense of peaceful nostalgia to great advantage. Zolotow's story is a mechanical juggernaut that repeats and repeats itself—repeats itself so constantly and regularly that it comes to sound as if it is being told by a computer with a loose screw. Furthermore, the repetitions tend to imply a slightly nasty snippishness in both Mr. Rabbit and the girl he encounters that might cause us to like them less than we presumably should; she always seems to be accusing him of being a little stupid, and he always seems to be just a little sarcastic about how of course her mother only likes birds in trees. But the mood of Sendak's light-filled pictures implies a calm peace that takes over and controls any of the possibly negative implications of the text. The characters come to seem appropriately pleasant, relaxed people when seen under a calming impressionist light; the pictures make it clear that neither of them could possibly be sarcastic. Consequently, the repetitions of the story cease to be annoying and become calming themselves, like the constant humming of bees on a hot summer day. The style of these sophisticated pictures, which at first seem to have nothing to do with this simple story, actually creates a mood that controls and makes bearable the tone of the words.

The distance between the original meaning of a style and the meanings we now find in it are nowhere clearer than in the use of the styles of primitive art in picture books. Because we identify the primitive with the simple and the childlike, numerous picture books make use of the conventional visual images of the cultures we call primitive, usually to accompany stories or legends derived from those cultures. When we assume that both those stories and those visual conventions will automatically be understood by and appeal to children, we neglect the vast differences between their original meanings and the meanings we now attach to them.

Both the pictures by Leo and Diane Dillon for *Why Mosquitoes Buzz in People's Ears* and Gail E. Haley's pictures for *A Story, a Story* have some similarity with African artifacts, particularly textiles. Gerald McDermott's pictures for *Arrow to the Sun* evoke the art of the Pueblo Indians who first told the story. Douglas Tait's pictures for Christie Harris's *Once More upon a Totem* and Elizabeth Cleaver's pictures for *The Mountain Goats of Temlaham* use the imagery of Northwest Coast native art. But the African and North American cultures that engendered these stories not only interpreted their own visual imagery differently from the way we do; they also had different conceptions of the purpose of visual images. And that led them both to engender different sorts of images and to use them differently. An exploration of those differences reveals how these images are neither simple nor childlike.

Before we even consider visual imagery, however, we must acknowledge that none of these cultures even thought of stories as we do. For us, the stories of *Arrow to the Sun* or *A Story, a Story* are entertaining fiction, products of the imagination that delight us the way the fairy tales collected by the Brothers Grimm delight us. For the cultures that originated them, however, some of the "supernatural" characters in these stories were actual beings—as much a part of the real world as a tree or a person. These were not "stories," then, any more than the events of the Bible are stories for Christians; they were *true*. For that reason, furthermore, their truth was more significant than the excitement of their apparent fancifulness. We may enjoy the story of *Arrow to the Sun* because its events seem so unlike ordinary life; for the peoples who originally told stories of this sort, such events were factual explanations of why ordinary life is the way it is. According to Alfonzo Ortiz, the Pueblos tell many stories about how the Sun as father and fertilizing agent and Earth as mother first become separated and then come together (144). But we are likely to interpret the story McDermott tells of such events in terms of our own story ideas, imagining that the story is about something specific and exciting that happens to a special, exciting hero and ignoring the mythic implications.

The Pueblos could not understand stories as we do because we place stories in a special category; they are a form of art, and none of the "primitive" cultures had an idea of "art" similar to our own. In her book on Canadian native art, Nancy-Lou Patterson does not deny "that 'primitive' societies . . . recognize aesthetic value or the value of the 'well-made' object. They do. But the making of artifacts for this end alone is as rare in primitive Non-Western societies as it was in Medieval Western society" (4). The objects made by primitive artisans that we have come to consider "art" almost always originally had some religious or social purpose; they were beautiful only incidentally—or rather, conceptions of beauty were so tied up with conceptions of the supernatural in the unified world views of their creators that they could not actually be separated. So, for instance, Frank C. Hibben says that the paintings found on the walls of ancient Anasazi kivas, which McDermott evokes in *Arrow to the Sun*, had ceremonial rather than decorative or aesthetic significance (34). And the split-figure representations of various birds and animals found on the totem poles and ceremonial screens of Northwest Coast natives had the primary purpose of identifying the lineage of those who displayed them; according to Viola E. Garfield and Paul S. Wingert, "The art was not essentially a vehicle for the recording of events and people of everyday life" (59).

Because its functions were so clearly defined, furthermore, none of this art admitted much in the way of innovation. The artist's job was to recreate conventional images in a conventional manner, not to express himself or to reveal his personal vision. Like the vast majority of human beings throughout history, none of these peoples considered personal vision significant or even interesting. Nor did they consider what their eyes actually saw as all that important. When the Northwest Coast natives depicted animals in their characteristic split-figure representations, with eye-shapes in all the bone sockets and with figures built of many empty spaces outlined by heavy formlines, they were clearly not very interested in showing what the animal might look like if viewed from a fixed point of view from a certain distance.

In *Once More upon a Totem*, Christie Harris says that people who wish to retell the stories of the Northwest Coast natives "need illustrators as dedicated as themselves to depicting the culture authentically" (195). But the impossibility of being both authentic and being an illustrator intent on depicting a culture different from one's own becomes clear in Douglas Tait's pictures for the stories Harris retells. While Tait uses the imagery of Northwest Coast art, he manipulates it according to the conventions of European art. His traditional figures consist of white spaces and heavy formlines and have eyes in their sockets; but he overlaps these figures as they were never overlapped in the tradition, and he provides them with backgrounds, so that they become representational figures in scenes with the depth of perspective. As symbolic representations "come to life," at least as life is represented in traditional European representational art, they turn into flat-looking cartoons—stick figures masquerading as people or animals. They are neither traditionally European nor authentically expressive of the tradition they purport to represent.

In her book on Canadian children's literature, Sheila Egoff suggests that Elizabeth Cleaver's pictures for *The Mountain Goats of Temlaham*, a legend of the Tsimshian people who lived in the same Northwest Coast area, *are* authentic: "the figures of people, animals, and birds are stylized in the totemic silhouette shapes of Indian art; they are frozen and static in a ceremonial, ritualistic sense. This aura of Indian mystery is also present in the linocuts of totem poles and longhouses, which are sombre, black, and dramatic against the white pages" (*Republic of Childhood* 260). But while *The Mountain Goats of Temlaham* accurately depicts many objects of Tsimshian culture—totem poles, ceremonial screens, blankets, and wooden hats that can be traced to specific objects now housed in various Canadian museums—it does not do so in the conventionalized style of the Tsimshian. Paradoxically, Cleaver's pictures become inauthentic simply because they do accurately represent these objects. We view them as we would see them in museums or photographs and in the context of their use.

Meanwhile, Cleaver represents the people and animals in her story not by the conventional details that specify what an image represents in Tsimshian art but by what conventionally represents figures in European art: their outlines. There are no formlines, no excess eyes except those depicted on the objects the "real" people wear and carry. Perhaps most significantly, and unlike the carefully balanced and equally filled decorative spaces of the Tsimshian, Cleaver's figures have a ground and occupy space. She uses the conventions of European representational art to depict people using the objects of Tsimshian art and thus reveals to people like ourselves who are interested in how things look how a Tsimshian village might have looked; she views that village with the detachment of a travelogue.

Franz Boas compares the conventional imagery of most Northwest Coast art with the realism of a head made by Northwest Coast natives for use in a ceremony depicting decapitation where realism was required (68). That they could make such representations but usually chose not to suggests that their "primitivism" was a matter of choice, not a matter of being unsophisticated or "childlike," and that their art was symbolic in purpose rather than illustrative—that an image most significantly represented a conventional meaning, not an appearance.

But picture-book illustration is inevitably a representational art, almost single-mindedly concerned with the ways things look and the meanings that attach to such appearances. In this sense, even the most simple and childlike of picture books is anything but primitive. In most North American native cultures, appearances are often less revealing than deceiving; supernatural beings often masquerade as mere men, and weak-looking people may have great power. But in Cleaver's *The Mountain Goats of Temlaham*, as in most picture books, we see both how the characters look and where they act. These figures occupy space because we believe that people are significantly influenced and explained by the spaces they occupy, and in fact the story in this illustrated version comes to be *about* the Tsimshian and their culture rather than expressive of Tsimshianian values—a documentary rather than a reconstruction. If Cleaver's images are symbolic, it is a symbolism demanding a relationship between appearance and meaning. The Tsimshian who knew the conventional imagery representing a mountain goat could identify a symbolic mountain goat in a confusing field of disconnected patterns, but having been trained to identify objects by standing back and perceiving their outlines, we can recognize Cleaver's mountain goat because it does in fact have the outline of a mountain goat.

Nevertheless, Egoff's faith in the authenticity of Cleaver's pictures is not entirely misplaced; the qualities she finds in them may not be Tsimshian, but there is a sense in which they are primitive. In fact, they are the qualities that European artists, chafing at the restrictiveness of traditional representational art a hundred years ago, came to admire in African art: clarity of structure and simplicity of technique. While the Africans who made these objects probably did not consciously intend such qualities, we see what we have been trained to see by our own art in the art of other cultures, and there is no doubt that Europeans could use the categories of European art to find these qualities in African art. Cleaver's work is primitive in the way that a Matisse is primitive, not in the way Tsimshian art is primitive. In fact, her work is frequently reminiscent of Matisse. In her version of the Micmac legend *How Summer Came to Canada*, the picture of the Fairies of Light and Sunshine dancing around their queen, Summer, directly echoes Matisse's *The Dance;* the figures form the same grouping, and Summer's face could have been drawn by Matisse. Ironically, then,

Cleaver evokes the primitive for those of us familiar with European art by evoking a style of our own culture that itself tries to evoke a different kind of primitive art. For those of us unfamiliar with the conventions of an alien culture, the remaking of the imagery of that culture in terms we can understand is inevitably more meaningful than the original.

In *Arrow to the Sun*, McDermott also remakes traditional imagery, but in a different way. Many of the elements of his pictures are similar to the elements of Pueblo Kiva art. He uses a traditional framing line of the sort that Hibben describes: "consisting of rainbow bands of color, this framing line crossed the walls of the kiva in a repetitive, fret-like border. . . . The figures either stood on the framing line or were enclosed by it" (28). McDermott's figures also stand on the framing line or are enclosed by it. Furthermore, his rainbows are like the curved bands of different colors found in Kiva art, his lightning and his serpents zigzag like Kiva art lightning and serpents, and his cornstalks are stylized like Kiva cornstalks.

On the other hand, McDermott's rainbow follows the order of the spectrum; the Kiva rainbows do not. His lightning always zigzags; Kiva lightning sometimes zigzags and is sometimes symbolically represented by sticks laid on top of each other. His cornstalks contain corn, each kernel of which is a geometric square; perhaps surprisingly, the Kiva corn is more representational. So are the Kiva mountain lions; they usually have the outlines of mountain lions, but McDermott gives his the zigzag shapes so prevalent in the rest of his pictures.

The figures of people McDermott draws also do not look much like the figures found either in Kiva wall paintings or on pottery objects of the various tribes of Pueblo Indians. While these figures are sometimes stylized, they also often look more like the outlines of human beings than do McDermott's geometrically symmetrical figures. Frank C. Hibben says that many of the figures in the Kiva wall paintings found at Pottery Mound "were drawn with a close eye to detail, so as to create a realistic impression. Musculature in shoulders . . . and legs . . . is well defined and occasionally exaggerated" (78). McDermott's figures are often too rectangular to seem muscular. They are composed of either square shapes or round ones and are often seen head on, so that their bilateral symmetry is emphasized. The traditional Pueblo figures are often seen in outlines and often composed of mixtures of both rounds and squares. They seem much less rigid than McDermott's, more like cartoons than like the carefully ritualized symbols McDermott creates.

But McDermott's figures do have the feeling of Pueblo art—not because they look like Pueblo figures, but because they look like extensions of Pueblo decorative elements. They are built out of the same elements of repetition and jagged angularity, the same step-shapes and Z-shapes and heavy black fields that we find in ancient Anasazi and in modern Hopi and Navajo art.

Ironically, then, while McDermott's pictures evoke the mood of Pueblo art for us because they consistently use the elements of Pueblo art, McDermott uses those elements much more consistently than did the Kiva artists themselves. Elizabeth Cleaver communicates the characteristic images of one alien culture by adopting a Europeanized version of the style of the primitive; McDermott conveys the characteristic mood of a different alien culture by exaggerating and regularizing the ways in which that artistic style is unlike our own. Cleaver deprimitivizes the primitive; McDermott's pictures are more primitive than his sources. But both change the meaning of alien imagery from the religious and heraldic to the narrative, and both powerfully communicate a meaningful and appropriate atmosphere by exaggerating and distorting the characteristics of an alien style. Above all, neither is simple or childlike; both communicate by means of a sophisticated knowledge of at least two complex sets of conventions, our own and those of another society.

In art, exaggeration and distortion are the characteristics of a specific form: caricature or cartooning. In a very real sense, both Cleaver's pictures and McDermott's pictures are cartoons, exaggerated and distorted versions of art in another style, and thus they are much like most picture-book art, which, as a genre, shares much with cartooning. Like cartoonists, picture-book artists are less interested in imitating styles than in evoking them—less interested in accuracy than in expression. A consideration of cartooning reveals much about the style of picture books.

Cartooning does not accurately depict the way things look and rarely excites our sense of beauty, but it always conveys attitudes toward its subjects. What Stephanie Ross says of caricature is true of all cartooning; "caricatures are those representations of people which are judged to be less realistic and which demand we see reality (which includes people *and* pictures) in terms of them"—that is, in terms of the caricatures (291). In fact, cartooning is better than any other sort of art at easily conveying two important aspects of stories: how somebody feels and how somebody moves.

It can do that in part because it simplifies; what is left after a cartoonist eliminates all the lines he or she considers unessential are those few lines that best evoke the object in question. A part represents the whole; cartooning is figurative rather than literal, and as Ross says, "Caricature is to realistic art as metaphor is to literal expression. . . . Neither turns on resemblance or likeness" (293). In "Depiction Considered as a Representational System," John M. Kennedy also insists on the figurative nature of caricature: "shouting and other noisy events may be indicated by tell-tale concentric lines. Pain, luminosity and fizzing drinks are shown by graphic means that pertain to the object. . . . Metaphor romps through caricature" (137).

Caricatures and other cartoons convince us of their interpretations of reality because the lines left after the simplification represent movement rather than shape, the smile rather than the lips that made it. Because our faces and bodies are always in motion, even when we sleep, conventional portraiture is often unconvincing; capturing a likeness depends less on capturing the shapes of individual features than on capturing all of them at a moment when they are characteristically related to each other. As I suggested earlier, we often believe that photographs of ourselves do not look like us; the camera has not lied so much as captured an uncharacteristic moment, a moment in which our features express the wrong information. Cartooning simplifies to convey the *right* information; it is a static representation of the body in motion. It offers illustrators the chance to depict both the individuality of people and the movement of things.

MacCann and Richard, who believe that the pictures in picture books have a primarily aesthetic purpose and that we should appreciate them for their beauty rather than pay attention to how they help to tell stories, condemn cartooning: "the cartoon illustrations have quite a different function from illustrations discussed so far in this study; they have a narrative function more than a truly visual one. The pictures are used by the child as he would use a toy, as a substitution for something with which his imagination is engaged, but he is not stimulated, stirred, astonished and delighted in a purely visual way" (*The Child's First Books* 79). This rather summarily dismisses the meaningful, interpretive aspects of pictures. *All* pictures in picture books have narrative functions. Their various structures and colors, their various lines and shapes and media, and, above all, their style, all have the potential to express the meaning and mood of a story; if this means they are like toys, then all narrative is like toys. And because the communication of narrative information, and not aesthetic beauty for its own sake, is their purpose, because they are more significantly meaningful than either accurate or beautiful, the pictures in picture books always have much in common with cartoons. In an important sense, they almost always *are* cartoons.

One reason for that is purely practical. Color printing requires that the pages go through the press a number of times, one for each different color. One of the major problems is to avoid poor registration, that is, to make sure that the different colors come out in the appropriate places—that the reds in the finished picture are not slightly to the left or the right of the blues. One way to do that is for the artist to make the base of the pictures a clearly perceivable cartoon—a set of strong black lines that will allow printers to control the registrations of the various plates of different colors.

Nevertheless, effectiveness nicely confirms practical considerations; the strong lines that allow accurate registration also assist in the telling of stories, and not just because strong lines can so effectively communicate movement and feeling. As my earlier discussion of perception suggests, a figure must be noticeably separate from its ground before we can remark it as a distinct object; strong lines mark out specific objects in pictures and thus call special attention to them. Without such outlines—as, for instance, in much impressionist painting—the various objects depicted in a picture all seem to require the same amount of attention, and that makes it difficult for viewers to consider the relative significance of the different objects and thus from becoming conscious of the varying relationships upon which all narrative depends.

Many of the pictures in picture books—the sort that MacCann and Richard specifically attack—are literally cartoons. Many of the great picture books are illustrated by cartoons pure and simple: the ones by Dr. Seuss and William Steig and Peter Spier, Jean de Brunhoff's pictures of Babar, Robert Lawson's pictures for Munro Leaf's *The Story of Ferdinand*, and Sendak's pictures for *Where the Wild Things Are* and *In the Night Kitchen*. Dr. Seuss's depictions of rather grotesque creatures who never actually existed cannot be accurate and are certainly not beautiful; but they do express the exuberant, cheerful ebullience of the accomplished doggerel they accompany. Sendak's simple drawings for his *Nutshell Library* express a Seussian ebullience but with an essentially Sendakian warmth, and William Steig's *New Yorker* cartoons are only slightly more bleak and cynical than his often disturbingly emotional pictures in picture books. In *Art and Illusion*, Gombrich singles out the simple clarity of de Brunhoff's *Babar* books for praise and speaks of "the final distillation of expression in the simple works of illustrators or of the designers of children's books" (334). It is that expressiveness, that ability to show how somebody or something feels, that makes cartooning so appropriate a style for illustrators of narrative.

The cartoon element of some picture-book illustrations is less obvious, probably because they are not particularly funny. Nevertheless, Burkert's *Snow White* pictures, McDermott's for *Arrow to the Sun*, and Sendak's pictures for *Mr. Rabbit and the Lovely Present* are all cartoons in one important sense—they are all caricatures of style. All exaggerate and simplify the characteristic mannerisms of another time or culture in order to express something about the stories they illustrate. They can be expressive because they exaggerate, because they are cartoons.

The characters in these and in many other children's books tend to be more like cartoons than are the spaces they inhabit. The exaggerated over-stylization of McDermott's figures is a case in point; the Pueblo looks realistic in comparison with the boy's geometric regularity. Mr. Rabbit moves through an impressionist forest, but he is hardly an impressionist rabbit. When Burkert's Snow White stands amid the authentic and min-utely detailed equipment of the dwarfs' kitchen, her face is a few simple, characteristic lines; even the detailed and comparatively photographic por-trait of her on the dust jacket gives her one strong line for a chin instead of the shading and modeling we might have expected of portrait art; if one did not understand cartooning techniques one might wonder how she got the cut on her neck.

Similar differences between character and scenery occur in many other books, even in Le Cain's rich evocations of art nouveau in *Cinderella* and in Young's pseudo-Persianisms in *The Girl Who Loved the Wind*. I suspect that happens simply because illustrations *do* have a narrative purpose. They must show us not just beautiful patterns and evocative atmospheres but what people look like as stories happen to them; that is, as they move and talk and think and feel. So their faces and bodies usually have the simplicity, and consequently the expressiveness, of cartooning, a sim-plicity at variance from the frequent richness and detailed accuracy of their backgrounds, which give us a different sort of narrative information. When faces and bodies do have the same solidity and detail of shading and lines as their backgrounds, they may come to seem static and inexpressive; that may be yet another factor that contributes to the dreamlike stillness of Van Allsburg's *Garden of Abdul Gasazi*.

The extraordinary expressiveness of cartooning seems to make it a par-ticularly appropriate means of communicating narrative information. To suggest that all picture-book art is a sort of cartoon or caricature is no insult; it merely stresses the extent to which the purposes and pleasures of this art differ from those we assume of other kinds of visual art.

■ ■ ■ ■

CHAPTER FOUR

Code, Symbol, Gesture: The Contextual Meanings of Visual Objects

While overall qualities such as style convey much about mood and atmosphere, most of the narrative information that pictures provide comes from the specific objects depicted—not just what they are but also how they relate to each other. The objects themselves become meaningful through the contexts they evoke, which relate them to our general knowledge and experience of life, of literature, and of visual art.

Objects in pictures become meaningful in relation to the extent to which we notice them and single them out for special attention. The more we notice them, the more visual *weight* they have. For instance, research reveals that human beings generally tend to find images of human beings more interesting than anything else and to give them more attention (Goldsmith, *Research* 282); consequently, most of us will assume that the person is probably the focus of a picture showing a person and a dog on a staircase. Furthermore, greater interest leads to more accurate perception: because we look at human beings with greater attention, we are more capable of seeing subtler visual distinctions in depictions of human faces than of anything else, and as a result, faces almost automatically have great visual weight. Because he is human, therefore, and also because we can interpret his facial expression, Maurice Sendak's Max dominates the pictures throughout *Where the Wild Things Are*—including the one in which he chases a dog down a staircase. Although he is relatively tiny, Max seems to be in control of the large, hairy monsters that surround him in many of the pictures—and the information we read from his face confirms that. Yet if the pictures showed one small Wild Thing surrounded by much larger human beings, we would probably assume that the humans were in control of the situation and feel sorry for the monster.

While there are many means by which the objects in a picture can be given weight, contextual information is the most significant one. Only someone familiar with European fairy tales would give much weight to the tiny image of a little girl in a red hood surrounded by trees and hidden in the corner of one of the pictures in *Anno's Journey*. Meanwhile, members of some imaginary society in which the depiction of the color green is taboo might be too shocked to even notice the one red object surrounded by horrifyingly green ones.

As I said earlier in relation to baby books, even our basic ability to distinguish objects from their backgrounds depends to a great extent on contexts external to pictures. The most basic of these is our previous knowledge of such objects in the world outside of pictures; an infant might not see the image of an apple as significantly separate from its background and thus worthy of separate attention if the infant did not already think of apples as a separate category of real objects. The infant must not just know apples but also think of them as important; an infant who knew about apples but did not find them particularly interesting might well give more weight to the intricate pattern of red stripes that the apple depicted in *Baby's Things* interrupts.

Consequently, the ways in which we interpret the relative weight of objects in a picture depends not just on our knowing what an object represents but on how much we know or are willing to know about the object represented. We need specific knowledge about apples to obtain all the information the photograph in *Baby's Things* contains—for someone capable of reading the specific details of its color and shape, it will appear to be a Macintosh. Similarly, viewers who share Nancy Ekholm Burkert's knowledge of fifteenth-century clothing and artifacts, or who have even a potential interest in such information, will certainly pay more attention to her accurate renderings of these things in her pictures for *Snow White* than will those who are ignorant of such matters; they will give weight to details that would probably remain vague background for less-informed viewers.

But pictures exist within many other contexts besides our own subjective interest in them. In picture books, of course, the most important context provided for the pictures is the text; the extent to which the words influence our understanding of the pictures is the key to the uniqueness of picture books as a form of art, and it involves much more than just the giving of varying degrees of weight to specific visual details—as I will show later. But my catalog of contextual guides to the meanings of visual objects would not be complete without at least one example of how a text can provide immense visual weight for even an exceedingly tiny object.

No one looking at William Steig's *The Amazing Bone* for the first time would be likely to notice the bone of the title the first time it appears; but this small undistinguished object is indeed there, depicted by a few vague lines and surrounded by a voluptuously springlike forest, in a picture that appears before the bone is even mentioned in the text. While the picture on the next page is almost an exact duplicate of this one, most readers probably treat it differently; rather than simply responding to the overall atmosphere of the forest, they probably explore the picture carefully in order to find the bone, which has, now, been mentioned in the text. Our attention having been attracted to it by the text, we will give more weight to this small detail—just as Steig wanted us to, for his heroine, Pearl, has been claiming to "love everything" about the beautiful woods she sits in, but she has not even noticed the bone; and when she does, her new awareness of the significance of apparently insignificant objects—small details— teaches her to mistrust appearances. That becomes a major theme of the story that follows, so that the focus provided by the text causes a reader's experience of the pictures to parallel the experience of the story's heroine.

In a sense, however, the actual text in a picture book is merely the most local and literal of a vast series of unspoken words that the pictures imply and depend on; although pictures are not literally manifestations of language, they imply and are sustained by many different codes of signification—orderly structures of meaning that are actually unspoken texts.

Knowledge of those texts allows us to comprehend any given picture's participation in what theorists of literature call intertextuality—the interconnectedness of all acts of communication and their consequent dependence upon each other for their strategies of meaning making. It is their specific participation in this interconnectedness that most clearly gives objects in pictures their weight and, thus, their meaning.

For instance, even our familiarity with the usual patterns of rational thinking causes us to apply contexts that affect the meanings of visual objects; we interpret pictures as subsets of the general categories we can apply to them. If a picture of a person with a dog on a staircase were found in the biography of the person it depicts, we would assume that the description of human life is the operative general category and read the staircase as merely background and the dog as just a possession, an object of secondary interest to the person himself; but if the same picture were in a magazine advertisement for a housing development, the staircase would attract most attention as a subset of architecture; and in a book about dog breeding, the same picture would inevitably seem most significantly to depict the dog.

In these cases, it is merely the topics in relation to which a picture occurs that create a context for its objects. But our differing expectations about the functions and, consequently, the significant content of pictures found in differing places also act as a context for the ways in which we pay attention to them. We look at paintings in a gallery differently from the way we view pictures found in the instructions for assembling a piece of furniture. Such expectations come into play when we look differently at the same picture in a magazine advertisement and in a biography; we expect the pictures in advertisements to focus on objects we can buy, the ones in biographies to focus on the appearances of people. When a picture of a person and a dog on a staircase actually does appear in *Where the Wild Things Are*, we expect it to depict most significantly not an object but an action, since that is the most obvious purpose of pictures in the context of a text that tells a story; consequently, we do not so much try to determine the most significant object in the picture as we try to understand the relationships between the objects—what is the dog doing to the boy, or vice versa?

Such contextual assumptions about the functions of pictures are always of great significance in giving meaningful weight to objects in illustrations. If we looked at Burkert's first picture for *Snow White* removed from the context of the book it appears in, we might merely see a woman dressed in clothing of another time and judge the picture in terms of whether or not it gives us pleasure; not knowing who this woman is, not thinking of the picture as an illustration, we would give no specific weight to any of its details—other than the human face, for, given human nature, human faces always attract our attention. We might be equally uninterested in details if we did look at this picture as an illustration but with the conviction that illustrations merely confirm the information provided by the words they illustrate; we will see only Snow White's mother looking out a window, just as we expected. If we expect pictures that illustrate stories to reveal something of the characters they depict, however, we might look at the same picture with more attention to details of facial expression. And with a further, more sophisticated expectation that pictures use all aspects of visual imagery to reveal narrative information about the characters they depict, we might give weight not just to this woman's face but also to the boxlike gray shapes that surround her. We might interpret them as a commentary either on how she is imprisoned by her royal life or else on how she is separated from its bleakness by her beauty.

As Burkert does in providing details of her characters' clothing and furniture, illustrators often offer more information than appears to be minimally necessary for conveying the meaning of an accompanying text. But in fact this extra visual information is almost never superfluous. Even the fact of its existence implies an attitude, an interest in details both in and for themselves and for their signifying capability. Burkert's fastidious attention to the textures and intricacies of visual objects gives her *Snow White* illustrations a focus entirely different from that in the illustrations by Jack Kent, where a lack of such detailed information oppositely suggests that such specifics are not important—that the meaning of the story has little to do with its specific setting in the past.

Furthermore, apparently superfluous pictorial information can give specific objects a weight beyond what the text suggests, and illustrators can use that difference to great effect. That the boy who goes out to play in Ezra Jack Keats's *The Snowy Day* is black implies an attitude of tolerant unconcern for such matters in a text that never mentions the boy's color; the apparently superfluous information in the picture gives the text a meaning it would not have on its own. More subtly, the bakers of Sendak's *In the Night Kitchen* all look like Oliver Hardy, for no reason that the text explains. But viewers who recognize the resemblance will pay more attention to the bakers and respond with pleasure to the mere act of recognizing them. Having recognized them, furthermore, knowledgeable viewers can then understand that these theoretically menacing-looking bakers are actually funny and rather harmless—like the original Ollie. Someone who did not recognize the bakers would certainly see them differently—assuming, of course, that the supposedly forbidding image of Oliver Hardy is not inherently funny. We can understand pictures, as we can understand any aspect of human existence, only in terms of the depth and subtlety of the contexts we are able to apply to them. As Bryson says, "the sign exists only in its recognition, 'dialogically,' as interaction between the signifiers presented by the surface of the image or of the text, and the discourses already in circulation: those sequences or collocations of signifiers that cannot link together with discursive formation never arrive on the scene, never cross the threshold of recognition, never acquire intelligibility" (151). The more knowledge we have, the richer and more complex even very simple pictures come to be.

The extent to which our knowledge of matters exterior to pictures causes us to give varying degrees of weight to the same visual objects becomes particularly clear in a consideration of the symbolic values of visual objects. Symbolism is the habit of mind through which physical objects come to represent abstract ideas other than their actual selves. Because the objects are not actually the ideas they represent, symbols are always attached to specific traditions—they evoke specific unspoken texts. Thus, when the shadow of a cross appears on the head of the boy in Keeping's *Through the Window*, those familiar with Christian imagery will understand his situation differently from those who are not.

As many studies of visual iconography have shown, traditional visual art is replete with such symbols. So, perhaps surprisingly, are many picture books. Throughout her version of *Snow White*, for instance, Burkert includes depictions of objects that traditionally possess symbolic value and which can then communicate information about the characters to those who know the unspoken text these images imply. As Snow White lies suffocated by the Queen's laces, we see what may be a grim reaper in the background; as the Queen prepares her deadly apple, her workbench is littered with every conceivable symbol of evil and death: deadly nightshade; the tarot card for thirteen, which shows a human skeleton shooting a bow; a skull; a spider in a web; a bat flying against the full moon. Trina Schart Hyman's version is equally symbol-filled. We can tell the difference between Snow White's mother and the new Queen because the first keeps living holly in a vase, the second only dried flowers. Furthermore, the good woman sits by a fragile bird, while the bad one fondles a black cat. And the dangerous temptation of caring too much for one's appearance is revealed by the snakes carved in the frame of the mirror.

That there should be so much symbolism in these books is surprising only because their intended audience is young and presumably unsophisticated. All symbols are inherently arcane. Only those in the know can interpret them, and a cross is just two pieces of wood to those who are not familiar with its implications. Knowledge and experience can provide that familiarity. Children provided with both the general information that symbols exist and specific information about the meanings of particular visual symbols will have the tools to appreciate the otherwise hidden subtleties of many picture books—even many apparently simple ones, for as William Moebius says, "the frequent depiction in picturebooks of gates, doors, windows and stairs, of roads and waterways, and the changing representation of light, artificial and natural, to accord with different degrees of character understanding, are not accidental or fortuitous phenomena, but downright basic to the symbolic force of the story" (146). The most typical of picture books tells of a journey that almost inevitably symbolizes a growth in understanding; in *Where the Wild Things Are* and *Outside Over There*, in *Peter Rabbit* and *The Garden of Abdul Gasazi*, doors and windows are symbolic thresholds, and roads and streams are symbolic paths to wisdom.

But knowledge of traditional symbolism will not open up all the symbolic meanings of the objects in pictures. Some of it is merely private. As Sendak has explained to a number of interviewers, his books are filled with visual references to objects meaningful to himself in ways that others could not be expected to share. For instance, he says to Jonathan Cott, "rain has become one of the most potent images of my new book [*Outside Over There*]. . . . It's such an important ingredient in this new work, and I've never understood what it meant. There was a thing about me and rain when I was a child" (65–66). He also suggests that *Outside Over There* is based on a picture of a girl in a yellow slicker that he saw as a child; that the presence of eggshells in it relates to the Grimm brothers tale "The Goblins," in which a woman boils water in an eggshell to get rid of a changeling and have her own baby restored; that there may be five goblins as a reminiscence of the birth of the Dionne quintuplets; and so on. Theoretically, this sort of private symbolism can affect the meaning of a picture only for its artist; but the artist's willingness to explain it provides contexts others can share.

At another point, Sendak tells Cott, "I'm sure that the things I draw— little boys flying and falling—reveal something. In one sense it seems very obviously Freudian, as if coming out of my own analysis" (53). In theory, Freudian symbolism is both private and communicable—communicable because we all share it. In fact, Freudian interpretations of picture books are eminently possible—and not just because picture books depict so many circles and circular objects and enclosed spaces that might well represent wombs, and pointed sticks and spears and fences and such that might be considered phallic. Many good picture books manage to capture a childlike guilelessness—a sort of defenseless and vulnerable fantasizing that comes very close to dream. Books like those by Sendak and by Chris Van Allsburg are capable of powerfully affecting viewers far more than their simple stories suggest they ought to, and I can only conclude they do so because they speak symbolically to a level of human understanding that is below consciousness—or at least below adult consciousness, for parents often report that children respond with great intensity to books like *The Garden of Abdul Gasazi* and *Outside Over There* at very early ages. Before she was two, my own daughter insisted that we read her *Outside Over There* again and again. She did not express the same obvious delight in it that she took in other books and could not be persuaded to discuss the book or her response to it, but she always listened to the story with great attentiveness and solemnity and carried the book with her wherever she went for some weeks. While many adults find such books disturbingly difficult, they seem to speak to children directly, presumably to a part of them that is eventually numbed by experience of the world and that may exist only below consciousness in adults.

It is possible to present detailed and persuasive analyses of the imagery of such books in psychoanalytical terms; for instance, in Sendak's *In the Night Kitchen,* a naked Mickey "kneads and punches and pounds and pulls" some soft dough until he erects it into an airplane, flies up with it, and ends up covered by a milky substance. All this has clearly masturbatory connotations—if one wants to think of it in those terms.

But alternatively one may want to focus on Mickey's problems in understanding his engendering and emergence from his mother's body; both milk and children are produced by female bodies, and the bakers blindly confuse Mickey with milk and put him in a "Mickey" oven—thus reminding us of the colloquial phrase that identifies being pregnant as having something in the oven. Not surprisingly, then, Mickey falls into the night kitchen only after awaking and hearing suspiciously sexual noises from his parents' bedroom, and the kitchen itself contains cans of baby food whose labels have pictures of infants. Eventually, Mickey declares his separate selfhood by emerging from the oven, refusing to be milk, and getting milk "the Mickey way."

I might also apply a different system of meaning making to the objects these pictures depict. I might associate Mickey's oven with the alchemist's idea that the crucible symbolizes the body; his encasement in bread dough with the ideas of societal imprisonment found in the psychology of Wilhelm Reich; his flying with Icarus of Greek mythology, and therefore representative of human aspiration; his milk bottle with the biblical Tower of Babel, a symbol of human vanity; and the stars in the sky behind him as lights shining in the darkness, symbolic of the spirit. Having combined various symbolisms from various sources, I would arrive at the conclusion that this story tells how the heroic Mickey escapes the attempts of mere ordinary men to hold his spirit down to mundane reality and that he aspires to and achieves a more-than-human spirituality because he has faith in himself.

That such different interpretations of the same visual objects are possible makes all such interpretations interesting but suspect—ways in which we attempt to make rational for our conscious minds the aspects of pictures that may well mean most to our unconscious. Speaking of claims that the story of Cinderella "is simply a surface manifestation of an underlying story of 'psychosexual development,' or 'an allegory of Christian redemption,'" Wallace Martin says, "The objection of structuralist critics to these conclusions is not that they are wrong but simply that there is no way to determine whether or not they are right or wrong—which is to imply that they can be produced forever without hope of definitive result. A similar complaint can be made about other forms of archetypal, symbolic, and psychoanalytic interpretation" (91). In other words, all such readings depend for their acceptability on one's having faith in the truth of their assumptions. They might well, then, be legitimately discovered in the works of illustrators who have publicly professed faith in certain specific sets of assumptions and who therefore might have deliberately chosen to offer narrative information through a particular system of symbols. It seems logical, for instance, to accept the Reichian implications of the work of

William Steig, who has told interviewers of his deep interest in Reich. But attempts to find them elsewhere will be convincing only to those who share, or who can be persuaded to share, the faith.

But there are other meaningful aspects of pictures that we may not consciously be aware of and that do not demand our agreement to that sort of faith. Those who claim to know no grammar nevertheless often can speak grammatically: they have absorbed the patterns and relationships of the language they use without being conscious of them. Similar patterns and systems of relationship govern all aspects of human existence—how we interact with each other, how we lay out the rooms in our houses, how we choose the colors of our clothing. Often, we act according to the demands of such patterns of signification without even knowing that they exist or that they matter to us. Pictures communicate much to us because they offer visual expressions of such patterns and relationships, whether we are conscious of them or not. The contexts we apply to pictures inevitably outnumber the contexts we are aware of.

Some of the more obvious narrative information implied by the objects in pictures relates to our most basic cultural assumptions. Dark tends to represent evil, light goodness; many picture books show evil characters in the shadows and good ones in the sunlight—or sad protagonists in the dark and happy ones in the light. Consequently, it tends to be the evil or unhappy characters in illustrations who wear hats that put their faces in shadows, whereas good or happy people most often have bare heads. In *The Garden of Abdul Gasazi*, the faces of the evil Gasazi appears to be in shadow even when he stands outdoors in the sunlight, and young Alan's face goes through a series of transitions from sunlight to shadow and back, depending on his relative degree of fear or content—and also, whether or not he has his hat on.

Other cultural assumptions also affect our understanding of the spaces the characters occupy. Particularly since the eighteenth century, we have tended to associate peace and joy with green, natural landscapes, sterility with man-made structures that exclude the natural world. Consequently, relatively empty, boxlike spaces like Max's bedroom as we first see it in

Where the Wild Things Are imply bleakness to those of us ingrained by our culture's values—our ideas of what sorts of deprivation make a room a prison. On the other hand, lush greenery like the woods that enter Max's room and like the forest in *The Amazing Bone* or in Sendak's pictures for Charlotte Zolotow's *Mr. Rabbit and the Lovely Present* bring with them all the implications of idealized paradise that we identify with poets like Wordsworth and that we as a civilization have probably derived from knowledge of the Garden of Eden and the entire European pastoral tradition. Even people who are unfamiliar with that tradition often share the attitudes it implies toward dense greenery, and such people will be influenced unknowingly by the visual information that Trina Schart Hyman's Snow White lies in her coffin as the last leaves fall from a bare tree but that her prince appears when the same tree is lushly green.

Similarly, there are rarely ugly heroes or handsome villains in illustrated versions of fairy tales—assuming, of course, our usual societal values about what constitutes beauty and ugliness. Indeed, picture books help to teach us such values: when an illustration shows us that the princess whom the text calls beautiful is slender and blond and has a small nose and large eyes, we are being given information about the nature of beauty. Traditionally, the young characters in picture-book illustrations have almost always represented that sort of idea of beauty; many adults were so used to the conventionally blond, perfectly proportioned angels of previous picture books that, when Sendak began to produce his books in the fifties, they found his large-headed, fat-bellied, dark-haired gnomes repulsive. Yet Barbara Bader quotes Ursula Nordstrom's comment that, by the early seventies, all real children had come to look like Sendak's depictions of children (*American Picturebooks* 427).

Nevertheless, picture books still depend to an astonishing extent on clichés of physical appearance. We are so conditioned to associating physical ugliness with spiritual evil that most illustrated versions of *Snow White* conveniently ignore the essence of the plot of the tale—that the evil Queen is supposed to be the fairest in the land. In many picture books, she is dark-haired, heavy-browed, and rather wild-eyed and has the sort of hooked nose and tight smile that we traditionally associate with witches. Only Trina Schart Hyman has been astute enough to depict the Queen as exactly the kind of woman whose very being so depends on her physical appearance that she might kill to preserve her reputation. Hyman's queen is blond, shapely, and fairly young; she looks much like the typical Hollywood image of a sex goddess.

But that is merely to say that Hyman, too, depends on cultural assumptions about physical appearance to convey narrative information; the fact that her prince, rough-hewn, bearded, and muscular, exudes traditional machismo merely evokes a different conventional image from that expressed by Burkert's prince, who is blond, pale, and slender—the sort of adolescent weakling who might match the gentle innocence of her timid-looking Snow White. The physical appearances of Hyman's characters evoke the melodrama of conventional romance, the awakening of young girlhood by aggressive manliness. Burkert's fragile youths so seem to be passive victims of fate that the story is less a romance than a moral allegory about the getting of just deserts.

Furthermore, it is surely no accident that so many of the evil queens in other illustrated versions of *Snow White* have faces that might well represent conventional ideas of male handsomeness—square chins, strong noses, and so on; here cultural assumptions about relationships between gender and aggression come into play and allow us to understand the wickedness of the Queen, who confuses orderly categories even in the way she looks. And it is also no accident that Hyman highlights the ironies inherent in the story of Snow White when she depicts the Queen, determined to defeat the advances of age and preserve her reputation for a sort of beauty that we almost always equate with youth, setting out to deceive Snow White by transforming herself with makeup into a conventional image of crabbed age. Here, cultural assumptions about relationships between age and ugliness come into play and allow us to understand the irony.

An astonishing number of the characters depicted in picture books are not people at all, but animals—or rather, humans who look like animals, for Horton the elephant of *Horton Hatches the Egg* and Pearl the pig heroine of *The Amazing Bone* are certainly more human than animal in their interests and motivations. In many picture books, indeed, only the pictures inform us that the characters are animals: to give just one example, Russell Hoban's Frances is a badger only in Lillian Hoban's illustrations of her; in the text, she talks and acts like an ordinary human child.

There are historical reasons for this concentration on animals who act like humans, among them the fact that some of the first stories considered suitable for children were the fables of Aesop, in which supposedly characteristic animal attributes are identified with human behavior. These identifications still operate in picture books today. The image of a fox in *The Amazing Bone* immediately evokes the idea of craftiness, and in picture book after picture book, we are meant to understand immediately that the lions depicted are arrogant, the peacocks proud, the pigs gluttonous, the mice timid, the rats nasty. As Leonard Marcus says in "Picture Book Animals," "animals as images in our everyday thought and expression are among the most association-rich classes of symbols. Just under the surface of picture book fantasies, cultural meanings may well be at work" (128).

Some of these cultural meanings are not traditional ones. In *Sylvester and the Magic Pebble*, Steig created a notorious visual joke when he borrowed an insulting term from common slang and gave the policemen who search for the missing donkey Sylvester the bodies of pigs. Given current slang, we surely do not have long to wait until a picture book appears about the adventures of an unintelligent turkey.

In some of the most interesting picture books, illustrators use our assumptions about the attributes of animals to create subtly ambiguous situations. In *The Amazing Bone,* for instance, Steig's text focuses on the delicacy and gentleness of his heroine, Pearl, so that the fact that she looks like an ordinary gluttonous pig is amusingly ironic; and Dr. Seuss's pictures hilariously point out how ridiculous an elephant looks sitting on a nest in a tree—Horton's human kindness does not accord with his elephant bulk.

In an essay in *About Looking* about why we look at animals, John Berger claims that the tradition which identifies animal images with human attributes divests animals of their animal qualities; he believes that in the works of artists as diverse as Beatrix Potter and Walt Disney, animals have been "transformed into human puppets. . . . In such works the pettiness of current social practices is universalized by being projected on to the animal kingdom" (13). There appears to be some truth to this accusation. Certainly Disney's animal characters are so absorbed in one specific human culture that even their physical images speak loudly of that culture's values, and bear little resemblance to animals; his mice and deer and birds all clearly express conventional American gender attributes of the thirties and forties. Potter, too, takes her specific human culture for granted, so that part of the charm of her animals now is their immersion in the values of a polite English society of an earlier time.

But like many later picture-book artists, Potter does not in fact lose sight of the unhuman characteristics of the animals she depicts, and that gives her books a surprisingly subtle richness that contradicts Berger's analysis. There is a basic ambivalence about all creatures who look like animals but act like humans, and instead of ignoring this ambivalence, numerous picture books actually highlight it, so that the stories in which such characters appear often hinge on confusions between their animal and human qualities. One of Arnold Lobel's stories about Frog and Toad explores Toad's embarrassment about how silly he looks in his bathing suit; the joke of the story is that he looks silly in his bathing suit because he is, as the pictures reveal, a toad, an amphibian creature, wearing a human outfit over his natural swimming outfit. A darker version of a similar joke is behind Mary Rayner's *Mr. and Mrs. Pig's Evening Out,* in which the pictures reveal that the new babysitter named Mrs. Wolf is in fact a wolf, just as the Pig family are actually pigs; when the babysitter decides on the most tender of her young charges for a snack, she is merely giving in to the truth of her essential nature, a truth not very well hidden by her human clothing.

In many of her books but particularly in *Peter Rabbit,* Beatrix Potter makes a consideration of clothing her central thematic concern. Although the story seems to be a moral allegory about why human children should obey their parents, it is Peter's human clothing that hampers his attempts to escape after he acts like a rabbit and steals vegetables from a garden, and the book as a whole subtly explores the question of whether Peter should act on instinct, as an animal, or do as his mother wishes and act like a civilized human. The dilemma is not resolved, even despite the apparent message about obedience implied by the conclusion, in which the sisters who acted like good humans get food that Peter is too sick to eat; for Peter is rabbit enough that he seems unable to resist the rabbitlike actions that get him into trouble, and we are told he has already lost his human clothing earlier in the same fortnight. The pictures add to the ambiguity: Peter looks and acts brave in his human clothing at the point when he is acting on natural rabbit instincts and stealing vegetables, but when he loses his clothes and feels a human desire for the safety and civilized comforts of home, the pictures of him express the timidity of a natural rabbit.

The story of Peter Rabbit sums up a central dilemma of childhood—whether one should act naturally in accordance with one's basic animal instincts or whether one should do as one's parents wish and learn to act in obedience to their more civilized codes of behavior. The importance of that dilemma may explain why picture books about creatures who look and sometimes act like animals but who talk and sometimes act like humans continue to be so prominent: these curiously ambiguous creatures actually represent our understanding of childhood better than any less ambiguous creature might. It is not surprising that the animals most frequently depicted in picture books are rabbits, mice, and pigs; rabbits and mice are small enough to express the traumas of small children in a world of large adults, and pigs have a sometimes disturbingly childlike pink chubbiness.

Annie Pissard, complaining that "not many illustrators of children's books have succeeded in representing a child," claims that "the children's pictures that are alive borrow traits from animals. Max of Sendak's *Where the Wild Things Are* has a human face but the body of an animal thanks to the clever disguise of his wolf costume" (71). Indeed, Max's problem is that he has given in to wild animal instinct and must learn a way to enjoy being "human" again; he is a boy in a wolf suit, just as ambivalent as Peter Rabbit, an animal in a boy's suit. The depiction of animal children acting like humans or of human children acting like animals is so centrally characteristic of picture-book imagery that it tends to disappear; we so take it for granted that we do not often consider its significance. Perhaps that explains why Berger could ignore it. One has to conclude that such depictions express not just our relatively unimportant assumptions about the attributes of animals but also our deepest convictions about children and the nature of childhood. Furthermore, they mark a significant difference between the world depicted in picture books and the world we actually see with our eyes—a world in which animals do not dress and live like humans. This difference makes clear how much all of the imagery of illustration expresses internal values rather than just uninterpreted external appearances.

Cultural assumptions also allow us to derive information from the gestures and postures of characters, both animals and humans. We understand that upturned lips mean happiness, slumped heads sadness, and so on. In her richly melodramatic pictures for *Snow White,* Hyman's characters place their hands on their foreheads in despair and grow visibly tense with anguish; anyone who lives in a histrionic family or who has seen enough soap opera will understand such gestures.

Some aspects of our understanding of gestures relate specifically to our responses to pictures. For instance, we tend to assume that pictures show characters and scenes in a typical state unless something about them specifically suggests otherwise. It is this assumption that allows us to associate characters with their environments and to read the rooms and furnishings depicted in picture books for information about their owners' personalities. Similarly, when we see Beatrix Potter's Peter Rabbit with his back turned to his mother and separate from the cozy group created by his mother and sisters, we assume that his independence is not momentary but typical—as in fact it is. Meanwhile, the rather overpoweringly huge rabbit whom the little girl encounters in *Mr. Rabbit and the Lovely Present* is shown in many of the pictures seated in unthreatening poses of the sort that usually signal repose and vulnerability. We assume he is typically lazy or at least unenergetic—in either case, no obvious threat to the little girl. Also, we are not disturbed by his presence simply because picture books so frequently depict animals. In a painting hung in an art gallery, an animal leading a little girl down the garden path might have powerful sexual connotations; in a picture book it hardly attracts our notice.

Perhaps it should, however. Speaking of pictures in versions of "Little Red Riding Hood" that depict a different animal, the wolf, meeting a different little girl in a forest, Jack Zipes finds surprising meanings in gestures much like those of Sendak's characters: "the girl in the encounter with the wolf gazes but she really does not gaze, for she is the *image* of male desire. She is projected . . . by male illustrators as an object without a will of her own. The gaze of the wolf will consume her and is intended to dominate and eliminate her" (107). It might seem outrageous to read similar significations into Sendak's gentle depictions of a rabbit and a little girl, particularly when the story told by the text they accompany has none of the implications of temptation and rape that can so easily be ascribed to the events of "Little Red Riding Hood." But Zipes's descriptions of depictions of "Little Red Riding Hood" do sum up with astonishing accuracy the gazes of both the rabbit and the girl as depicted on the title page of *Mr. Rabbit;* he seems to be looking at her devilishly out of the corner of his eye, while she gazes out at the viewer with a smile that seems to accept and invite our perusal of her. Perhaps Sendak allowed such undercurrents to disturb the placid waters of this simple story as a joke, but there is no doubt that bodily and facial gestures throughout the book give it a surprisingly rich ambivalence.

In seeming to invite our gaze, moreover, Sendak's little girl merely expresses in an obvious fashion one of the least obvious but most compelling ways in which the objects in pictures have significance—they are available for our pleasure. As I said earlier, it is in the nature of pictures that they imply our freedom to enjoy what they depict. Consequently, we assume when we open a picture book that we are allowed to stare at Max's wildness in *Where the Wild Things Are* or Snow White's beauty in Burkert's

Snow White without the restrictions that apply to viewing people in real life—that we can guiltlessly peruse the image of Max surrounded by monsters without feeling the need to involve ourselves in the potentially dangerous situation, the image of Snow White without feeling any embarrassment or concern for how a living Snow White might feel about being regarded so remorselessly.

As the picture of Snow White suggests, this freedom to view can amount to a metaphoric rape. Without even being conscious of it, we view the image with a rudely voyeuristic frankness, a possessiveness we would surely find distasteful if applied to viewing the actual girl that the image represents. Yet our assumptions about our relationships with images do in fact often seem to transfer over into attitudes toward the objects the images depict. Julia Kristeva asserts that, in the Western tradition of realistic representation, an artist works at "reproducing bodies and spaces as graspable, masterable *objects,* within reach of his eye and hand" (246); consequently, the images of representational art inherently imply an interest in the power of possession, a desire to gain control through ownership: "Body-objects, passion for objects, painting divided into form-objects, painting-objects: the series remains open to centuries of object-oriented and figurable libido, delighting in images and capitalizing in artistic merchandise" (246).

Whether or not it is inevitable that our possessive attitude to images transfers to objects, it often does seem to happen. Earlier I suggested that the pleasure infants are meant to take in the images of objects depicted in babies' word books seems to suggest and support a pleasure in the objects themselves as things to enjoy—an early introduction to the sensual joys of material possessions. Our free enjoyment of Burkert's picture of Snow White also seems to imply a possessive right to enjoy actual physical beauty.

Furthermore, like the smiling image of the girl on the title page of *Mr. Rabbit,* pictures often imply through signifying gestures that the victims of our gaze are willing victims. We all know that we should "smile for the camera"—show a facial gesture that signifies pleasure to those who will eventually see the picture, and who will view it with a relentless attention that would cause us to stop smiling and feel abused if we experienced it in reality. The covers of many picture books ape such photographs and show their main character in a sort of introductory portrait that implies an acquiescence in the right of viewers to observe and to enjoy what they see. There are also, of course, many picture books whose covers show their protagonists simply getting on with the business at hand, whatever that business may be. But interestingly, those who smile and invite the gaze of viewers are most often female, the others usually male. When Ray Cruz depicts Judith Viorst's *Alexander, Who Used to Be Rich Last Sunday* on the cover, he shows him in a pose that sums up the book: grimacing over his empty pockets. But even though Ben Shecter's *Hester the Jester* is about a liberated girl who wants an unusual job for a female, she smiles out at us in a fashion-model pose on the cover as she shows off her jester's hat; the liberation here does not extend to the implications of the visual imagery. The cover of Shirley Hughes's *Lucy and Tom's Christmas* contains both these stereotyped gestures: Tom looks in his Christmas stocking while Lucy sits on the bed and smiles out at viewers.

The same distinction also occurs in the pictures inside picture books; for instance, on the last page of Susan Jeffers's *Hansel and Gretel,* Hansel is hugging his father, his back toward us, whereas Gretel, also hugging her father, has her smiling face turned toward viewers of the picture. In Terry Furchgott and Linda Dawson's *Phoebe and the Hot Water Bottles,* Phoebe directs a smile toward viewers not just on the cover but also on the title page and on the first page of text. She smiles out of the picture when she takes her hot-water bottles for a walk and again when she teaches them how to swim in a pool filled with other children of both genders, none of whom appear to be conscious that anyone might be looking at them. One might well assume that, since the pictures in picture books are illustrations, they will depict the characters performing the actions of the story. But Phoebe is like a bad actress in an amateur play, conscious of her audience and unable to stop flirting with it.

In allowing characters like Phoebe to smile at us, picture-book artists merely indulge in the conventional facial gestures which traditionally signal desirable femininity and delighted acquiescence in being viewed in visual imagery, and it is not just facial gestures that do that. In *Ways of Seeing*, John Berger suggests that the characteristic poses of nudes in paintings imply the superiority of the viewer, presumably male and dressed, and the subservience of the person they depict—inevitably female, totally exposed, and apparently delighted by her vulnerability in the face of superior power. While the naked human body is not as significant a subject of picture books as it is of conventional painting, its depiction in picture books deserves some discussion. Not only does it reveal much about the kinds of narrative information implied by the depiction of postures and gestures—above all, the communication of attitudes toward characters—but also it suggests how even cultural assumptions we believe we have outlived survive in surprising ways in literature and art.

As Berger defines it, nudity can be distinguished from mere nakedness by means of gestures. Naked people simply have their clothes off; nude people take on certain postures that suggest their availability, their passivity, their willingness to be vulnerable and to put themselves at the disposal of a superior viewer who has the right to survey them. They tend to be supine, relaxed, smiling sensuously with an implied consciousness of a viewer or with their eyes closed. If such poses and gestures represent nudity, then the unclothed children of picture books are, surprisingly often, nude—and not, surely, because artists wish to suggest the sexual availability of young children but more likely because the gestures of nudity are so conventional and so interiorized that artists use them unconsciously when they come to depict naked bodies.

For instance, Jessie Wilcox Smith's illustration for "He felt how comfortable it was to have nothing on him but himself" from *The Water Babies*, reprinted as plate 1 of David Larkin's *The Fantastic Kingdom*, shows a presumably male baby in a pose familiar to viewers of nude female pinups—supine, with his knee coyly lifted to mask his maleness. The gesture of this male baby makes him a typical nude.

There are few female nudes in picture books, simply because there are relatively few pictures of unclothed girls in picture books—it seems that we so associate feminine nakedness with sexual availability that artists tend to forbid its appearance in the theoretically sexless atmosphere of children's books. Nevertheless, the rare female nudes in picture books tend to sit in bathtubs or hold towels around themselves or hide behind trees; they almost always take on the traditional gestures of nudity, and they almost always smile out at viewers. For instance, Carl Larson's "Bedtime Scene," reproduced in William Feaver's *When We Were Young*, shows a young girl in nothing but black stockings, facing the viewer; she stands and looks at us without modesty but clearly not without consciousness of her full frontal nudity. Her gesture implies that she knows she is being looked at and clearly assumes that her viewers have the right to look at her, and her pout makes it clear that she enjoys being looked at.

Even rarer than female nudes in picture books are naked females. The only two I have encountered are both infants, and thus, presumably, representations of a safely asexual innocence, and both were drawn by Maurice Sendak. When Sendak depicts the Princess of MacDonald's *The Light Princess* as a naked baby with exposed genitalia, her facial gesture is unlike those we associate with nudity; she is neither smiling nor pouting nor in repose with her eyes closed; she looks a little drunk. Of all the naked goblin babies depicted in *Outside Over There*, only one reveals her genitalia and only once, and that happens when she is too busy dancing to Ida's wonderhorn to look very enticingly available. The other naked babies in *Outside Over There* do often take the poses of nudes, but their doing so establishes an ironic tension both with the fact that they are dangerous goblins and the fact that they are "just babies."

There are more naked boys than girls in picture books, probably because we unconsciously accept that boys can have their clothes off without implying their availability for our pleasure. In fact, pictures of naked boys almost all show them clearly doing something—moving, active, *not* posing. One of Caldecott's illustrations for "The Farmer's Boy" shows a naked boy cavorting on his nurse's knee while a nude girl with the pouty mouth of many pinups sits quietly in the tub, her voluptuous back awaiting our inspection. When male frontal nudity occurs—more often than does female frontal nudity—the boys in question are too involved in intense activity to be passive pinups. The action lines at the elbows and knees of Carlos Friere's depiction of the unabashedly naked Simon in Daniel Wood's *No Clothes* make it clear he is in motion even though he directly faces viewers.

Sendak's Mickey of *In the Night Kitchen*, probably the most famous naked picture-book child, has his hands aggressively on his hips as he howls "COCK a DOODLE DOO!" He also is too active to be nude. Yet some of the pictures of the naked Mickey in *In the Night Kitchen* are more pinuplike. They give little sense of movement and have little energy. They show Mickey floating through the air, asleep, unconscious that anybody might be looking at him; we can, in fact, observe him freely. The same is true of Sendak's pictures of David in Jarrell's *Fly by Night;* these pictures of a naked boy asleep are close to traditional cheesecake. In fact, the naked male body in repose and unconscious of a viewer seems to be a favorite subject of Sendak's: not just Mickey and David but also Mr. Rabbit, splendidly nude in *Mr. Rabbit and the Lovely Present* as he lies on a green hillside, his eyes closed. Mr. Rabbit is one of the few animals in picture books who can talk to humans but who does not wear clothing, and this scene of him as a nude centerfold sitting beside a clothed girl is almost a reversal of *Dejeuner sur l'herbe,* Manet's painting of a naked woman at a picnic with clothed men. In fact, this sensuous rabbit assumes pinup poses throughout the book, and that helps create the fascinating tension that Sendak brings to Charlotte Zolotow's minimal story.

It is not only nudes whose conventional gestures convey meaning to viewers, but the gestures of nudity do differ from the other meaningful gestures of picture books simply because they exist only within the realm of visual depiction. A hand on the forehead symbolizes the same thing in reality as it does in a picture, but a supine body and a smiling face do not necessarily mean in life what they have come to mean in art. Finally, then, what is most revealing about the depiction of naked children in picture books is the extent to which they evoke the characteristic gestures not of life but of earlier art. In doing so, they assert the intertextuality even of nontexts—of the conventions of visual imagery—and make clear the extent to which even the most apparently simple of picture books exists in the context of the entire history of visual depiction.

Burdened by the weight of that history, pictures not only communicate richly, but also sometimes send messages that their artist may not have consciously intended and that we may not wish ourselves or our children to receive. Knowing how the illustrations in picture books can evoke such messages—not just dehumanizing assumptions about sexuality and gender relationships like those implied by depictions of nudes but also shallow ideas of beauty and masculinity and the desirability of attractive objects that are implied by many other pictures—can only serve the liberating purpose of diluting their effectiveness.

■ ■ ■ ■

CHAPTER FIVE

———

Visual Weight and Directed Tension: The Relationships
of Visual Objects to Each Other

While much of the meaning of visual objects is imposed from without, in terms of the contexts that give them significance, much of it comes from within a picture itself, in terms both of the visual qualities of individual objects and of the varying weights of different objects in relation to each other. In *Art and Visual Perception*, Rudolf Arnheim says, *"Visual experi-ence is dynamic. . . .* What a person or animal perceives is not only an arrangement of objects, of colors and shapes, of movements and sizes. It is, perhaps first of all, an interplay of directed tensions. These tensions are not something the observer adds, for reasons of his own, to static images. Rather, these tensions are as inherent in any precept as size, shape, loca-tion, or color" (11). That last statement is suspect: both the theories of semioticians and the findings of cognitive psychologists suggest that there is no reason to believe—and for that matter no logical need for wanting to believe—that our perception of "directed tension" is not merely another code of signification that we learn as we learn all such codes, through specific teaching or just from experience. What is certain, however, is that pictures do indeed express such directed tensions and that illustrators make use of them to convey information about characters and situations.

Discussions of the dynamics of visual art usually concentrate on the ways in which the qualities and relationships of various elements of paint-ings and drawings create balanced compositions and thus provide the aes-thetic satisfaction of wholeness. But the individual pictures in a picture book do not in their nature possess that kind of wholeness, for each picture is conceived as only part of a larger whole that also includes a text and other pictures; and as William Moebius rightly asserts, "Unlike the framed settings of a Biblical text of a Raphael or Rembrandt, the pictures in a picturebook cannot hang by themselves" (141). Indeed, because no single picture in a picture book is complete, most such pictures actually violate the usual principles of unified visual composition. Their purpose is to show just one part of a continuing action, a moment of tension and imbalance; and pictures can most successfully convey such information by diverging from conventionally balanced visual patterns in such a way that they attract attention to their most obviously imbalanced parts. Since stories characteristically achieve a state of balance only at the end, and only by moving beyond the disruptions and tensions that constitute their plots, it is often only the last picture in a picture book, the one depicting the resolution, that satisfies traditional ideas of balanced composition.

Lyn Ellen Lacy unintentionally reveals the divergence of picture-book art from conventional ideas of aesthetic wholeness in her discussion of a picture in McCloskey's *Make Way for Ducklings*, in which she tries to show that a depiction of boisterous activity achieves visual balance. Her analysis actually shows that the picture in question deliberately defies conventional principles of balance in order to focus attention on the unsettled energy of the activity, so that finally she has to insist, unconvincingly, "And balance there most certainly is in this picture because, despite the flutter of activity (imagine the noise!) everyone is momentarily frozen in place for this most charming family portrait framed within an oval" (44). Freezing does not automatically create balance, especially when what is frozen is itself so excitingly imbalanced. The discussion that follows focuses on carefully conceived violations of pictorial unity rather than on successful examples of it.

■ ■ ■ ■

Perhaps because we associate certain emotions with certain shapes, the shapes of visual objects as they relate to their background and to other objects can create specific tensions and thus imply meaning in themselves.

We tend to assume that squares are rigid and that rounded shapes are accommodating; Burton probably makes her supposedly square little house surprisingly round for this reason. On the other hand, Burkert places Snow White's mother inside a series of constricting rectangular boxes, and Sendak places Max inside a bedroom of harsh rectangular shapes. As Peter Rabbit crawls under a fence, Potter shows his rounded body partially hidden by the severe rectangular shape of a picket, in the process of escaping constriction and indulging in freedom.

More surprisingly, however, Sendak's Wild Things are comfortably round; the only sharp, jagged things about them, their claws and their horns, are actually rounded crescent shapes, and when Max tells them to "be still," the shape of their horns merely echoes the mysterious crescent moon in the background. But Max himself is a jagged object. His toes, his fingers, his ears, his whiskers, all form points; his boat, its flag, and its sail all bristle with points. This paradoxical relationship between bristly child and accommodatingly curvaceous monsters helps us understand that the child has little to fear from the monsters.

As the relationship between the rounded shapes of the Wild Things and the bristly lines of Max suggests, spaces—lines joined together to enclose an area—affect us differently from the way disconnected lines do. Joined to form spaces, lines develop solidity and seem stable; lines that do not connect enclose no space, create no solidity, and seem to have more energy— to be disordered. Thus, Dr. Seuss's Horton in *Horton Hatches the Egg* is a solid citizen, always firmly enclosed in a black outline; but the flighty Mayzie has her shape defined inconclusively by a series of disconnected lines, which imply both feathers and emotional instability. In *Outside Over There*, Sendak consistently uses the jumbled lines formed by folds of cloth to suggest disorder. Both Mama in despair and the horrifying goblins are enmeshed in broken lines of folded cloth; and Mama's yellow rain cloak becomes progressively more line-filled as Ida's experiences while wearing it grow more intense. Meanwhile, the backgrounds are more or less devoid of lines; they tend to a Seurat-like pointillist vagueness that focuses our attention on the more intense activity of the lined areas within them.

As well as drawing attention to themselves, the shapes and textures of objects can make us pay attention to other objects in a picture. For instance, an object that comes to a point tends to focus our attention less on itself than on what it points toward, no matter how big it is or what surrounds it. Throughout McDermott's *Arrow to the Sun*, the pistol-like hand of the boy points toward the focus of the action. Leo and Diane Dillon use this aspect of pictorial dynamics to particular advantage in *Why Mosquitoes Buzz in People's Ears*. The pictures in this book have a flat, two-dimensional effect; they are filled with confusingly juxtaposed areas of pattern and color that make them hard to interpret. But in each picture, the Dillons provide a small red bird with a pointed beak. It plays no part in the story, but its beak always points toward the significant object the story is at that moment focused on; at one point, for instance, the bird's beak points at the mosquito, which has carefully hidden itself behind a leaf.

That is merely one way in which objects may be related to each other. As our original lack of attention to Steig's little bone suggests, the sizes of various objects as they appear on the two-dimensional surface of a picture influence the way we understand their relationships in the three-dimensional space they signify. Larger figures tend to overpower those that occupy less space—even though they might represent smaller objects. For instance, we pay as much attention to the objects on the Queen's worktable in Burkert's *Snow White* as we do the Queen herself in the background, simply because their images are literally as large as hers is.

That tendency of large figures to dominate is useful in story situations involving small creatures threatened by large ones—as, for instance, when Beatrix Potter's Peter Rabbit is threatened by Mr. McGregor. The first time we and Peter see McGregor, he is a large brown bulk that dominates both the tiny cucumbers he is setting out and Peter.

Since, like *Peter Rabbit*, many picture books are about small animals who win out over larger creatures, the greater weight of bulkier objects can be problematic for illustrators. In good pictures we *do* focus our attention on smaller figures that occupy less space—as we do on Max instead of the Wild Things and on the bone instead of the bulkier trees around it. As these two examples suggest, in the hands of a good illustrator, other aspects of visual imagery can make up for the effects of size—our special interest in humans, the focusing power of words, or the fact that a solitary object usually has more weight than a number of similar ones. The figure of Max attracts special attention not just because he has a human face but because there is only one of him and many Wild Things, and the weight of our attention on him contrasts with and thus emphasizes his relative lack of size in relation to the many bulky creatures. Another way to solve the problem is to make the figure of a smaller object as large as the figure of a large one; in two later pictures in *Peter Rabbit,* which depict the tiny Peter escaping from the large Mr. McGregor, Potter uses the effects of perspective to make Mr. McGregor in the background smaller than Peter in the foreground.

The size of objects in relation to their background may imply relationships between characters and environment. In Burkert's picture of Snow White in the forest, the figure of Snow White occupies only the middle of the bottom half of the left side of a picture that covers both halves of the spread; she is clearly threatened by the dangerous wilds that surround and diminish her. But depicted inside the security of the dwarfs' house, she is not only taller than the dwarfs themselves but about twice the size she was in the forest; her image fills most of the page from top to bottom. Similarly, the ark Peter Spier gives Noah in his *Noah's Ark* fills most of two pages as it is being built, which implies the immensity of Noah's task in building it. But as the flood grows, the image of the ark gets smaller and smaller, until one two-page spread is occupied entirely by sky and rain and water, with the ark only a small black silhouette on the horizon.

The extent to which space relationships can be symbolic is particularly clear in *Where the Wild Things Are.* Whereas the first picture of Max's bedroom after he has been sent there by his furious mother conveys isolation, the last picture of the same room makes it seem cozy. Part of the difference is caused by differences in composition: in the first picture Max is front and center, isolated from and intruding upon the balance created by the lines of the furnishings, and in the second he is to one side and more directly related to the bed beside him. Another difference results from a change in color tone, so that the second picture seems warmer than the first. But it is particularly revealing that the furniture in the room is significantly larger in this picture—and not just because the picture itself is in a larger scale. In fact, the furniture actually fills up more of the space; the gap between the table and the bed is not larger, as we might expect if we consider the larger scale of the picture but, in fact, a lot smaller. Sendak was obviously more concerned with conveying a mood in these pictures than with representational consistency.

As the effect of Max's varied position in these two pictures suggests, the location of objects in relation to other objects can affect the way we understand them. Discussions of composition in art center frequently on the shapes created by the layout of figures in a picture—the various triangles and squares that form the composition. Since such configurations create balance and order, the disruption of them can imply imbalance and disorder; and both balance and disruption can contribute to the meaning of pictures. For instance, three figures related so that they form a triangle with a stable base create less tension than three figures that form a triangle that stands on a point. Thus, the final picture of Max in his bedroom, with Max at the bottom right point of a triangle and the moon and the corner of his room at the other points, communicates stability and implies the release of tension. But in the earlier picture of Max in his bedroom, Max not only disrupts the basic triangle of the composition but is himself the bottom point of another triangle, the upper points of which are the window and the bed; the tension created by this discordant and top-heavy arrangement helps to define Max's feelings. As in these two pictures, balanced geometrical composition is found more often in the last picture of a picture book, in which resolution has been achieved, than in the earlier depictions of moments of tension.

Max stands out from his bleak room when the composition is imbalanced, and he is less isolated when he appears against his bed; objects in a field of other objects stand out less than isolated ones. Peter Spier's pictures for *Noah's Ark* are crowded with groups of animals; it is clear that none is more important than any of the others, and our inability to find a focus expresses the general chaos of life on the ark. But when Noah sends out the dove, we see it alone against an empty background—it becomes the focus both of the story and of our attention.

The dove is a figure, the sky its ground. As I have said, the ability to distinguish between figure and ground is basic to perception: to say, "I see a dove" is to say, "I can separate this one part of the field of my vision from the rest." So basic is the performance of such separations that we tend to assume that the figures in pictures have grounds even if none is depicted. For instance, Beatrix Potter's picture of Peter Rabbit hiding in a watering can shows only Peter and the can—no sky, no ground, no shed; we assume these backgrounds without even thinking about it. Furthermore, if pressed, we would probably say that the white area below the watering can represents ground, and that above it sky. Our basic assumption that visual gaps should be filled with normative conditions unless we have evidence otherwise would cause us to perceive one white space as two quite different areas.

When Pearl is captured in *The Amazing Bone*, we see Pearl and the three robbers, and then Pearl and the fox, against an empty white background. We can assume that the lush and pleasing spring forest of previous pictures is still there, but its actual absence seriously changes the mood. Most picture-book artists use the occasional absence of background for a much simpler reason: it focuses our attention on the action of the figures rather than on their relationship to their setting. Thus, we see Peter Rabbit within a background when his feelings about the garden are a central concern and against white space when he is running or hiding or otherwise enmeshed in intense emotion. In *Why Mosquitoes Buzz in People's Ears*, the Dillons have a more practical use for the ability of figures to imply grounds. They use the same edge to represent a figure for part of the picture and to represent the ground for another part. When the crow describes its actions, the animals appear against a black background; but in the depiction of what the crow is saying in the corner of the same picture, this black ground becomes the figures of trees against a blue ground. This discontinuity between two parts of the same picture clearly marks off the depiction of the storytelling from the depiction of the story being told; it provides basic information we need to understand a complex picture.

The crowded pages of Richard Scarry's books often show numerous animals involved in many different activities against a white background; and the meaning of the background adjusts in terms of the figures in front of it. The figures both float in space, quite cut off from each other, and also are related to each other by their shared background of white. So these pictures paradoxically both isolate every figure they depict and make it merely one of numerous equal objects in a group. That echoes Scarry's usual purpose: to show the various individual objects or activities that make up a certain category. It also helps explain why his pictures tend to annoy adults, who are likely to find the discontinuities of the implied background disturbing. Children, less experienced in reading implied ground from the figures they view, may merely see Scarry's figures as quite separate from each other.

The relative isolation of objects from backgrounds is often meaningful. Peter Rabbit against a white ground as his mother gives her instructions stands out more than do his three sisters in the same picture, who appear against the background either of their mother or of each other; in the next picture they blur into a hazy background, while Peter is separated from the ground by heavy black lines. Both these pictures make clear which of these rabbits we are supposed to be interested in. According to Graham Collier, "the heavier the weight of a line, the more frontal dominance it and the surrounding space will have" (34). As we see Mama in her arbor near the beginning of *Outside Over There*, Ida, her mother, and the goblins are outlined in black and stand out; but the dog at the center of the picture, where we might expect to focus, is not outlined in black and becomes merely part of the background.

In *The Little House*, Virginia Lee Burton depicts the transformations the story is about by the extent to which each of the pictures isolates the little house from its backgrounds. In the first picture, the house stands proudly alone against a white background. Then the white space around the house gets smaller, as its harmonious relationship to the natural cycle is depicted by the way seasonal changes affect the fields around it. Nevertheless, the white space is always there, making the house stand out as an object of special interest. But as the city grows around the house, the white area grows narrower still, and as the house becomes closer in color to the buildings surrounding it, it ceases to occupy its own space altogether and becomes part of an undifferentiated mass. Then, in the picture that shows how the great-great-granddaughter of the original owner saw the house, the white space between the house and the ugly city surrounding it has grown again; the house is set apart, once more an object of special attention.

The house in *The Little House* remains our focus throughout the book, even though it remains boringly more or less the same while the backgrounds change in an interesting fashion; in a diametrically opposite case, the various pieces of folded cloth are the focus of the pictures of Ida's bedroom in *Outside Over There* not just because they are more line-filled than the vaguer backgrounds. In both cases, the object at the center of the picture is the most important. By visual convention, the center of a picture is also the center of our visual attention; the location of an object will attract our attention to a greater or lesser degree to the extent that it is closer or farther away from the center of a picture.

In picture books, artists vary the location of their characters in order to inform us about whether we should be more interested in the action or in a character's response to it. In *Where the Wild Things Are*, Max is at the edge of the picture as he sees the Wild Things for the first time, for at this point, what Max sees is what matters. But once we are familiar with the creatures, Max's own action becomes more significant, and he moves to the center as he joins their wild rumpus. Peter Rabbit is at the center of almost every one of Beatrix Potter's pictures of him; the focus is less on what Peter encounters than on how he reacts to it. But he moves out of the center when he sees a cat and each time he sees Mr. McGregor; as the text refers to what he sees rather than to what he feels, we see it with him.

A more unusual use of central focus is the picture in *Wild Things* in which Max makes mischief by building a tent. The tent is on the left of the picture, Max on the right; the center is empty. Max faces out of the picture to the right, and his teddy bear faces out of the picture to the left; the focus is away from the center rather than toward it, and the mood is as unsettling as Max's tantrum.

Obviously, then, the relationship of an object to the top and bottom and to the left and right edges of a picture is also significant. Given our experience of gravity in the actual world, we seem to assume that an object of the same size has more weight in the top half of a picture than in the bottom half; it is for that reason that the two parts of a number three or eight seem equal only if the top part is actually smaller. Spier shows Noah's ark, suspended on a rock as the waters recede, in the top half of the picture, and that defiance of gravity by such a large object makes it seem all the more precarious. But as Noah releases the dove, the ark is in the lower half of the picture; its relative inertia makes the bird's release all the more unconstraining.

Since gravity pulls objects down in pictures as in life, the top halves of pictures tend to be less occupied than the bottom halves; and as a result, objects that do appear in the top half are surprising enough that they tend to attract us more. The Queen in Burkert's *Snow White* occupies the top half of the picture of her workroom and attracts our attention even though, compared with the brightly lit and very interesting objects on the table in the foreground, she is in relative darkness. Furthermore, she seems to be defying gravity as she floats in a swirl of wide skirts, and that makes her indulgence in witchcraft particularly mysterious and magical; there is no evidence that she has feet or that there is a floor in the room to place them on. In *Art and Visual Perception*, Arnheim suggests that many modern painters fill the top half of the canvas because "the stylistic preference for overcoming the downward pull is in keeping with the artist's desire to liberate himself from the imitation of reality" (31). Burkert's Queen, afloat in defiance of gravity, defies convention also, and in fact that is the comment made about her in one way or another by all of Burkert's pictures.

In terms of actual physical size, Burkert's *Snow White* is higher than it is wide. Most picture books are wider than they are high; even Burkert's

Snow White is wider than it is high once the book is opened, and the two-page spreads of conventional picture books tend to be more than twice as wide as they are high when opened. Consequently, distinctions between top and bottom are much less noticeable than distinctions between left and right. We tend to read pictures from left to right, as we have learned to read print. As I show in more detail later when I discuss the ways in which pictures imply action and the passing of time, that means that we tend to assume a chronological order within individual pictures that has a profound effect on their storytelling capabilities; we assume that time moves as our eyes move, from left to right, so that we assume, for instance, that Max lands his boat on the left and *then* sees the Wild Things on the right.

But our tendency to read pictures from left to right has other effects also. In a discussion of how pictures seem quite different if we reverse them photographically and look at their mirror images, Mercedes Gaffron suggests that we conventionally look at pictures in terms of "a certain fixed path which we seem normally to follow within the picture space" (316). Gaffron calls that path the "glance curve" and suggests that it moves from the left foreground back around the picture space to the right background. Because we look first at the left foreground, we tend to place ourselves in that position and to identify with the objects or figures located there: "we not only feel that the objects represented here are near to us, but also that they have greater importance to us. People represented here belong to our side in the figurative sense of the term, in contrast to the people on the right side" (321). In fact, the protagonists of many picture books—the characters we are asked to identify with—do tend to appear on the left more often than not. Burkert's Snow White is on the left of a picture showing the frightening forest on the right. In illustrated versions of *Little Red Riding Hood,* the young girl almost always stands to the left of her mother in the first picture—at least in the many versions of the story in which the first picture shows Mother holding up a finger while she offers her daughter instructions. The boy usually appears to the left throughout *Arrow to the Sun,* the only exceptions being at the beginning and the end of the book, where we identify with him less because in the first instance he is new to us and in the second, he has become godlike. In *Rosie's Walk* the text suggests that Rosie ought to be the center of our attention; the pictures tells us that the fox, who always appears on the left, is the *real* protagonist, Rosie merely the object of his attention.

As is often true, the ignoring of a convention can be as meaningful as the use of it. Throughout *Wild Things*, Max is usually to the left, but when he appears to the right of his dog as he makes mischief, it is most likely the dog we want to sympathize and identify with—Max is the villain in this picture; we come to sympathize with him only when he stands to the left of the picture on the next page, after he has been sent to his room. Furthermore, Gaffron suggests that a character on the lower left with his back turned to us will receive the most sympathy, for his position is most like our own in relation to the picture. Our empathy with Max grows as he gets what he wants and his room turns into a forest, and in this sequence of pictures he gradually turns from the left to the right; finally, he turns his back to us. Alan also stands on the left and with his back to us as he first confronts Gasazi.

Since we tend to empathize with a character on the left, the move of a previously established protagonist to the right can suggest that the protagonist is in some sort of difficulty; now we must glance past a dangerous figure who occupies the position on the left we would like to identify with and toward the figure we have learned to identify with, now displaced from his or her "rightful" position. So we have Max to the right of the first Wild Thing he encounters but moving back to the left as he makes it clear that he will not be cowed by this theoretically scary monster. A similar tension develops in the sequence in *Outside Over There* in which Ida is to the left in all the pictures showing how the goblins steal her sister but then moves to the right as she notices the loss; in the picture showing her doing that, we must follow our glance curve past the melting ice baby on the left.

On the other hand, once a dangerous event is over, the positioning of a protagonist on the right might in fact suggest rest rather than tension—particularly in the last picture in a book; that probably happens because our habit of reading from left to right means that the right side of the last page will be the last thing we look at and thus signifies an ending. In *Outside Over There*, as we first see Mama in her arbor, we must glance past the goblins on the far left before we rest on Ida on the far right, and that creates a discomfiting tension; but the similar picture at the end of the book gives us the rescued baby sister in the dominant position on the far left, and that makes our final glance at Ida on the right a matter of resolution rather than tension. Similarly, Max returns to his room and stands on the right in the last picture of *Wild Things*, and Rosie, who left her coop on the left of the picture on the title page of *Rosie's Walk*, nearly walks off the right side of the last picture in order to reenter it.

In Evaline Ness's *Sam, Bangs, and Moonshine*, we see Thomas walking on a beach near some fences. The small child in the left half of the picture is isolated against a large bare space but connected by his shadow to a jarring series of differing sets of parallel lines on the right side that represent fences and their shadows and that all seem to point out toward the edges of the page, away from the center. This radial movement outward is typical of depictions of confused or intense emotion; it is often used to represent explosions, and Ness here seems to use it to imply the child's disturbed state of mind.

A quite opposite effect is achieved by the unifying spirals of roads and hills that surround the satisfying central house in every picture in Burton's *The Little House* and obviously symbolize the unity and continuance of life. These spirals all echo each other and are the same in every picture. They are pleasing because their repetitiveness creates a visual effect like the quality of music and poetry we call rhythm. Such repeated visual shapes can be either maintained or broken for the same purposes as they are maintained and broken in poetry and music.

The atmosphere of *Rosie's Walk* is clearly not dangerous, despite the threatened violence of the situation, at least partially because so many of the objects it depicts consist of repeated patterns: a pear tree is a round green circle filled with carefully arranged rows of similar pears, and even the fox's fur consists of the same shapes repeated to form patterns. These images are ritualized, repetitive, and therefore unsurprising, like wallpaper. No true danger could take place in such a comfortably decorative world. No danger is implied, either, in the decorative world of Errol Le Cain's *The Twelve Dancing Princesses*, in which various elements of the scenes depicted on one side of the two-page spread turn into repeated, ritualized elements of the border around the text on the other side. As the King peruses his daughters' worn shoes, we are told he does so in words surrounded by a balanced pattern of the same shoes; the border around the description of the Princesses dressing is a simplified version of the pattern on one of their dresses in the picture opposite. A little more dangerous is the occurrence in many of the pictures in Van Allsburg's *Jumanji* of a living object that echoes the pattern on an artificial object. A snake bears the same pattern as an armchair; a pot of flowers mirrors the pattern on Mother's dress. This combination of living objects and dead patterns heightens the eerie atmosphere of this book.

Broken rhythms suggest the opposite of stillness. In *Arrow to the Sun* the boy's emotional distance from the other boys in the first picture that shows him grown up is expressed by the fact that his body inclines to the right, breaking the pattern of their three bodies, all the same shape as his but all inclined to the left. But at the end of the book, a harmonious order is expressed by the fact that the boy's body is inclined in the same direction as the four others to his left, who are shaped like himself; meanwhile, the women to his right also all incline in the same direction as each other, are gradually diminishing versions of each other, and have on their heads objects that echo in appearance the one in the boy's right hand. Furthermore, the concentric circles of yellows and oranges that represent the sun at the top left of this picture are echoed both by the rainbow of similar shades upon which the people dance and by the concentric circles of vibrant colors upon which the boy dances at the bottom center. This picture depicts joyful order; the only element not echoed is the boy's mother, who still sits isolated in the background.

Perhaps less obviously, when the Wild Things make Max king the crescent shape of the moon is echoed by the curved backs and by the crescent-shaped horns of the Wild Thing closest to Max. Furthermore, the curves of Max's crown turn its spikes into more crescents, the position of the first Wild Thing's legs and arms make them into crescents, many of the leaves of the tree behind Max are crescent-shaped, the ground has suddenly developed a semicircular rise, and the line formed by the tops of the heads of the group of Wild Things on the right forms an arch also. The rhythmic unity of this picture evokes a much quieter moment than those depicted before and after it, both of which seem to put more emphasis on the points of crescents than on their roundness.

One particular sort of repetitive rhythm is of particular significance in picture books. If a picture-book artist chooses to extend his picture across facing pages, then the picture automatically breaks into two different parts—nothing of significance can appear in the middle, called the gutter, because it might be hidden or distorted in the binding process. Consequently, picture-book artists have the problem of joining the two parts so that they do indeed form one cohesive and unified picture. Burkert does that in the picture of the Queen in her workroom in *Snow White* by creating a triangle of centers of attention that joins the two separate parts of the picture—the moon and the book on the left and the Queen on the right. But even though the entire picture is a unified composition, each half of the picture also has its own self-contained patterns, and the patterns of the two halves rhythmically echo each other. The major thrust of each side of the picture is a diagonal from top left to bottom right; in the left half the diagonal is formed by the window and the edge of the book and in the right half by the lines of the Queen's body and the edge of the table. Furthermore, there is a sort of bilateral symmetry in this picture: there are windows at top left and top right, rounded utensils at bottom left and bottom right, glass utensils to the right and to the left of the gutter; even the Queen's veil on the right is mirrored by the bat's wings on the left. I suspect the cohesiveness of this complex depiction of many different objects is created by the rhythmic relationships of the two halves. As Stephen C. Pepper suggests, such pictures are like folded inkblots: "the blot alone was a confused blob, but the symmetrical pair of blobs you now have is a clear and ordered pattern" (78).

But the connection between the bat and the Queen's head suggests that such bilateral symmetry can also contribute to the communication of meaning. The Queen occupies the space the bat occupies on the other side of a bilaterally symmetrical pattern; therefore, she is like the bat—and bats are evil. Similarly, there are obvious symbolic connotations in the last picture in this same book. The dark arched door on the left, with steps going down, is echoed by the brightly lit door on the right, with steps going up. The figure of justice in a dark square appears over the dark stairs; it is echoed by the bright square depicting a life-filled space on the right. The triumphant Prince and Snow White occupy a space on the right equivalent to the cowering dog on the left; and the iron shoes on the left, symbol of the Queen's defeat, are echoed by the joyful dwarf musician on the right, symbol of joyful victory.

Even artists less prone to visual symbolism than Burkert sometimes use double-page symmetries to comment on their characters. In *The Amazing Bone,* for instance, Steig shows Pearl returning home with her newfound bone on a two-page spread that shows a huge butterfly in the foreground occupying more or less the same position on the left as Pearl herself occupies in the middle distance on the right. She is just about to be robbed; her heedlessness is signaled by her implied relationship to the butterfly.

Not all pictures that display bilateral symmetry are symbolic. But even if they lack other sorts of symbolic meaning, they almost always seem to suggest repose or peacefulness. After a series of pictures in which Max and the Wild Things have their wild rumpus, we see Max in a tent on the right. The triangular shape of the tent is echoed by the triangular shape of the Wild Thing on the far left; the two Wild Things toward the center of the picture almost mirror each other across the gutter, and the entire picture is framed by trees at the left and right edges. While the pictures that precede this tend to divide into two groupings, one on either side of the gutter, they are not nearly so symmetrical; they are wild, not relaxed. Even less relaxed is the picture at the beginning of the book that this one so obviously echoes, which is divided in half even though it occupies just one side of the two-page spread. On the left is the tent Max has made out of a sheet, on the right Max himself, his body forming a similar triangle. But this picture is unsettling rather than relaxing, because it leaves the center of the page empty; the same picture spread across two halves of a spread would have a quite different effect.

In *Outside Over There* the most symmetrical of the pictures occurs at the important climax of the story: when Ida tumbles into a goblin wedding and discovers that the goblins are just babies. Both sides of this picture contain a triangular relationship of three bodies. Each side has a figure in a rounded hood at the top (Ida on the left and a baby on the right) and a baby in a pointed hood both to the right and to the left. In both halves the baby to the left has a cloak that trails into a point heading left and a foot beside the top half of an eggshell and immediately below a hand (Ida's on the left, a baby's on the right). The relative stasis created by this repeated composition might merely suggest the end of Ida's anguished journey, but it also accomplishes much in terms of the rhythm of the story as a whole, as a relatively stable moment, a climactic pause between the frenzied action depicted in less balanced pictures both before and after it.

Of all the variations in the picture plane, those of color are the most immediately noticeable, and, like shapes, colors have emotional connotations that allow them to act as signifiers of states of mind. As I suggested in my earlier discussion of the overall color schemes of pictures, red seems warm or dangerous, blue strikes most of us as a calm color. Sometimes, then, picture-book artists give the specific objects they depict colors with emotional resonances of this sort. Burton's little house is innocently pink—and Peter Rabbit's sisters wear pink, although probably just because they are girls; Peter himself wears blue. Witches tend to wear black. Whereas Hyman's Snow White favors clear, innocent blues, the evil Queen tends to the regal imperiousness of purple.

But the specific colors of specific objects within pictures usually have less significance than the overall color scheme of a picture as a whole, which I discussed earlier; indeed, given the nature of color itself, the color of a specific object often becomes important only because of the mere fact that color is present at all.

Color differs from other aspects of perceivable reality that sustain systems of meaning in that, while differing colors and combinations of color can and do act as signs within a conventional system of visual signification, they also still communicate their original essence directly to the eye; whereas it is hard to hear the nonsense in sounds that we have learned to use to signify ideas, or to see two crossed sticks as just lumber once we have learned to think of them as a cross, a red light can both tell us to stop and offer us a basic sensual arousal in our mere perception of it that exists beyond and apart from the meaning we attach to it. Artists most significantly use color, then, for its potential for arousal; Julia Kristeva, who sees color both as a signifying code and as a liberating eruption of the unconscious into the undeniably limiting conventional codes of art, quotes Matisse's demand for colors that can "stir the sensual depths in men" (221).

Paradoxically, however, the fact that color appeals so strongly to our senses without reference to meaning can contribute to the meaning of pictures. The mere presence of a vivid color is so likely to give weight to visual objects that illustrators forced to work within the constraints of one- or two-color printing almost always use it to focus on the significant details of otherwise colorless pictures. The egg that Horton hatches in *Horton Hatches the Egg* is often the only red object on a page otherwise black and white; the only other color in the book, a bluish green, is usually used for background. In these circumstances, a small amount of red is so attractive that Dr. Seuss even uses it to give weight to objects that could not possibly be red—for instance, to highlight lightning flashes during a storm. Similarly, illustrators often draw attention to significant objects by depicting them in colors unlike those of the remaining objects in the picture—for instance, Anno's tiny figure of Little Red Riding Hood as a girl in a red dress surrounded by green trees in *Anno's Journey*. On the other hand, blank white areas tend to stand out as blocks of pure color when they are surrounded by a mixed palette of blended colors, and that may explain why Sendak makes Max's wolf suit the only relatively blank area in the pictures in *Wild Things*.

Color can also create important relationships between different parts of a picture. In *Wild Things*, Sendak often implies connections between the objects he depicts by making them the only white spots on an otherwise colorful page. As Max makes mischief, his white suit associates him with the white dog; they are two beasts. The white of the moon throughout connects it also to Max's wolf suit, an appropriate connection not just because it helps to relate the elements that create the basic composition of the picture but also because of the moon's traditional stature as a symbol of behavior beyond the pale of normalcy. Max is most isolated when he becomes the only white object on the page, as he does when he sits alone in his tent and feels homesick.

In *The Amazing Bone*, Steig connects Pearl's pink complexion and pink and purple dress with the many pink and purple blossoms of the spring forest; she seems to belong there more than she did in the mainly yellow and brown town. The thieves who intrude into this pleasant pastoral scene wear brown, yellow, and red—reminiscent both of the town and of autumn. The fox has a yellow shirt and brown fur, and a brown and yellow house—so the pinkish purple of his tie is clearly just an attempt to deceive.

A more subtle use of color to make connections is that in Burkert's panoramic view depicting Snow White laced into unconsciousness by the wicked Queen and the effects of that action on the kingdom as a whole. The image of the dragon with a rabbit in its mouth on the right clearly balances the small insert on the left, showing Snow White unconscious as the Queen flees: in fact, given the emblematic quality of this entire picture, the dragon and rabbit could hardly be interpreted as anything but a symbolic interpretation of the Queen and Snow White. But the dragon is the same orange-red as Snow White's dress. So just who is in whose clutches? At this point in the story, the Queen seems to be winning and to be dragonlike in her vengefulness. But the story as a whole lets us know that Snow White is never really in danger, simply because she is good and innocent and weak. Her passive goodness will eventually triumph over the Queen's self-seeking and self-indulgence, and this moment of apparent triumph for the Queen is merely one step in her inevitable progression toward painful death and Snow White's toward a happy ending. In that sense, Snow White is the dragon who stalks and eventually triumphs over a creature who is weaker than herself because she presumes to think herself stronger. As the strange repetition of color suggests, perhaps things are not what they seem; the rest of the picture is equally ambiguous in its depictions of the sun either rising or setting, the Queen's castle either being hidden by clouds or about to emerge from them, and the reaper at the center, who can imply either the rewards of harvest or the punishment of death.

Warm colors—reds, oranges, yellows—seem to advance, and cool ones—blues and blue-greens—to retreat, and as result, reds tend to have more weight than blues. It is probably for this reason that, when Dr. Seuss is limited to just red and blue-green in *Horton Hatches the Egg*, he uses the red to highlight objects and the blue-green for backgrounds. Burkert clothes Snow White in blue as she is lost in the forest, and later at her wedding, but in reddish orange as she supervises dinner at the dwarfs' house and then later as she lies unconscious, laced too tightly by the Queen. The blues cause her to blend in, either because she is dominated by the forest or unguarded in her moment of happiness; the reds enforce her isolation from the background—as does the Queen's red dress as she prepares her instrument of death in the workroom. In fact, red is a favorite color for the clothing of picture-book protagonists—it makes them stand out.

Perhaps the most carefully worked out use of color to suggest the meaning of a picture-book story is McDermott's *Arrow to the Sun*. The book does not so much make use of conventional connotations of colors as it creates and sustains its own internal system of color significations. For the most part, the pictures in this book are in the earthy tones of brown, yellow, and orange that we associate with Pueblo Indian art. Consequently, the few figures in solid black stand out and are all related to each other. The "spark of life" shot to earth by the Lord of the Sun travels down against a black rainbow-shaped background; the woman it enters is herself a black figure, and so is the child she gives birth to. In fact, the boy and his mother are always distinguished from the other characters by differences in color quality; the painted blacks used elsewhere in the pictures are softer than the intense black ink of their bodies, and they are always totally black, while the other characters are depicted with the oranges and browns of the backgrounds. Furthermore, the boy is incomplete, merely a black outline; the colors of the background can be seen in the holes made by the patterns of his body. Unlike other humans, he is isolated and in need of fulfillment.

Finally, the boy meets another character whose body contains some of the same black, the arrowmaker. Only his face and forearm are the intense black that connects him to the boy, but it is his eyes and his arms that give him his skill at archery and thus allow him to play a special part in the boy's story.

As the boy, transformed into an arrow, heads toward the sun, he passes through a zone of other colors against a field of black. These appear to be stars, sources of light, and some of them are blues and greens and pinks quite unlike the only colors we have seen up to this point—the Pueblo colors of earth and sun. Their sudden appearance at this point in the book makes these colors symbolic of the superhuman and superearthly.

When the boy lands on the sun, the Lord is not, as we might have expected, as black as his child; in fact, he contains no black at all. Instead, he is a combination of the colors of the stars and the colors of the earth, half earthly, half divine, the sum of everything. But as the sum of everything, he is not like the boy, who is half human, half divine, and who thus stands out from everybody in his isolated black uniqueness.

Not surprisingly, the various kivas of the boy's testing contain the star colors, the blues and pinks and greens which seem now to represent the more-than-human. And as the boy leaves the last kiva in triumph, having proven that he is more than human, his transformation is represented by a rainbow containing all the clear colors of the book but no browns. Transformed, he is as colorful as his father, a similar combination of colors and contrasting darkness, but he is still different, for he is black and the rainbow colors, not brown and the rainbow colors. He seems to combine not the earthly and the divine as his father does but divinity and his own uniqueness; like the Christ his story is clearly modeled on, the boy is unlike anyone divine or human because he combines the attributes of both. Finally, in the most interesting transformation of the book, the people who dance with the boy at the end take on some of his divine sun colors; as do all participants in rituals, they take on the attributes of the god they worship during their act of celebration. While the boy's mother does not take part in this unifying celebration, she has lost her intense blackness and has become a grayish brown that makes her less isolated.

■ ■ ■ ■

The various focusing elements I have discussed thus far involve relationships between portions of the two-dimensional plane—the surface of a picture. But as a visual representation, that two-dimensional plane implies a three-dimensional space: the space of the scene depicted. The techniques that help to imply three-dimensional space can also give different weight and significance to different parts of pictures. These techniques are like the equivalent elements of stagecraft and filmmaking: the way directors use light, block their actors, or vary camera angles to attract attention to certain aspects of what an audience sees on a stage.

Unless qualities like those I discussed earlier create a different balance, objects that seem to be farther away from us in perspective pictures often attract our attention more than those that are closer up—even though they tend to be smaller than objects in the foreground (in perspective, of course, smaller objects are interpreted as being farther away). The diagonal lines that indicate perspective seem to form arrowlike shapes that focus our attention on the objects they lead toward—the ones in front of the vanishing point. An obvious example is the picture of Alan heading into Gasazi's garden in *The Garden of Abdul Gasazi,* in which the perspective lines formed by the pedestals of the statues, the steps, and the gate all point to the vanishing point, and meanwhile, the curved trunks of the trees we see through the garden gate form a pattern of ever-diminishing circles around the small oval spot of light at their center. Together, these lines form a tunnel something like the barrel of a rifle, pointed at the small but attractive spot of light, and that spot is itself the vanishing point. Stephen C. Pepper suggests that linear perspective of this sort is rare in paintings because the lines that create it make a hole in the picture, and because the artist has no choice but to make most of the lines of the picture head toward that empty and therefore unimportant space (219). Van Allsburg's picture shows how such a hole can have narrative potential: here everything draws us through the gate and toward the mystery of Gasazi's garden.

But such pronouncedly obvious uses of perspective are as rare in picture books as in other forms of art. Usually, the use of perspective to create focus is more subtle. In *Where the Wild Things Are*, for instance, Sendak takes advantage of perspective lines to focus our attention on the moon, which gradually develops more weight in the series of pictures in which Max's bedroom changes into a forest. In the first picture, the moon occupies a point close to the vanishing point, but it is hazy, and the unsettling upside-down triangle made by Max, the door, and the bed focuses our attention on Max and his anger. In the next picture, the moon is more distinct from the background, while the heavily outlined trees make the bed and window stand out less. The original triangle has faded, but no definite focus replaces it, and the picture demands our attention to many of its elements: the more prominent moon, the trees as new and therefore automatically interesting, and still, if only because he is human, Max himself. In the third picture, the bed fades, and the trees lose their harsh outlines; only Max stands out. But the moon, now exactly in front of the vanishing point, demands some attention; furthermore, its whiteness echoes Max's whiteness, so that a relationship between the two is suggested. The last picture in the sequence makes the relationship clear. Max, his back turned to us, is in shadow, and the moon, at the vanishing point, is the only really bright object left. As the focus of our attention and Max's, it communicates the key meaning of the picture, the mysterious unreality traditionally associated with moonlight; it creates an atmosphere of freedom from restriction that might imply anarchy, of wonderful but potentially dangerous things about to happen. As a whole, this sequence of pictures shows how subtle changes in focus can make what is basically the same composition express different meanings. The pictures so economically move our attention from Max's state of mind to the potential excitement of a moon-bathed forest that few words are necessary.

Burkert similarly uses a moon in a window in her picture of the Queen preparing the poisoned apple for Snow White; the window is so deep that a quite long perspective line representing its inside corner focuses attention on the moon. But this picture has two vanishing points, and the one on the right also has a window in front of it. Its perspective lines draw our attention to the Queen, who is farther back in the picture than the table of interesting objects in the foreground. Meanwhile, the brightest object in this generally dark picture is neither the Queen nor the moon but the book in the foreground open to the picture of an apple, and that has enough weight to form the third corner of a triangle of relationships—the evil act done by the evil person under the mysterious light of the moon. Interestingly, the apple depicted in the book is half as red as the one the Queen holds aloft and half as white as the moon itself. Burkert has cleverly used perspective to help unify two halves of a wide picture that has, like many double-page spreads in picture books, nothing at its center; furthermore, the points of the triangle I have described here are also important parts of the bilateral symmetry in this same picture that I described earlier, so that the picture makes sense both as two halves and as one whole.

Most children's picture books tend to downplay perspective, or to use it only as a convention—merely one of a repertoire of stock tricks of depiction. As I suggested while discussing pictures in baby books, perspective used in this way becomes merely one more of the list of attributes that help to offer a visual definition of an object and create a stereotyped image of it; the illustrator is less interested in capturing a representation of reality than in evoking the idea of an object through a sort of visual shorthand. Consequently, different ideas about objects can be evoked by varying the list of stock attributes; and for this reason, the pictures in picture books often depict some objects in perspective and others not in perspective. The fox and Rosie in *Rosie's Walk* are two-dimensional images, but they walk through a barnyard that has a sort of conventional perspective which does not so much create depth as it satisfies our conventional idea about what barns and wagons look like.

Like the vast majority of picture books, *Rosie's Walk* places more emphasis on action than on atmosphere. The lack of detailed perspective suggests that Hutchins's pictures are meant to be quickly scanned for their narrative information, not inspected for the implications of their settings. On the other hand, the complex three-dimensional spaces of books like Burkert's *Snow White* or Van Allsburg's *Garden of Abdul Gasazi* invite viewers to peruse and consider the implications of settings. The difference between these two different demands on a viewer's attention explains why pictures like Burkert's and Van Allsburg's seem so different from those commonly found in more typical picture books.

Nevertheless, even books with little perspective use perspective techniques for the narrative purpose of focusing attention. In *Arrow to the Sun*, which is generally unrepresentational enough to seem unrealistic, McDermott places the Lord of the Sun in the foreground of the picture, so that he dwarfs the much smaller figure of the boy, who stands farther back in the implied space. Even cartoonists occasionally use perspective for focusing; in *Horton Hatches the Egg*, Dr. Seuss uses perspective lines to focus attention on Horton throughout the book—especially when Horton is in the background and there are interesting things to look at in the foreground.

By definition, perspective drawing shows what can be seen from a fixed point of view. The choice of a particular point of view can greatly affect the way we understand the situation a picture depicts. On the dust jacket of *The Garden of Abdul Gasazi*, its publishers claim that the artist is "manipulating the position of the viewer to create a more dramatic picture." Throughout the book Van Allsburg changes point of view to focus attention. We see Alan asleep on a sofa head on in a picture devoid of dramatic focus and therefore quite rightly devoid of tension. But we move down below and look up as Alan falls down a flight of stairs, and that seems to make him fall toward us in a rather threatening way. We are below and to the side as Alan stands insignificantly at the edge of the picture of Gasazi's imposing residence, and we are below whenever Gasazi himself appears, so that we feel dwarfed by *his* imposing presence. But Alan lost in a pleasant pastoral landscape is seen from above, and as he is about to enter the garden he is also seen from above, his body and the arms of two statues pointing to the hole created by the vanishing point that he seems to be about to fall into, just as Carroll's Alice fell into the equally magical garden of Wonderland.

Generally speaking, figures seen from below and against less patterned backgrounds stand out and seem isolated from their environment and in control of it; figures seen from above become part of an environment, either secure in it or constrained by it. Also generally speaking, illustrators who make significant use of changing angles tend to be those who emphasize the intense drama of the stories they depict; Van Allsburg and Trina Schart Hyman, both of whom tend to depict highly charged emotions, use extreme views from above and from below in book after book.

As Alan heads into Gasazi's garden, his back is to us; we focus less on him than on what he faces toward, so the picture creates anticipation. His back is to us again when he stares up at Gasazi's huge house and again when he stares up at Gasazi; in all three cases, what he sees is more important than anything else. But a fourth picture, the one in which Gasazi tells Alan he has turned his dog into a duck, shows Alan with his head toward Gasazi, again turned away from the front of the picture. We might expect to see his face at this distressingly emotional moment, but the picture implies a moment of arrested movement that suggests Alan's shock better than any facial expression could.

In *Peter Rabbit*, as Peter's mother gives her children instructions, we see Mother's and Peter's fronts, the girls' backs. We know whom we should be paying attention to already, even though Peter has not yet become the focus of the text. In fact, the only time we are positioned in a way that lets us see the front of the girls is the last picture of the book, at the one and only moment when they actually do something interesting. We see Peter from the front throughout the book, except for the two occasions when we see past his back to a sight that alarms him, in both cases Mr. McGregor. Throughout the book, furthermore, we see Peter from below or head on when he feels in command; but when he overeats we see him lying against the ground, from above; and the same thing happens when he is caught in the netting and nearly gives up.

Leo and Diane Dillon make an ironic point in *Who's in Rabbit's House* by suddenly changing the point of view. All through the book we have seen a group of lions in the background, watching as the people perform a play in which they act the parts of animals. In the last picture, the actors move into the background, and the real animals in the foreground look at each other in utter bewilderment about what the people have been doing. This sudden shift in point of view confirms the sense of playful artifice that all the illustrations in this sophisticated book communicate.

As well as viewing their characters from varying angles, picture-book artists can place them against differing sizes of backgrounds, much as movie directors do, in order to focus our attention on specific aspects of their behavior. Long shots, which show characters surrounded by a lot of background, imply objectivity and distance; they tell us about how a character's actions influence his environment, or vice versa. Middle-distance shots, which show characters filling most of the space from the top to the bottom of a picture, tend to emphasize the relationships between characters. Close-ups generate involvement with characters by showing us their facial expressions and, presumably, communicating the way they feel.

In picture books, close-ups are rare—not surprisingly, for the width of most picture books makes it difficult to show a face without any background behind it. In any case, this is a literature of action rather than of character, and the emphasis is on events and relationships rather than on subtleties of feeling. If close-ups are used at all in picture books, they tend to be on the front cover or dust jacket and to operate more as an introduction to a character's appearance than as a way of revealing character. Burkert's close-up of Snow White on the jacket of her version is like a portrait photograph; it shows us what Snow White looks like, suggests she is young and pretty, and has next to no emotional impact; even though Snow

White gazes sideways out of the picture, her facial gesture conveys no sense of her response to what she sees. The same sense of a portrait photograph is conveyed by the close-up (or more accurately, "two-shot") of Hansel and Gretel on the dust jacket of the version illustrated by Susan Jeffers; while the tree in front of their faces indicates that they are lost in the forest at the moment this picture depicts, the faces themselves suggest nothing but youth and innocence and prettiness. As I said earlier, a surprising number of picture-book characters appear on the covers or dust jackets smiling the way we all do in portrait photographs, an expression that speaks more of emotion and attitude than these pictures by Burkert and Jeffers do but that still has little to do with the stories such pictures preface.

Middle-distance shots and long shots predominate in picture books, and most picture books depict the actions they describe in a series of pictures that all imply the same distance from the scene; as I will show later when I discuss sequencing, the characteristic effects of that unvarying point of view from picture to picture are a significant aspect of picture-book narrative as a whole. Nevertheless, occasional shifts to a very long shot often indicate a change in the narrative situation—as it does, for instance, in Burkert's *Snow White* in the difference between a long shot of an endangered and isolated Snow White surrounded by forest and a middle-distance shot of Snow White enjoying the secure domesticity of the dwarfs' house. The bakers of Sendak's *In the Night Kitchen* bulk large enough to fill the middle-distance shots in which we first see them; they are rather frighteningly massive. But when Mickey frees himself from them, Sendak pulls back into a long shot, a panoramic view of the entire night kitchen that makes the three bakers seem relatively insignificant. In *Oh! Were They Ever Happy!* Peter Spier cleverly shows children painting their house in every color of the rainbow in middle-distance shots; he saves a long shot, in which we can finally see the astonishing overall effects of their efforts, until the very end.

In perspective drawings, the spaces that depictions of objects occupy on the page inevitably interfere with each other; something that is presumed to be in front of something else will prevent us from seeing part of the object behind it. Artists can use the way objects overlap each other to imply something about their relationships. In *Art and Visual Perception,* Arnheim suggests that "occlusion always creates visual tension. We sense the occluded figure's striving to free itself from the interference with its integrity" (252). That is clearly the point of Potter's depiction of Peter struggling with the fence picket in front of him as he enters the garden. As Max relaxes after his rumpus with the Wild Things, he is overlapped by the edge of the tent and occluded by the shadow; at this point, the text implies that he feels hemmed in by his newfound freedom. Not surprisingly, the Wild Thing to the far left is also overlapped, by a row of imprisoning trees—the first time this has happened in the book. Burkert's Snow White is overlapped by the trees in the wild forest that seems to threaten her (although not nearly so overlapped as are Hyman's and Jack Kent's Snow Whites, whose forests are both like prison bars that occlude and imprison them). But in the dwarfs' house, Burkert's Snow White is overlapped by the tables and chairs, just as her mother was earlier overlapped by the window; in both cases, these women are protected by being constrained; the overlapping suggests security rather than imprisonment. More symbolically, the evil Queen is overlapped by the apparatus of evil on her worktable, and her vileness is symbolized by a bat which overlaps the pure white light of the moon.

Overlapping shadows tend to suggest the power of the objects that cast them over the objects they overlap. Errol Le Cain cleverly suggests Beauty's father's fear of the Beast in his *Beauty and the Beast* by showing the Beast's unusually shaped shadow overlapping the father's foot. Later in the book, the father turns his back to a window through which light streams, but he casts no shadow, as he ought to, on Beauty sitting at his feet, for such a shadow would imply the wrong symbolic meanings. Shadows are so obviously symbolic that they usually appear only when illustrators need them to symbolize something.

That shadows can cause overlap effects suggests the importance of light sources for creating relative weight and focus. Not all pictures imply a source either inside or outside the picture for the light that illuminates the scene—books like *Rosie's Walk* deliberately avoid any hint of darkness, and everything is bathed in the same even, cheerful light. But pictures that do imply a light source focus our attention on the objects in the light—and, if it is depicted in the picture, the light source itself. In Peter Spier's picture of Noah by candlelight, for instance, the small circle of light thrown by the candle and the light it casts on Noah's face are the only objects that emerge from an overriding darkness. The picture communicates Noah's isolation and despair.

Throughout *Wild Things,* depictions of the moon attract attention both to themselves and to the objects they cast light upon—usually on Max himself. But surprisingly, the moon is not the only source of light in many of the pictures in which it appears; Sendak invents other invisible light sources to make the objects he wants us to focus on stand out. When Max stands in his bedroom with his back to the moon, his front is lit from the left front; but when he turns his back and focuses his attention—and ours—on the moon, this apparent source of light in the front disappears and Max's back is shadowed. Something similarly strange happens in Ida's bedroom in *Outside Over There:* the light shining through the window causes the table leg to cast a shadow, but as the world outside darkens, the shadow remains. Perhaps, as Stephen Roxburgh suggests in "A Picture Equals How Many Words?" this is Sendak's way of telling us that all that happens here is a daydream that occupies only one brief instant.

Such inconsistencies suggest that light sources, like shadows, are more significantly meaningful than representational. In fact, they are often used symbolically. Burkert surrounds Snow White with light despite the darkness of the forest she is presumably lost in, and when she and the Prince finally marry, they walk up into a symbolically joyful light, whereas the Queen has presumably gone down another set of stairs into an equally symbolic darkness. Throughout her *Sleeping Beauty,* Trina Schart Hyman depicts light shining in the background, so that characters standing in the foreground stand out against it; as the Prince enters the palace, for instance, he stands out powerfully as a dark figure against cheerful yellow backgrounds, imposingly seen from below. In an alternative use of the same technique, in Ezra Jack Keats's *Apt. 3* we first see the boy, Sam, as a dark shape against a lit window, the weak light behind him not doing much to cast light either on him or on a rainy, gloomy world. Throughout the book, characters are thrown into darkness by the shadows cast by bare, feeble light bulbs. But when a blind man plays his harmonica, and the text says, "All the sights and sounds and colors from outside had come into the room," the blind man is suffused by a yellow light from above—from an unseen light source that presumably has no real existence. In traditional paintings, in fact, light from an unseen source above often implies a heavenly glow.

Gyorgy Kepes suggests that we expect light to fall from above, so "every shift from this standard light condition is registered and interpreted by us as an exaggeration of spatial dimensions" (145). That helps explain the magical quality of *The Garden of Abdul Gasazi*, in which Van Allsburg switches the light source from picture to picture. As Alan falls down the stairs, he is lit by a harsh bright light from above and in front; not only is the surprise on his face spotlighted but he seems to float on his own shadow in this curiously still depiction of fast activity. In a later picture, he is lit from above as he reaches out to the duck that flies away with his hat, and his alarmed face is again spotlighted. But in less-surprising moments, his face is usually in shadow. As he talks to Gasazi, the light from the left not only puts his face in shadow but creates a shadow of his body on the carpet that gradually fades as it reaches toward the fearful Gasazi; meanwhile, Gasazi's fearfully imposing face has light shining directly down on it from the upper left.

Effects such as these are the results of the artistic techniques which illustrators use to represent three-dimensional space on a two-dimensional surface. But illustrators often also use techniques similar to those with which directors manipulate the three-dimensional space of a stage. The characters in picture books often form what stage directors would call "stage pictures," achieved on stage by blocking the actors; they take positions in relationship to each other that create a pleasing and informative visual image rather than mirror the ways in which people orient themselves to each other in reality. For instance, the characters in picture books often converse with each other while standing with their bodies and faces at ninety-degree angles from each other, both to create a balanced picture and so that we can see and read their facial expressions—as in Hyman's *Snow White*, when the Queen persuades Snow White to wear her magic comb. And they often dine at tables at which no one sits on the side closest to the viewer or form other unlikely patterns to prevent obstruction of important objects—as again in Hyman's *Snow White*, when the dwarfs all stand behind Snow White, rather than all around her, as she lies on the ground apparently dead. As always in visual imagery that has a narrative purpose, narrative informativeness is more significant than visual accuracy.

In the theater such "stage pictures" often have the purpose of indicating something about the relationship of characters to each other—as in the first picture of the rabbit family in *Peter Rabbit*, for instance, in which tight groups imply contact and solitary figures isolation. In other words, both stage directors and picture-book illustrators suggest the relationships of their characters by placing them in ways that make use of the directed tensions of visual imagery. In fact, once a three-dimensional picture space has been created, the relative positions of characters within it can become meaningful through all the various means of directed tension I have already described. Important people can appear at focal points or wear brightly colored clothing or be heavily outlined; insignificant ones can appear toward the edge of pictures or have their backs turned or stand in shadow. And relationships between characters can be implied by their sharing or nonsharing of shapes or colors or perspective lines.

Hyman makes a particularly dramatic use of directed tension to create stage pictures in the scenes in which she shows Snow White lying in her coffin. In the first of these, Snow White is isolated near the center of the picture. Two dwarfs sit in despair, also in isolation from each other and with their backs turned to Snow White. One looks out toward the left edge of the picture, the other out toward the bottom edge—and an owl looks off toward the right edge. All of this focusing of attention away from the center of the picture isolates Snow White even more and creates an intense feeling of bleak despair. But in the next picture, as the Prince stands over Snow White's coffin, he and six of the dwarfs stand in a tight group surrounding it, and two of the Prince's men that stand in the shadows point toward this central group; while the seventh dwarf looks away from this group and faces the viewer, his image is close enough to the group to occlude the feet of one of the dwarfs, and he looks not out at us but down at a small flower—a fragile image of vitality. The image as a whole implies an end to grief. Finally, as Snow White awakens and sits up, four men and a horse stand around her, and all five incline toward her to create a stage picture that implies both surprise and the ending of tension.

As these examples show, picture-book art is a rich blend of the techniques of a variety of forms of visual information—not just the directed tensions of visual art and the stage pictures of theatrical blocking but also the camera angles of film, the conventionalized action lines of cartoons, and the stock types of stereotypical diagrams. It is because these techniques all offer differing forms of information that the combination of them in picture-book illustrations can contribute so much to the telling of stories.

■ ■ ■ ■

CHAPTER SIX

———

The Depiction of Action and the Passing of Time:
How Pictures Imply Events and How Sequence
Affects Meaning

Stories, which are about movements and changes, necessarily take place in time, whereas most pictures depict only how things look at one moment separated from the flow of time. A picture can show us a rabbit underneath a sieve held by two human hands, but it requires an accompanying text to add time to that frozen instant—a text that tells us, for instance, that the hands belong to Mr. McGregor, that he is about to pop a sieve upon the top of Peter Rabbit, and that Peter wriggles out just in time. Had we not known that text, furthermore, we could not accurately interpret all of the information about the situation revealed graphically in the layout and style of the picture—the kinds of information I discussed in previous chapters.

In a revealing comment in *The Responsibility of Forms*, Roland Barthes says, "the single photograph is very rarely (i.e. with great difficulty) comical, contrary to the drawing; the comic requires movement, i.e. repetition (which is readily obtained in the cinema) or typification (which is possible in drawing), these two 'connotations' being denied to the photograph" (14). It is not just the "comic" that requires movement or typification—in fact, as I suggested in my earlier discussion of cartoons, any visual story-telling does, and that accounts for the prevalence of cartooning in picture-book art, even in books that are not comical. But while the individual pictures in a picture book can, unlike most photographs, convey narrative information through the expressive distortions and typifications of cartooning, no single one of them can depict actual movement—neither the "repetition" Barthes speaks of that engenders the comic nor the changing series of actions that make up a narrative plot.

Nevertheless, picture books do imply movement. The sequence of pictures offers enough repetition—images of the same characters in different postures or of the same settings under different conditions—to convey a sense of continuing action, and even an individual picture *can* convey motion and the passage of time, implying what it cannot actually depict. As Roland Penrose says, "Art has the unique quality of being able to halt the march of time while still giving the illusion of movement" (265)—and that is as true of Beatrix Potter's picture of Peter and the sieve as it is of Marcel Duchamp's *Nude Descending a Staircase*.

Of course, it is not through actual depiction that such pictures convey the passage of time but, rather, through the use of established conventions—through "typifications" that represent movement. The limitations of duplicating the actual are clearly revealed by stop-action photographs, which can show us how objects in motion actually do look and which ought to convey motion better than any other sort of image. Yet pictures of horses galloping or of people high-jumping most often seem motionless, as if the figures were awkwardly stopped and held up in midair. In fact, even photographers must resort to conventions of pictorial representation in order to capture persuasively the characteristic motions of objects—conventions common to all sorts of pictures. Or else they must invent conventions of their own, such as the use of blurs; for many decades after the invention of photography, blurred objects represented inferior work, for we do not actually see fast activity as a blur, and people therefore did not understand the blurs in photographs. But now we have learned from photographs to interpret blurs as objects in motion, and the conventionality of conventions is confirmed by the fact that even illustrators now sometimes imply speed by *drawing* a blur.

The most obvious means by which a picture implies motion is by manipulation of viewers' assumptions about context. Since pictures are unlike life in that they stop time, we can relate them back to life by guessing about what must come before and after what we actually see. We assume that a sieve in a picture that is held in midair by two hands is either going down or up, not standing as still as it is actually depicted to be. Because the hind legs of the rabbit under the sieve in Beatrix Potter's picture in *Peter Rabbit* are up in the air, where gravity could not keep them, we assume they must be going down too. And since the rabbit's legs are up and going down, the sieve could not be going up—or else how could the rabbit have been underneath it with his legs in midair?

We see the sieve *about* to descend but not yet down, and in imagining the inevitable follow-through of what we actually see, we ourselves create the motion. Picture books are filled with pictures that show an action just before it reaches its climax. In *Where the Wild Things Are*, we see Max's hammer *about* to hit the nail, Max in midair *about* to land on the dog, Max's foot in midair *about* to stamp the ground. The few pictures showing Max with both feet planted firmly on the ground are the least energetic ones in the book; they either suggest that he is resting or else give him a strong, stable position of authority. In *Arrow to the Sun*, McDermott gives movement to the otherwise static geometry of his figure of the boy by showing him poised precariously on one leg as he climbs the ladders of both the pueblo and the kivas, and also as he turns into an arrow; in the dance at the end of the book, all nine figures stand on one leg. In fact, a quick glance through any group of typical picture books might suggest that the entire population of the known universe spends most of its time with one foot in the air; in this storytelling medium, the evocation of action is of the essence.

According to Gyorgy Kepes, "linear continuance arrests the attention and forces the eye into a pursuit movement. The eye, following the line, acts as if it were on the path of a moving thing and attributes to the line the quality of movement" (174). This is not in fact literally true; with the possible exception of the glance curve I discussed earlier, the actual order in which we look at the parts of a picture may not be the ordering of the actions or events they imply. In fact, the experiments Guy Thomas Buswell reports in *How People Look at Pictures* show that the sequence of actual eye movements with which people inspect pictures has little to do with the dynamics of pictorial composition; we can look at a picture that suggests a circular motion without our eyeballs actually going around in circular patterns, and then we can rightly say that the circular pattern leads our "eyes" to understand the picture in a certain way. The dynamics by which pictures convey relationships among their parts demand activity of the mind, not of the physical eye. We must relate the various objects to each other not in terms of the order in which we actually do look at them but in terms of how we understand they ought to be looked at—in terms of the temporal sequences we determine they suggest.

Given that proviso, then, we can find uses of linear continuance in picture books that interestingly imply action. In *Arrow to the Sun*, actual arrowheads point our eye onward, and the boy's pistol-like hand points out the direction of the implied movement. The parallel "action lines" of cartoonists are another use of this convention, and illustrators often make subtle use of it in pictures where lines representing other objects act as action lines. In the picture of Peter Rabbit and the sieve, for instance, the lines of the net in the background are so arranged that they might easily be understood as action lines representing Peter's movement; and the lines of Peter's whiskers suggest the flight of the three sparrows that hover around him. As the boy and the snowman fly in Raymond Briggs's *The Snowman*, similarly, the shading lines that depict the darkness of the sky also slant in a direction that implies the characters' flight.

Earlier I suggested that pictures in which disconnected lines are emphasized over the solidity of shapes seem to indicate a lack of order; they do so by implying more energy, more activity. Such lines represent a different use of the principle of linear continuance: they seem to pull our eyes in a number of different directions at once and thus create a sense of unsettled chaos. Jon Cech suggests the energy inherent in broken lines as opposed to solid shapes when he describes Randolph Caldecott's sketchbooks: "Everywhere they are daubed with white ink to remove detail and, in essence, to release the energy of the work" (113).

In *Wild Things*, Sendak implies various levels of energy by using two different sorts of shading. In the pictures of Max making mischief at the beginning of the book, the shading on the figure of Max is composed of hatching, disconnected lines all in the same direction, but the rest of the picture is shaded with crosshatching, which creates numerous small, enclosed, stable squares. The crosshatching holds the objects down; Max is clearly in motion, while nothing else is. As the forest grows in Max's room and he calms down, his shading comes to consist of more crosshatching. Later in the book, during the wild rumpus, *all* the shading but that on Max is crosshatching, and he becomes more filled with crosshatching as the sequence goes on. That helps create a curious dreamlike stasis even in spite of the exuberant action in these pictures.

Distortion of bodies and even of objects is another conventional means by which pictures convey motion. As Peter runs from Mr. McGregor in another picture in *The Tale of Peter Rabbit*, his head seems almost bullet-shaped, his ears apparently held down by air resistance, his body at an impossible slant that conveys great speed. As Peter jumps out of the window of the shed, the threat of Mr. McGregor's descending boot is implied by its disproportionately large size. The convention by which the motion of drops of water is represented by elongating them into a shape they never actually have in the real world appears in the picture of Peter jumping into the watering can. Yet interestingly, while this teardrop shape is like a backward arrow, we know the movement is *away* from the point only because we know the convention; Peter is himself a teardrop shape in this picture, but we assume he is entering the watering can, not leaving it—that he heads in the direction his body is pointed toward.

In his description in *Ways of Seeing* of Rubens's *Hélène Fourment in a Fur Coat*, John Berger speaks of another sort of distortion; he suggests that the fur coat draped across the middle of the otherwise naked woman in this painting disguises the fact that her thighs are too far to the left to join her hips. Berger suggests that the disjunction creates the sense that she has been caught in a quick movement, so that she is unlike the lethargic nudes of the main European tradition (60–61). Sendak uses such distortions often in *Outside Over There*. As Ida floats in the sky in the midst of her twirling yellow robe, her legs point in the opposite direction from her torso; and as she plays a frenzied jig for the goblins, her feet emerge from her gown in positions that suggest that her legs could not possibly join her body. Either Ida is a contortionist or else Sendak makes clever use of distortion to imply motion.

Since we tend to "read" the pictures in picture books by moving our glance from left to right, we usually assume that figures of characters pointed toward the right are moving forward. Rosie heads to the right throughout Pat Hutchins's *Rosie's Walk*, while the goat, who appears in a few of the pictures, turns to the left and is clearly not moving anywhere.

In fact, action usually moves from left to right in picture books; and obviously, then, time conventionally passes from left to right. If there are two pictures on facing pages of a book, then we must assume the one on the left depicts action that comes first, and even one picture will sometimes show events on the left that must logically have happened before the events depicted on the right of the same picture. Adrienne Adams's illustration of the words "Jennie burst through the window in a shower of glass—snarling! Squink hid under the bed" in Jan Wahl's *Cabbage Moon* shows Squink's house as a continuous setting across both pages. But Jennie is in midair on the left and so is a lot of shattered glass, and Squink is already under the bed on the right. Either he moves astonishingly quickly, or else the picture actually shows two consecutive moments rather than just one.

Even when pictures do show only one moment, the characters (and the time in which their actions occur) tend to progress from left to right throughout a book. In *Cabbage Moon*, Squink's bicycle heads to the right as he dashes home, and Princess Adelgitha follows him in the same direction. The boy in *Arrow to the Sun* heads to the right when he goes home to the pueblo and then right again when he leaves home to seek help; he is shot to the right to reach the sun, even though the spark of his life had first arrived on earth from the sun from the left (it too was moving to the right). The boy leaves the various kivas to the right; finally, he is shot to the right again as he returns to earth. The old man in Wanda Gag's *Millions of Cats* heads to the right both when he goes to look for a cat and when he returns home; Anno always journeys to the right, whether he is in Britain or Italy or the U.S.A. The ducks head to the right in McCloskey's *Make Way for Ducklings*. Max travels to the right to get to where the Wild Things are, the protagonist of Blair Lent's *Funny Little Woman* travels to the right to get to the home of the Wicked Onis, and Raymond Briggs's Snowman takes the boy flying to the right.

But in the last three cases, the return journey is to the left. A different convention seems to be operating here—not simply that one always moves to the right but that one voyages away from home to the right and returns to the left. Given this variation, it is interesting to note that early filmmakers used a different convention, based on mapmaking: according to Huss and Silverstein, one traveled from east to west by moving from the right to the left of the screen (63).

In picture books, however, the convention that movement proceeds from left to right is so strong that, in a series of pictures in *Freight Train* that first show each of the cars separately and then finally show the train as a whole, Donald Crews depicts the caboose first. Presumably, he wants to show the train in the conventional order, from left to right, but he also wants it to be moving toward the right. It might have been more logical to start with the engine, the front of the train, but then either the train or the direction of the illustrator's movement across it would have to have been from right to left.

Leo Lionni's *Swimmy* offers another interesting contradiction of the left-right convention. When Swimmy addresses the other fish, he is on the left and they are on the right, as we might expect in terms of Gaffron's theory of the glance curve; we move from action to response. But when Swimmy becomes the leader of the other fish, he is to their right. That seems to happen simply because the fish are now on the move and must, therefore, move toward the right; for Swimmy to lead them the other way would imply that he was not a successful guide.

In fact, characters frequently move to the left when the story suggests that their progress is impeded. Sylvester moves to the left as he is stopped by a lion in Steig's *Sylvester and the Magic Pebble*. The fox in *Rosie's Walk* turns left even though the wagon he stands in moves to the right and, disastrously, into some beehives. Peter Rabbit, who enters the garden toward the right and also leaves it toward the right, is always to the left of Mr. McGregor as he is chased by him. Furthermore, characters often turn to the left in leisurely circumstances, in which time seems suspended; Mr. Rabbit and the girl frequently do so in *Mr. Rabbit and the Lovely Present*. More surprisingly, Alan faces left in *The Garden of Abdul Gasazi* whenever the pictures depict fast activity—falling down the steps, reaching for the duck that holds his hat; in these pictures, the sense of mystery is heightened by the paradoxical relationship of quick movement and time suspended; something similar happens when Ida tumbles backward into Outside Over There to the left, even though her movement up to this point has been to the right.

A more complicated use of directional conventions is the mixture of movement from left to right and from right to left, which tends to imply hectic confusion—lack of direction. Speaking of Caldecott's *Three Jovial Huntsmen*, Jon Cech suggests that Caldecott breaks the rule of left-to-right movement: "The pictures, the visual action of the book, are multidirectional like a hunt. The chase doubles back on itself, seeming to force the reader's eye back on the left margin where he has begun to read" (118).

Another complication occurs when the direction of an implied movement does not parallel the top and bottom edges of a picture. Directional convention intermixes with ideas about gravity: we tend to assume that diagonal lines joining the bottom left and top right of a picture are moving upward, and that diagonals joining top left and bottom right are moving downward. The boy in *Arrow to the Sun* is lofted toward the sun in part because he starts at the bottom left; not surprisingly, he returns to earth by moving toward the bottom right. Earlier in the same book, the boy goes upstairs toward the top right and, on the next page, downstairs toward the bottom right; while it would be more logical for him to go down the same stairway he came up, it would look awkward and confusing. Less obviously, Spier's Noah lets the dove go at the bottom left of a diagonal formed by his arm and by the action line behind the bird at the top right; the bird returns at the top left of a diagonal made by Noah's arm.

Because these left-right distinctions are conventional, those unfamiliar with the conventions are not likely to understand their meanings. As a three-year-old, one of my own children once pointed to the right-hand side of a two-page spread in Wanda Gag's *Millions of Cats* and said, "The pond is empty." Then he pointed to the left-hand page and said, "Now somebody filled it up." The text tells us what most of us would have guessed anyway, that the pond was full before it was empty, but since my son happened to glance at the right-hand page first, he simply assumed it came first in a sequence. A year later, having learned from looking at numerous picture books that time conventionally passes from left to right in these books, my son understood what Gag had intended. He had learned a competence he needed, even though he was not conscious of having done so. Similarly, a student who had lived much of her life in Israel once told me that she never understood why so many pictures in picture books had made her feel uncomfortable until we talked in class about movements from left to right; she showed me picture books printed in Israel in which moving objects tend to move to the left. As Joseph Schwarcz suggests in *Ways of the Illustrator,* we seem to learn pictorial direction in relation to the direction of the language we know best (30).

At the same time as my son reversed the right- and left-hand pages of a book, his response to Wanda Gag's picture for "Every day they gave it plenty of milk—and soon it grew nice and plump" was, "Let me count all the cats." In fact, Gag's picture does show ten different cats, but if we understand the appropriate convention, we will understand that it actually depicts one cat in a series of moments that move from left to right; the fat cat on the right is the skinny cat on the left at a point later in time. Many picture books make use of this convention and show the same characters more than once in the same picture; Joseph Schwarcz calls this "continuous narrative" (*Ways of the Illustrator* 24).

Arrow to the Sun and *Why Mosquitoes Buzz in People's Ears* both use "continuous narrative." The backdrops are continuous, but if we read the pictures from left to right, we will discover the same characters in a series of consecutive actions. We see McDermott's boy first running from friends on the left, and then being consoled by his mother on the right; later he turns into an arrow in a series of images on the same page. In *Why Mosquitoes Buzz* we also see the same characters twice in different locations and must understand that the depiction on the left comes first in order to understand the story, but here the figures are sometimes immediately beside each other and sometimes even partially superimposed on each other. The rabbit is seen in his hole as the snake enters it and also leaving his hole an instant later, and these two images share one edge. The crow's caw is depicted as a series of superimposed crows, each larger and brighter than the one to its left; later, the owl hoots in two images so superimposed that the left wing of one forms part of the right wing of the other.

The Dillons carry this sort of superimposition even further in their pictures for Aardema's *Who's in Rabbit's House?* in which we see the same person, sometimes three, sometimes four, and at one point even fourteen times in the same picture, in a series of actions that form one large movement. There is no narrative reason why we need to see three moments of Rabbit's attempt to enter her house, three moments of Leopard's leap onto the roof, seven moments of Caterpillar's flight; the actions could as readily be communicated by one figure. But the Dillons gain more than they lose here, for these pictures have an astonishingly fluid grace. The black arms and legs of the characters playing the parts of the animals in the story, repeated so many times, create subtle visual rhythms so that, paradoxically, these pictures which show so many stopped actions seem filled with energy. They are like the frames of a film all superimposed on each other and seen at once; they achieve some of the effect of graceful motion that Matisse achieves in his painting *The Dance*, in which we see a circle composed of what looks like the same naked body in a series of consecutive motions.

Yet despite their energy, neither *The Dance* nor the pictures in *Who's in Rabbit's House?* convey any sense of time: rather, they convey a sense of time "typified"—of time *depicted*. They transform temporal movement and rhythm into visual movement and rhythm, actual activity into patterns on a two-dimensional field. They convey the *effect* of movement by finding an equivalent for it in unmoving visual imagery—in the conventions of a motionless medium.

That it is pictorial conventions that convey energy or activity in picture-book art becomes particularly clear in a comparison of two picture books that contain many pictures of people at rest. In the decidedly restful pictures in *Mr. Rabbit and the Lovely Present*, the characters keep their feet firmly on the ground even while they are walking, and the only actual lines amid a riot of small daubs of paint of different colors are the firm outlines that pin the characters to the background. But in Evaline Ness's *Sam, Bangs, and Moonshine*, even though Sam is continually shown lying on the ground or sitting dejectedly, the pictures actually convey the emotional turbulence of the situation, for they look anything but relaxed. Ness uses a wide variety of the techniques I have mentioned to suggest motion. Numerous parallel lines draw our eyes past and through the figure of Sam, such as the lines of the boxes in the background as she feels bad about Bangs and the lines of rain on the window in front of her as she quietly peers through it. And as Sam sits holding a gerbil and imagines it a kangaroo, Ness places her father's boots directly over her head, so that they seem about to descend and crush her, just as his anger crushes her imagination.

The depictions of still figures that convey intense emotional activity in *Sam, Bangs, and Moonshine* distinguish it from many other memorable picture books, which depict intense activity but actually convey a sense of stillness. For all their visual excitement and implied energy, the Dillons' pictures for *Why Mosquitoes Buzz in People's Ears* and *Who's in Rabbit's House?* both enforce the sense that time has stopped by showing us so many images of stopped activity. Ed Emberley's pictures for *Drummer Hoff* and Pat Hutchins's pictures for *Rosie's Walk* have a different sort of stillness; and different again but equally still are most of the work of Nicola Bayley, Nancy Ekholm Burkert, and Errol Le Cain; Sendak's *Where the Wild Things Are* and *Outside Over There*; and Van Allsburg's *The Garden of Abdul Gasazi*, *Jumanji*, and *Wreck of the Zephyr*.

The Dillons, Emberley, and Hutchins all make much use of bright colors in large, unshaded areas that focus attention on shapes rather than lines, on the two-dimensional surfaces of the pictures rather than the action they imply in a three-dimensional space. These pictures are not without energy; their compositions are unsettlingly bold, and they convey excitement even if they stop motion. But they have the energy of abstract art, not that of depicted action; it is a matter of compositional dynamics rather than of narrative information about the events depicted.

The others are another matter altogether. They are intensely and accurately detailed, and they have depth and a sense of solidity, yet they seem surprisingly still—even, sometimes, mysteriously immobile. Van Allsburg's Alan floats fixedly over the stairs of Gasazi's garden rather than seeming to fall on them, and when Sendak's Max swings from a tree, he and the Wild Things look as if they have been hanging in that same position for some time rather than being actively engaged in the act of moving from branch to branch. These pictures convey a dreamlike stillness, something like the logical conclusion of those sequences in motion pictures that slow down the movements of horses or athletes to make them look as if they were being resisted by the air itself; in these picture books, the air seems heavy enough to have stopped the movement altogether.

Sendak and Van Allsburg achieve that effect by doing everything possible to contradict and repress the intense activity they depict. In both cases, the protagonist's eyes are almost always shown shut—as if he were asleep, still instead of moving. In both cases, intense light sources make strong contrasts between shadow and light; the deep shading gives tremendous solidity to both objects and people, so that they look lumbrous, sculptural, hard to move—just as do the objects and people in the paintings of Picasso's classical period, which share the stilled fixity of these figures of Max and Alan. Also, Van Allsburg densely textures the surfaces of the objects he depicts, and Sendak makes much use of crosshatching; both these uses of line tend to act as grids that hold the characters down and make them seem still even when they are depicted in motion. While the pictures of both artists have some of the simplified feeling of cartoons, they are cartoons filled in, richly colored or shaded in a way that contradicts their energetic use of line—and neither uses action lines where we would expect to find them in cartoons.

The result of all this is a sense of dreamlike mystery, evoked most completely by one picture in each book. Sendak's depiction of Max and the Wild Things against a dark blue sky under a full moon shows their wild rumpus as a frenzy of activity that seems absolutely still; the one Wild Thing with no feet on the ground seems to be suspended in midair, balanced forever on nothing. Much the same feeling is evoked by Van Allsburg's picture of Alan, theoretically falling, but looking as if he were floating in suspended time above the stairway. And interestingly, Sendak conveys almost exactly the same sense of time suspended in his pictures of David floating over the landscape in Jarrell's *Fly by Night* and of Ida floating over the landscape in *Outside Over There*. All these pictures have some of the mystery of magic realism—an appropriate mood for the dreamlike situations they depict.

A similar feeling is engendered, albeit less intensely, by the fairy tales illustrated by Burkert and Le Cain and by many other illustrators who make use of rich colors and patterns and textures that draw attention away from the actions they depict. Such pictures are very much in the tradition of the richly detailed illustrations of fairy tales by artists like Edmund Dulac and Kay Nielsen, which focus so much on the splendid objects they depict that it becomes hard even to notice the people. Svetlana Alpers suggests the effect of such pictures when she says, "There seems to be an inverse proportion between attentive description and action: attention to the surface of the world described is achieved at the expense of representation of narrative action" (xxi). These illustrators most characteristically convey meaning through details of surface rather than through depictions of action.

The figures drawn by artists like Dulac and Nielsen, and by too many contemporary illustrators in this sumptuous tradition, are themselves often merely beautiful objects to admire; their positions are often the relaxed, passive ones of nudes in pinup photographs. But such is not the case with the people depicted by Burkert, or even the ones depicted by Le

Cain. They *are* doing interesting things; they *are* more than decorative. Like Sendak and Van Allsburg, Burkert and Le Cain combine effects that stop motion with depictions of activity, and thus create the paradoxically unsettling stillness that characterizes many of the best picture books.

■ ■ ■ ■

If a picture can, by means of various conventions, convey motion and the passage of time (or startle us with the apparent lack of those qualities), then it can, obviously, also suggest the organized events of a story—the interconnectedness of cause and effect that makes up a plot. It can do so because its evocation of motion and time's passage suggests cause-and-effect relationships among the objects it depicts. In *Rosie's Walk* we understand that the motion implied by Rosie's right-facing image causes the fox to follow her; in *Arrow to the Sun* the arrow shape that tells us the boy is flying toward the sun also suggests a cause-and-effect relationship between the boy and the bow. Furthermore, many of the various narrative implications of size, space, color, and so on that I discussed earlier depend on the way in which they evoke cause-and-effect relationships; to give just one obvious example, the shadows of characters that overlap the figures of other characters imply how those characters affect each other.

Even a picture of a set of visual objects that have no apparent temporal relationship with each other may evoke a story—as long as we assume that the figures we see in it are effects of causes not shown in the picture. For instance, even though the picture of Peter Rabbit's mother walking down the path shows only her holding her basket and walking through the forest, the details are interesting enough that even a viewer who looks at this picture divorced from its context in the book is likely to ask questions about them that evoke a past and a future and thus demand a narrative. What caused this rabbit to be clothed, and in this particular clothing? What led her to be carrying a basket and an umbrella? Where is she going to or from? Where does the path we see her on lead to?

Knowledge of the usual connections between similar objects and people in real life may help us to answer such questions, as can knowledge of the conventions that make pictures meaningful. Mrs. Rabbit's umbrella suggests that she has considered the possibility of rain, and the vague outlines and weak colors of the background behind her force us to acknowledge her sharply outlined and brightly colored figure as the central focus and most potentially meaningful element in the picture. The same factors particularly influence the cause-and-effect relationships we read into a picture that more clearly implies movement. As I said before, our knowing that rabbits do not usually jump up into sieves helps us to interpret the picture of Peter Rabbit and the sieve. We will also realize that pictorial gravity makes objects near the tops of pictures usually move down onto the objects beneath them, so we will assume that the sieve is moving down onto Peter, not that Peter is jumping up at the sieve. In picture books, of course, we also base such guesses on what we know about the story so far; even before we read the words that accompany the picture of the rabbit and the sieve, we will assume on the basis of information on previous pages that this particular image of a rabbit still represents Peter and that the hands on the sieve belong to Mr. McGregor.

Even then, though, we might not get the facts straight—at least, we might not understand them in the same way as the words tell us about them. For instance, from the picture of Peter and the sieve we might guess that something needed to be said about the birds we see in it—after all, they were mentioned prominently on the previous page when they urged Peter to exert himself. But in fact the text here says nothing about them and thus informs us that they do not matter very much at this moment. We also might assume from our knowledge of the story so far that Peter is too disheartened to find the strength to escape; the picture does not disallow that possibility, for we do not know where the sieve will land, and it looks as if it might well land on Peter. It takes the text accompanying the picture to tell us that in fact Peter has found new courage and that he does get away. Both differences are enlightening. In one case the picture shows a detail that amplifies the text and makes the situation more specific—something that pictures often do; but that detail is not as essential to the narrative thrust as the picture alone might suggest. In the other example, the picture shows a stopped action but communicates neither its outcome nor its emotional significance—in this case, courage instead of fear. Pictures do not convey such emotional information easily—especially when they show the incommunicative faces of creatures like rabbits.

Even so, we can use our store of previous knowledge to create a cause-and-effect relationship among the various parts of the picture that postulates the existence of time within it and lets us guess at the story it might be conveying. We can assume that appearances speak of actions and emotions—that they are, indeed, effects whose causes can be guessed at—and we can then "read" pictures for the meanings they suggest. Charles Lamb emphasized the linguistic nature of this sort of reading when he said of Hogarth, "His graphic representations are indeed books: they have the teeming, fruitful, suggestive meanings of words. Other pictures we look at—his prints we read" (449).

Raymond Lister's descriptions of a similar sort of art, Victorian narrative painting, imply much about the nature and the limitations of such reading. He sees Thomas Webster's *A Village Choir* as "a picture of a moment, as if fixed by a lens of a camera . . . but the painter's obvious invitation to us to speculate on the various elements of the scene makes it a narrative picture. Why does the 'cellist look so grim? Why is the clarinet player quizzically eyeing the farm worker? These, and many more questions pass through our mind as we look at the picture—and we can only guess at the answers" (44). That last phrase is particularly revealing. The picture can show us a stare that excites our interest and makes us ask questions, but it cannot provide us with the history that led to the stare or the feeling behind it. Unaccompanied by detailed texts, Victorian narrative paintings do not so much tell stories as they allow viewers to make them up. As Lister suggests in talking about Richard Redgrave's *The Poor Teacher,* viewers "can, in fact, work out a dozen different interpretations of many of its details" (22). Lamb suggested that this was just the quality he appreciated most in Hogarth: "it is peculiar to the confidence of high genius alone to trust so much to spectators or readers" (45).

Because there is usually a text to guide us in our reading of their pictures, picture-book illustrators do not trust their spectators quite so much. But they must in fact trust us, presume our knowledge of both societal and pictorial conventions; Potter must trust us to understand why a female would wear a cape and carry an umbrella, and Virginia Lee Burton must trust us to understand that the flowers, orange leaves, and snowflakes she shows on one page of *The Little House* are symbolic representations of the passing seasons, not a realistic depiction of highly unsettled weather.

Sometimes illustrators cleverly make use of this need for trust by deliberately depicting objects in startling contexts; the pleasure of such pictures is that we can indeed work out "a dozen different interpretations," and probably be satisfied with none of them. In Nicola Bayley's *Book of Nursery Rhymes*, for instance, the single picture for "Goosey Goosey Gander" depicts an ornate boudoir in which a goose with spread wings stands beside some spilled powder and a pair of lady's shoes. On the wall is a picture of a woman in eighteenth-century dress, yawning. Through the open doorway of the room, we see the legs of a man in carpet slippers suspended above a flight of stairs. Without the text to guide us, we might imagine any number of explanations for this picture; we might even assume that the man is floating up the stairs instead of falling down them. But even with the text, many details must still be accounted for. We do not know why the powder spilled, or how, or if it has anything to do with the shoes or the goose; we must acknowledge that there is something odd about a portrait of a yawning woman hanging on a wall, and we must cope with the incommunicatively gooselike appearance of the goose.

We must guess about two important aspects of this picture: what the characters it depicts are thinking and feeling and what sequence of events is implied by the particular moment we actually see—what happened before it to lead to the spilled powder and what is likely to happen after it. Not surprisingly, these are the aspects of stories that the *texts* of most picture books convey to us; Bayley creates a pleasurable game by breaking the rule and creating a picture which demands textual information the text does not supply.

On the other hand, Bayley's picture does communicate some definite information—it does focus our attention on what specifically demands our explanations. It *is* a very ornate house in which these events take place, and any interpretation would have to account for the elegant setting. The woman *is* yawning; any interpretation would have to accommodate the traditional emotions we connect with that open mouth—tiredness or boredom. The powder *is* on the floor, where it ought not to be; any interpretation will have to take into account this divergence from the ordinary. And so on. What this picture succinctly reveals is the extent to which all pictures provide images that demand further explanation and thus engage our talent for story making. As I will show later, the ability of pictures to imply and require information exterior to themselves explains the characteristic relationships of pictures and texts in picture books.

Certain kinds of pictures arouse narrative expectations more than others. We can most successfully find stories in pictures like the one by Nicola Bayley mentioned above and Burkert's of Snow White in the dwarfs' house, both of which provide many effects for which we may imagine causes—many details to attract our attention and require explanation. Because we need information before we can interpret a situation, we need pictures of people *in* settings and preferably in groups. Burkert's picture of Snow White on the dust jacket of her book and her picture of Snow White's mother at her window have less detail, less potential for a viewer's reading of relationships, and less narrative import.

There is also no picture of the same situation preceding these, and there is no picture preceding or following Bayley's single depiction of the goose. Simply because a sequence of pictures implies a cause-and-effect relationship that introduces time in between the fixed moments we actually see, a sequence is more capable of implying a story than a single picture. Each depiction of an object indicates one particular moment in time—the moment at which the object looked that way. Even within a single picture, consequently, duplicated figures indicate the time that passes between them: when we see one of the characters more than once in each picture of *Who's in Rabbit's House?* we assume the existence of the time it would take to move from one position to the next, and thus we assume that the character actually occupied the infinite number of theoretically separable and therefore depictable, but in fact undepicted, positions between the ones we do actually see. The picture implies both times and actions that it does not actually depict. Similarly, we assume the existence both of temporal movement and of an entire series of actions which we do not actually see but which would logically fill that imagined time in a sequence of different pictures; such actions would, for instance, logically lead Sendak's Max through a series of undepicted moments in which he would proceed from hammering a nail into a wall in one picture in *Wild Things* to a flight toward a dog in the next picture to a dead stop behind the door of his room in the next picture.

As we imagine the movements between the events actually depicted in a sequence of pictures, we tend to interpret each of the pictures differently from the way we might have if we had seen it by itself. Thus each picture in Burton's *The Little House* is a landscape, and by itself each would suggest little but atmosphere. But seen as a sequence, the pictures imply a number of changes that would have a powerful narrative effect even without the words that accompany them. As the work of cognitive psychologists suggests, we perceive new experiences in terms of the experiences preceding them. As I show later, the words in picture books are an inseparable part of that experience, yet even if we ignore those words, as we do in a first glance through a new book, each picture in a picture book establishes a context for the picture that follows—becomes a schema that determines how we will perceive the next picture. It establishes certain expectations, and the story we guess at to connect a series of pictures will depend on how they both fulfill and thwart our expectations. As Ulric Neisser says, "we cannot perceive unless we anticipate, but we must not see *only* what we anticipate" (43). A picture of a house surrounded by a rural landscape provides the context for a picture of the same house in the same landscape but with a road being built across it; it is the difference between the two pictures, the road, the thing that is left over after the schema is applied, that attracts our attention and causes us to invent a story that will explain the change.

puppy

Stereotypical images like this one of a puppy are less representations of actual appearances than collections of intellectually defined attributes. Consequently, interpreting them is an act of verbal rather than visual dexterity—a matter of giving names to the generalized ideas represented: the dots that signify eyes and the solid mass of one color that represents variegated fur. (From *A First Book Open and Say*. Copyright © 1978 by Brimax Books Ltd. Reprinted by permission of Brimax Books Ltd.)

Our knowledge changes our understanding of even the simplest of images: someone ignorant of the existence of apples might have trouble separating this figure of an apple from its complex background; someone with more specialized knowledge might identify it as a MacIntosh. To conform to the apple stereotype, this one is seen with its stem at the top. But since the image is a photograph of an actual apple, we might bring our assumptions about realism into play and wonder why the apple doesn't roll away. (Illustration from *Baby's Things*. Copyright © 1966, 1972 by Platt & Munk, Inc. Reprinted by permission.)

"Or maybe," she said, "it's asleep on the sand. Somewhere, anywhere on the beach."

Wherever Sam sent Thomas, he went. He climbed up trees, ran down steps, and scoured the beach, but he never found Sam's baby kangaroo.

While Thomas searched, Sam sat in her chariot and was drawn by dragons to faraway secret worlds.

Composition implies emotion. The small child, alone and looking for something he cannot find, is isolated against white space but connected by his shadow to the jarring sets of parallel lines formed by the fences, lines which imply some turmoil. (From

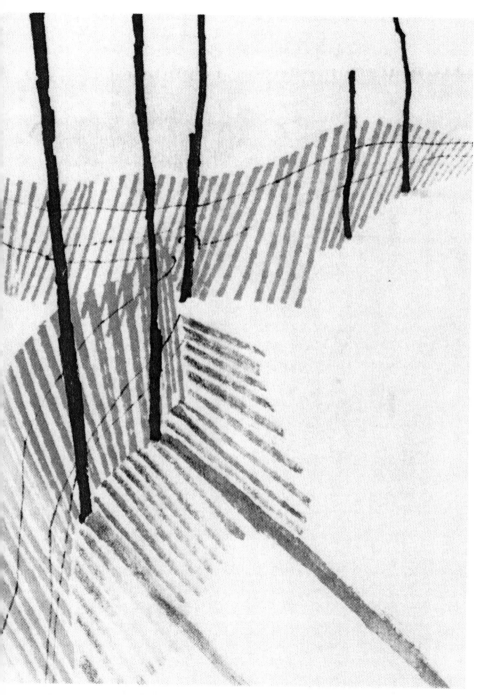

Sam, Bangs, and Moonshine written and illustrated by Evaline Ness. Copyright ©
1966 by Evaline Ness. Reprinted by permission of Henry Holt and Company, Inc.)

In the midst of a scene of boisterous childish activity, one female child takes the pose of a conventional nude, her voluptuously curved back turned to the viewer. (A Randolph Caldecott illustration for "The Farmer's Boy.")

The horrors of Alexander's horrible day are confirmed by pictures that report their truth. The pictures show not just the situation he describes so subjectively in his first-person narrative but also Alexander himself *in* those situations, viewed from an objective distance. The pictures imply a different point of view from the words; their comic style undercuts and makes humorous the seriousness of Alexander's own report. (Reproduced with the permission of Atheneum Publishers, an imprint of Macmillan Publishing Company, from *Alexander and the Terrible, Horrible, No-Good, Very Bad Day* by Judith Viorst, illustrated by Ray Cruz. Pictures copyright © 1972 Ray Cruz.)

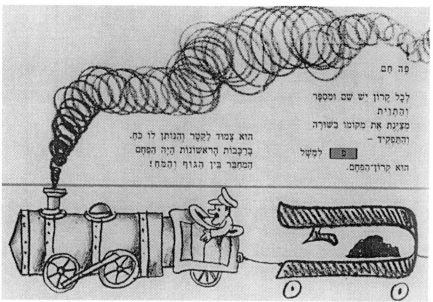

In this picture book published in Israel, the direction of the train's movement is the same as that of the Hebrew text—from right to left. (Illustration by Dani Kerman from Abba Kovner's *Journey to the Land of Words*. Reprinted by permission of the illustrator.)

While the text accompanying this picture reports dreams as literal truths, the picture shows more of the actual situation by revealing the peculiar meeting of reality and dream. Here we see not only the moment in which a real quilt turns into a dream landscape but also the arm of the dreamer's body. We are in the dream and in the

room with the dreamer at the same time. (From *The Quilt* by Ann Jonas. Copyright © 1984 by Ann Jonas. Reprinted by permission of Greenwillow Books—William Morrow and Company.)

Both pictures illustrate the moment at which Snow White's mother sits at a window, pricks her finger, and wishes for a daughter. But each adds further information about the situation; thus, each tells a different story and causes the same words to tell a different story. Nancy Ekholm Burkert's queen, *left*, is framed like a painting, an object of aesthetic appreciation. Trina Schart Hyman's queen, *above*, is viewed from a significantly different angle; thus, the reader comes to know her better through her possessions and empathizes with her. (Burkert illustration from *Snow White and the Seven Dwarfs* © 1972 by Nancy Ekholm Burkert. Reprinted by permission of the illustrator. Hyman illustration from *Snow White* by the Brothers Grimm, translated by Paul Heins. Translation copyright © 1979 by Paul Heins. Illustrations copyright © 1979 by Trina Schart Hyman. Reprinted by permission of Little, Brown and Company.)

"Mirror, mirror on the wall,
Who is the fairest of them all?"
asked the Queen.

Supposedly the "fairest of them all," the Queen of "Snow White" is evil, and convention demands that evil people be ugly (or, at least, that evil women have features of the sort traditionally assumed to be masculine). (From *Now You Can Read . . . Snow White and the Seven Dwarfs* by Eric Kincaid, adapted by Lucy Kincaid. Copyright © 1980 by Brimax Books Ltd. Reprinted by permission of Brimax Books Ltd.)

This picture uses a potential liability to support the theme of the story it accompanies. The block of white on which the words appear is the central focus of the right-hand side of this two-page spread but tantalizingly hides the possibility of action, just as the prose hides the rhymes of poetry within it. Are the statues actually chasing the boy? Careful use of perspective, contrasting backgrounds, and the pointing hands of the statues focus attention on the small figure of the boy and create a tension through our natural tendency to look first at larger objects like the white block of the text. (Reprinted with permission of Macmillan Publishing Company from *The Changing Maze* by Zilpha Keatley Snyder. Illustrated by Charles Mikolaycak. Text copyright © 1985 by Zilpha Keatley Snyder. Illustrations copyright © 1985 by Charles Mikolaycak.)

The theoretically straight walls of the house are gently curved, as is almost every line in the picture. The predominant shape creates a nonthreatening atmosphere, and if the house's windows look like eyes, then the curved front step implies a cheery smile. But the picture is visually ambivalent: understood as words, the words have no visual depth; but understood as part of the picture, they imply a walk drawn in perspective, which grows wider as it gets closer to us. (From *The Little House* by Virginia Lee Burton. Copyright © 1942 by Virginia Lee Demetrios. Copyright © renewed 1969 by George Demetrios. Reprinted by permission of Houghton Mifflin Company.)

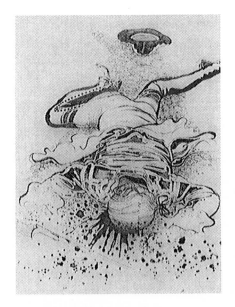

Even in death, Charles Keeping's bold highwayman expresses intense energy. The explosive lines of force created by blood and limbs make the figure seem to burst from the confining page; the peculiar angle from which it is viewed makes it seem to fall toward us. The energetic rhythms of the picture balance the regular beats of the poetic text. (From *The Highwayman* by Alfred Noyes, illustrated by Charles Keeping. Published by Oxford University Press 1981. Illustration © Charles Keeping 1981. Reprinted by permission of Oxford University Press.)

The chief's painted mask changed into a goat head and his whole body became
that of a mountain goat. The Temlahams watched in frightened silence. The
dancing goat stamped its hands and the lodge trembled. Suddenly a sharp crack
thrust its way through the floor and the goat chief leapt upon it. Now the
Temlahams screamed with fear.

In *The Mountain Goats of Temlaham*, Elizabeth Cleaver depicts figures and objects in a
conventional European representational style; her goat has the outline of a goat, not
the form lines and eyes sockets of the native tradition. Cleaver uses the stylized
shapes of traditional Northwest Coast native art only where they would have been
found traditionally—on native artifacts. Even though it is not authentic, the picture
has an affinity with the work of artists like Matisse that gives it the feel of primitive
art. (From *The Mountain Goats of Temlaham* by William Toye, illustrated by Elizabeth Cleaver. Copyright © 1969 by Oxford University Press. Reproduced by permission of Oxford University Press Canada.)

Overleaf: Disturbingly realistic dragons and witches like these do not allow us to dismiss such creatures as cute or endearing fantasies; we must confront the horror they
so graphically represent. Meanwhile, a very human-looking hero requires us to see the
implications of the events the story describes in terms of our acquaintances and ourselves. (From *King Stork* by Howard Pyle, illustrated by Trina Schart Hyman. Illustration copyright © 1973 by Trina Schart Hyman. Reprinted by permission of Little,
Brown and Company.)

The next night the princess flew away to the house of the one-eyed witch again, but there was the drummer close behind her just as he had been before.

"Uff!" said the one-eyed witch. "Here is a smell of Christian blood, for sure and certain." But all the same, she saw no more of the drummer than if he had never been born.

"See, Mother," said the princess, "that rogue of a drummer answered my question without winking over it."

"So," said the old witch, "we have missed for once, but the second time hits the mark: he will be asking you a question tomorrow, and here is a book that tells everything that has happened in the world, and if he asks you more than that he is a smart one and no mistake."

After that they sat down to supper again, but it was little the princess ate, for the drummer helped himself out of her plate just as he had done before.

They set out toward the prince's castle with the glass coffin on their shoulders. But they had not gone far when they stumbled and dropped it.

It is Jack Kent's decision to depict the moment in which the theoretically dead Snow White slides out of a dropped coffin amidst a shower of broken glass that defines his version of this fairy tale as comic. (From *The Happy Ever After Book* by Jack Kent. Copyright © 1976 by Jack Kent. Reprinted by permission of Random House, Inc.)

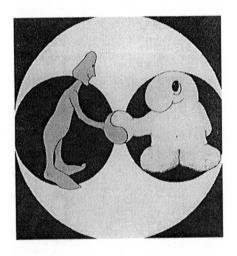

Conventional symbolism specifies the meaning of a picture unaccompanied by words. The two figures still occupy the separate circles that have isolated them from each other in previous pictures; but now those circles are inside a larger one that contains them both, and the mandala formed by their touching hands confirms the significance of the meeting of opposites. (From *Your Own Story* by Barbara Salsberg. Copyright © 1977 by Annick Press. Reproduced by permission of Annick Press Ltd.)

In many picture books, the last picture suggests a harmonious order. Here, the slant of the central figure is mirrored by the four figures to the left. The four figures to the right also all incline in the same direction, and each is a diminishing version of the other. Their headdresses mirror the object held by the central figure, and the concentric circles in the upper left mirror those in the bottom center. (From *Arrow to the Sun* by Gerald McDermott. Copyright © 1974 by Gerald McDermott. Reprinted by permission of Viking Penguin Inc.)

The static geometric shapes of Gerald McDermott's depiction of a boy imply energy because the figure stands precariously balanced on one leg. The energy becomes forward movement in the conventional left-to-right direction because the boy leans toward the right and also points toward where he is going. (From *Arrow to the Sun* by Gerald McDermott. Copyright © 1974 by Gerald McDermott. Reprinted by permission of Viking Penguin Inc.)

35

Through clever use of pictorial dynamics, Beatrix Potter's picture allows the viewer to create the motion it cannot actually depict. Implied action lines, assumptions about logical movement, and previous contexts help to tell us that the sieve is moving down onto Peter Rabbit. (From *The Tale of Peter Rabbit* by Beatrix Potter. Copyright © 1902 by Frederick Warne & Co., p. 35. Reprinted by permission of Frederick Warne & Co.)

It is an ordinary cloudy day in Manhattan—except the Empire State Building has lost its top. The precise documentary style creates a matter-of-fact tone that confirms the possibility of what has not yet happened. (From *Unbuilding* by David Macaulay. Copyright © 1980 by David Macaulay. Reprinted by permission of Houghton Mifflin Company.)

That happens only because, as I said earlier, we assume a temporal relationship that implies cause and effect; not only does picture A precede picture B, but something we see in picture A (or assume about the events we imagine to have occurred between picture A and picture B) led to something we see in picture B. A "picture sentence" found in Grady and Luecke's *Education and the Brain* reveals how firmly established that assumption is. The picture is a cartoon showing two bones on the left, then an arrow pointing to the right, then a dog with a bone in its mouth, then another arrow pointing to the right, followed by a question mark. Grady and Luecke offer the "sentence" as an example of how teachers might make use of their students' propensity for "visual thinking" as opposed to the more conventional verbal thinking that they believe to be overstressed in education. It is meant to represent a question about subtraction: if there are two bones, and a dog comes along and eats one, then how many bones will be left? While Grady and Luecke incorrectly assume that the arrow and the question mark are visual representations rather than conventional (and verbally oriented) symbolism, what is more revealing is their apparently unconscious assumption that viewers will automatically read the various images in a certain sequence and assume a cause-and-effect relationship among them.

Yet even though both the sequence and the relationship are purely conventional, it seems that Grady and Luecke were not wrong in making that latter assumption. Convinced that pictures without words to explain them cannot communicate such a specific meaning, I showed this "picture sentence" to a hundred or so people, of all ages from three to seventy, and asked them only, "What is the answer?" While these viewers were often just as confused and frustrated by my unhelpful instructions as I had expected, they almost always came up with an "answer," all the answers did postulate a cause-and-effect relationship among the pictures, and almost all of them suggested a story that connected the two images in a conventional left-to-right sequence and led to a third one. One person said, "If you have two bones and a dog comes along, then you have three bones and a dog." A number of people familiar with the effects of bones on dogs drew pictures of dog leavings after the arrow. One symmetrically minded person wrote, "If you have two bones and then a dog and a bone, then next you have to have two dogs." The habit of reading cause-and-effect relationships among pictures in a sequence is clearly a deeply ingrained one.

In order to postulate such relationships, we must understand that the meaning of each succeeding image actually changes the meaning of the images that preceded it. First we see two bones, and that is all; but after we see the dog, we must think of the bones in terms of the relationships of bones with dogs. In his structural analysis of *Anno's Counting Book*, Stephen Roxburgh says that the first picture in the book does not mean anything: "Finally, we simply don't know enough" (49). But "as we turn the page . . . all hell breaks loose"; in fact, the difference between this picture and the one before it changes the meaning of the first one. It is no longer just a snowscape; the very absence of activity in it makes it significantly different from the picture that follows it, which depicts numerous people and objects. In retrospect it comes to seem deliberately and noticeably empty—an appropriate image of the nothing that precedes the number one.

Something similar happens in *The Little House*. As the urban blight depicted in the succeeding pictures leaves the original bucolic peacefulness far behind, the merely pleasant pastoral of the first picture becomes modified in the viewer's memory into a paradise lost, a place particularly desirable because it is no longer obtainable. A little more subtly, we come to understand the implications of Max's joyous anarchy in the first pictures of *Where the Wild Things Are* more completely only when we see the picture that shows him alone in his room; the anarchy is now not merely fun but appears to have significant social implications. Furthermore, it is not until much later in the book that we may recall the picture "by Max" hanging on the staircase wall in those earlier pictures and come to understand its implications: we learn that Max drew not just a monster but a creature he might visit in his imagination, and we understand how very much the place where the Wild Things are is indeed a product of Max's imagination. The model airplane hanging over Mickey's bed in the first pictures of *In the Night Kitchen* has a similar function. Such examples suggest how very much the later pictures in a book become a context for the earlier ones in rereadings. It is impossible to reread a book as we first experienced it.

In juxtaposing a series of pictures in order to imply the sequence of a story, picture-book artists act much as filmmakers do. André Bazin suggests that montage, assumed by many to be the essence of film art, is "the creation of a sense of meaning not proper to the images themselves but derived exclusively from their juxtaposition" (90). In films, the arrangement of a succession of shots provides the events depicted with their significance; not surprisingly, filmmakers often prepare themselves for shooting by using storyboards, sequential drawings of the various shots they intend to make of the scenes they will film that look much like picture books.

Conversely, picture-book artists use techniques of visual storytelling borrowed from films to make aspects of a sequence of pictures meaningful. In *Tikki Tikki Tembo*, for instance, Blair Lent's first picture is much like what cinematographers call an "establishing shot"; so is the picture on the title page of *Rosie's Walk*. Both these pictures show the entire area in which the story takes place, as seen from a distance. The succeeding pictures duplicate small areas of the establishing shot; we can understand the geographical connections between the various specific locales we see throughout these books because we first saw them together. Since the first picture establishes the geographical relationships of all the others, these illustrators are free to concentrate on depicting the emotional high points of the story, the narrative connections rather than the geographical ones. The final picture of Peter Spier's *Oh! Were They Ever Happy!* showing an entire house we have previously seen only in small sections as children paint different parts of it in different colors, is a clever reversal of this technique; our inability to see the total effect of the house in all the different colors creates a suspenseful tension that only the final picture resolves.

Another type of film editing is the "form cut." According to Huss and Silverstein, "This consists merely of framing in a successive shot an object which has a shape or contour similar to an image in the shot immediately preceding, the two shots together creating a rhythm based on their geo-metrical congruity and balance" (67). In picture books, the visual rhythms created by sequential images of similar shapes often have a strong effect on the meaning of stories: they use the action of turning a page and viewing a series of pictures to support the meaning of the actions in the pictures.

In *The Garden of Abdul Gasazi*, for instance, the round back of the sofa Alan lies on is replaced by the curve of the bridge in the next picture. That curve narrows into the round shape made by the trees surrounding the square gate in the next picture, and that is followed by the square steps and curved rails of the stairways in the next picture; meanwhile the leaves that surrounded the gate are here replaced by two trees, one at each side of the picture, and similar trees occupy similar positions in the next picture, in which the curve of the stairway is replaced by the curves of the stream bank and the path. Later in the book, Gasazi is seen standing inside the arch of a doorway and then, on the next page, beside the arch of a fire-place, and Alan reaches for his hat at the top of a flight of stairs that is echoed by the similarly positioned flight of stairs in the next picture. All these connections imply a mysterious unity in a series of diverse land-scapes; they suggest something like the crazy logic that provides the se-quence of many dreams and thus help to express the mood of the events depicted.

More repetitively, the arches found in similar positions on each page of Hyman's *Sleeping Beauty* operate as form cuts that create a more static sequential rhythm; they provide a sort of visual subplot of orderliness that undercuts and works to balance the almost excessively sentimental depic-tions of people who stand in front of them in various highly romantic or melodramatic poses. The spiraling lines found in the same locations in each picture of Burton's *The Little House* also create a regular rhythm that binds the book together, but in this case the repetitive form cuts amplify the overall insistence on repetitive natural cycles.

The constant presence of form cuts also supports the narrative by mak-ing the differences between each picture clear, as does the constant square, pink shape of the house in the same position on each page. A similar use of a fixed position to anchor narratively significant changes surrounding it—a constantly repeating form cut that focuses attention on that which differs from itself—appears in the pictures for many accretive stories. For instance, Pat Hutchins depicts the same tree in each picture of *Goodnight, Owl* but adds a new set of birds each time; the old birds always remain in the same position, so that the point of the story, the ever louder and more annoying noises of an ever larger number of singing birds, is given a visual equivalent. And in Marie Hall Ets's *Elephant in a Well*, the fact that the elephant always appears in the same position makes clearer the addition on each spread of a new animal to help pull it out of the well. In *Where the Wild Things Are*, Sendak uses a variation of the same technique during the transformation of Max's room into a forest; Max stays in the same position in the picture even though his posture changes, and the posts of his bed turn into trees that occupy their former position; even the bushes in the forest seem to grow from the potted plant which occupied their position in the original room.

Another technique of filmmaking—the dynamic frame—is more common in picture books than it is in films. Filmmakers who use dynamic framing actually change the size and the shape of the image on the screen. But this obvious control of the message by the artist has gone out of fashion in moviemaking, and when there is dynamic framing in contemporary movies, it is done by shooting through doorways and such, so that the lighted area we see is shaped even though the shape of the screen itself does not change. Hyman uses a technique much like that in her many views through arches in *Sleeping Beauty*. But in picture books, a sequence of actual variations in the size and shape of pictures is also common and often adds to the meaning of the action depicted. I earlier discussed how the pictures gradually grow in size and then become smaller during the course of *Where the Wild Things Are*. Many picture books contain sometimes one, sometimes two, sometimes even more pictures per page. In Steig's *The Amazing Bone*, there are two pictures on pages that depict intense activity, only one at more relaxed moments. In Spier's *Noah's Ark*, there are as many as seven and as few as one picture on each set of facing pages; the seven are crowded pictures that together convey the confusion and activity of life on the crowded ark, and the one shows nothing but the ark itself, seen from a distance against a field of pure blue, which conveys the immensity of the flood. We do not find these changes in the size of frames distracting, as we probably would in films; they are merely an acceptable convention of current picture-book technique. What is rare in one medium is acceptable in the other.

That became particularly clear to me when I decided to borrow the techniques of film analysis and attempt a "shot analysis" of the pictures in some well-known picture books. A shot is a single sequence in a film; a "shot analysis" is a description of the sequence of shots. In film, shots can vary from each other by means of the way the camera moves—from left to right, from up to down; by means of the way the actors move before it; by means of the angle from which the camera shoots—from above, from below, or from eye level; and by means of the distance between the camera and the subject—close-ups, middle-distance shots, long shots. As I have shown in both this chapter and the last one, picture-book artists do make use of such variations, particularly differences of angle and distance, to convey meaning in individual pictures; like Van Allsburg in *The Garden of Abdul Gasazi*, they may present views from different angles that imply interpretations of the actions depicted, and like Burkert in *Snow White* or Spier in *Oh! Were They Ever Happy!* they may sometimes use a long shot to reinforce the meaning of a particular moment.

Significantly, however, my shot analyses of picture books revealed only one book that consistently used a wide repertoire of variations of both distance and point of view throughout: Robert Lawson's *The Story of Ferdinand*, which includes very low shots (the castle on the first page), long high shots (the little bulls butting their heads together), reverse shots (we first see Ferdinand in the foreground under his tree, then on the next page we see his mother in the foreground looking at Ferdinand in the background, a change that matches the changing focus of the story), close-ups (the five men from Madrid), even detail shots (the bee that Ferdinand is about to sit on).

Barbara Bader suggests that "*Ferdinand* is only one of many picture books that, in its choice of vantage points, its quick cuts, its total flexibility, would have been unthinkable before motion pictures" (*American Picturebooks* 145–46). She is right about *Ferdinand*, certainly, but for the most part my shot analyses revealed only what I said in the last chapter—that most pictures in most picture books are middle-distance or long shots, showing full figures in settings, usually seen at eye level; my shot analysis of *Where the Wild Things Are* repeats the words "long shot at eye level" seventeen times—once for every picture in the book. In point of fact, the sequences created by picture-book artists do not take advantage of the variety of shots common in films; they tend to express the significance of the actions they depict by other means, and they have quite a different sort of rhythm.

Even when picture-book illustrators do vary from eye-level middle-distance or long shots, the effect of the variation is not cinematic. In films, we see the same scene from a variety of angles; in most picture books, indeed even in *Ferdinand*, every picture marks a different point in the story, in effect a different episode. My attempts to do shot analyses of picture books were thwarted from the beginning by my quick realization that almost every picture in most books represents a different scene. The whole point of film montage is that we come to understand action by means of the various ways the action has been broken down into smaller bits. But that does not happen in picture books. That, I believe, is the major difference between the depiction of action in picture-book narrative and in all other sorts of visual media; we see only a few carefully selected moments out of numerous possibilities, whereas on film we see many different ones of those possibilities, and on stage in any given scene, we see all of them. Because picture-book artists are restricted in the number of moments they can depict—usually it is fewer than fifteen, including the title page—they must choose their moments carefully and vary them more than do film-makers. If the angles remain the same, the actions depicted are always different; Max may make mischief in two different pictures, but they are two different sorts of mischief. Furthermore, on these few occasions when we do see the same action in a sequence of pictures—the four shots of the transformation of Max's room into a forest, for instance—it is the action that changes, not the angle from which we view it. The fixed angle forces us to focus on the transformation itself rather than on how it might feel, on what is new and changing rather than on what the person experiencing the change feels about it.

Not surprisingly, perhaps, picture books which contain more sequences of shots of the same action tend to provide more variation in point of view. Considered in these terms, comic books can be located somewhere between picture books and films; they almost always show many different pictures of the same sequence of actions, and they tend to make use of every conceivable sort of shot, every possible angle. The subtle variation of high and low shots and of various distances in some contemporary comic books is highly sophisticated and not much different from film. When picture books show more shots, they tend to take on the conventions of comic books and films. Like most picture books, Sendak's *In the Night Kitchen* tends to show us the action in long shots from the viewpoint of a fixed camera at eye level, but this book is enough like a comic book that some of its many images do imply a pan shot by a camera as we follow Mickey's movement across a fixed background.

Raymond Briggs's *The Snowman* contains even more images, seems even more like a comic book, and contains even more cinematic conventions. The ten pictures on its first page include close-ups; middle-distance shots; long shots; and high-angle, eye-level, and low-angle shots. The relationships between consecutive pictures imply that the camera-viewer has dollied in or out between them at least five times. Furthermore, these ten pictures include six shots of the same scene, as do six of the ten pictures on the next page. The many variations continue throughout the book, as they do in most comic books. And as in most comic books, there is much use of dynamic framing: the pictures sometimes come ten to a page, sometimes one, depending on the emotional intensity of the action and on whether it is action or feelings that matter.

The Snowman is a wordless picture book. The fluidity of its style makes up for the lack of words—it implies variations in our relationships with the characters that create a specific sort of involvement with the action depicted. Obviously, the best way picture books can convey narrative information of that sort is the one way I have not yet discussed: by using words. But the large number of picture books that contain no words at all raises important questions about how well pictures by themselves can depict events that we can recognize as stories.

When Hogarth or various of the Victorian narrative painters created a sequence of pictures, they always provided titles for them—words to specify what viewers should look for in them. The Victorian painters often also provided detailed descriptions in catalogs; Ford Madox Brown told viewers of his *The Last of England* that "the husband broods bitterly on blighted hopes and severances from all that he has been striving for" (Lister 27). The titles of contemporary wordless picture books also pay a large part in determining our response to them. Having read its cover, we open a book called *The Mystery of the Giant Footprints* knowing that the footprints we see in it *are* mysterious and are therefore important. So when the characters in Fernando Krahn's wordless book see the footprints, we understand that they are seeing them for the first time—that the footprints are not regular occurrences and that these characters are as mystified as they are frightened by them. Similarly, the title *Sir Andrew* is a comment on the donkey whom we assume bears that name and whom we see in the pictures that follow, and we are more likely to perceive the snobbishness of Paula Winter's character than if he were identified merely as Andrew or had no name at all.

But like *The Mystery of the Giant Footprints* and *Sir Andrew,* many books contain no words except their titles. The mere existence of such books disturbs some adults, who fear that these books will encourage illiteracy— that, like television, they encourage a visual orientation at the expense of a verbal one.

The flaw in that argument is that the comparison is not a just one: television is not merely a visual medium. Words (and music, and just plain noises) pour out of television sets as rapidly and as aggressively as pictures do; for that matter, printed words appear on the screen constantly, in commercials, as captions, as the titles of programs. Television is a highly verbal medium whose pictures by themselves communicate next to nothing—a fact easily discerned by anybody who makes the experiment of watching television with the sound turned off. In fact, television is like most picture books, a medium dependent upon the interrelationship of words and pictures. In his attack on wordless books, Patrick Groff suggests that, given the predominance of television in their lives, children are "'prewired' to see plots in pictures—but not in writing" (296). Given the predominance of television, I suspect that children are actually "prewired" to see plots in pictures accompanied by words. If Groff believes that pictures without words prevent children from learning to respond to the more complex demands of words on their own, then his attack ought to apply equally to picture books *with* words.

In fact, children of the television age ought to have as much or as little trouble with the pictures-without-words of wordless picture books as they have with the words-without-pictures of the stories we tell them orally. Both forms require some training, but if the words are rhythmically pleasing or interesting, even very young children can learn to understand and enjoy stories told in words without pictures; and if the pictures are interesting or attractive, even very young children can learn to interpret and enjoy stories told in pictures without words. Furthermore, children tend to express their enjoyment of wordless books by telling, in words, the stories the pictures suggest to them; they themselves turn purely visual experiences into verbal ones, a practice that surely must aid in the development of literacy.

But that is not to say that wordless books are anything like conventional picture books. They are very different, and one of their major differences is that, like the single images unaccompanied by texts that I discussed earlier, the "stories" in them can be told by many different children in many different ways. Because these books have no words to focus our attention on their meaningful or important narrative details, they require from us both close attention and a wide knowledge of the visual conventions that must be attended to before visual images can imply stories. These are the conventions I have outlined: the choices of media and color and style that communicate mood and atmosphere; the conventional meanings of gestures and facial expression, and also of dress and furniture and such, that communicate information about social status and interior attitude; the various uses of color and line and shape that point to important figures in pictures and imply their relative significance; the underlying assumptions about left and right and cause and effect that allow us to read meaning into a sequence of pictures; and so on. Because there are no words to help us, we have special need of these skills if we are to find stories in a sequence of pictures.

In fact, finding a story in a sequence of pictures with no help but our eyes is something like doing a puzzle. It cannot be done if we do not know that it is meant to be done, so we must first understand that there is indeed a problem to be solved. And it must be done as puzzles are done; we must search for clues and put together apparently disparate bits of information. And we must provide meanings to complete the pictures out of our own storehouse of information; as does Bayley in the picture for "Goosey Goosey Gander," the illustrators of wordless books depend on the ability of pictures to suggest information they do not actually offer.

At the most basic level, books like Tomi Ungerer's *Snail, Where Are You?* are pure puzzle. The pictures in this book have no connection with each other except that each of them contains a snail shape. Once the words of the title tip viewers off to the problem, the pleasure is in the search for that shape and in discovering that now it can be found in the horns of a goat, now in the eyes of an owl. These images are very much not a goat and an owl but merely *pictures* of a goat and an owl; our focus must necessarily be on how they are drawn rather than on what they depict.

More subtle versions of the same game can be found in books like *Anno's Animals* or Susan Jeffers's *Three Jovial Huntsmen*, which contain depictions of animals carefully hidden in foliage, and in Molly Bang's *The Grey Lady and the Strawberry Snatcher*, in which the Grey Lady continually disappears against gray backgrounds. In *Anno's Journey* and the other travel books in the same series, the Japanese illustrator plays a still subtler version of the same game: hiding stories in the pictures, not just objects and people. The most obvious story is the one of Anno himself; as he travels through these crowded locales, we must find him on every page. Then, we must place ourselves in his position as a traveler in a strange and exotic place and *observe* all the ways in which it is strange and exotic. Among the strangenesses are whole stories implied by various groupings of figures. One such group in *Anno's Journey,* posed like the figures in Millet's *The Gleaners,* evokes the entire story evoked by the painting; another group on a different page, a number of people pulling a giant turnip from the ground, evokes the whole story of the Grimm tale "The Enormous Turnip." There are also stories suggested by tricks of perspective: how is it that the man on the other side of the square appears to be holding the reins of the statue of a horse on top of the column on this side of the square? There are yet more stories suggested by sequences of pictures; a balloon that three children lose floats away over three pages, a declaration of love on one page seems to lead to a duel a few pages later, a race that begins on one page ends three pages later. The number of stories implied by these pictures seems to be limited only by the extent of a viewer's visual competence.

But it is the perception of them, the realization that they *are* stories and that one has discovered them to be stories, that makes them pleasurable— not the events themselves or the people they are happening to. Since wordless picture books by their very nature force us into some distance from their characters, they tend to tell the sorts of stories that depend on distance rather than involvement. In fact, many stories without words require superiority as well as distance and imply a satirical, or at least a comic, point of view. Since the actions of wordless picture books must be clear in line and focus in order for us to understand them, the pictures tend to be in a cartoon style that exaggerates not only actions for the sake of clarity but also appearances for the sake of humor.

We must stand back and feel detached from the family of cats in John S. Goodall's *The Surprise Picnic* if we are to enjoy the various slapstick plights they get into: choosing a rock to set their lunch on that turns out to be a turtle, being pulled aloft by an umbrella in a rain storm, and so on. To allow ourselves to feel sorry for these characters would spoil the point of the book, which is slapstick rather than empathy. The same is true of some of the most successful wordless books: Mercer Mayer's books about a boy, a dog, and a frog are filled with visual jokes, and it is not surprising that Spier's *Noah's Ark*, which provides all the words at the start and then retells the story in pictures without words, should focus on the comic implications of a boat full of animals. Even in a book as visually complicated as *The Grey Lady and the Strawberry Snatcher*, the focus is on slapstick. Once we have involved ourselves in the game of finding the Grey Lady, we might expect to sympathize with the Strawberry Snatcher, who has the same difficulty finding her that we have, but he gets himself into the sort of slapstick messes that demand laughter rather than sympathy.

While it tends to be more subtle and sophisticated, satire requires the same distance as does slapstick. There is a long tradition behind the use of visual narrative for satiric purposes, beginning with Hogarth's depictions of the various failings of his own society and including the comedies of the silent era of movies. The differences between Hogarth, the Keystone Cops, and Paula Winter's *Sir Andrew* are more in the relative savagery of the attack than anything else. The donkey Sir Andrew becomes involved in a series of slapstick situations because he spends so much time enjoying his own reflection: in the side of a toaster, in glass doors and windows, even in mirrors. Winter obviously does not expect us either to identify with him or even to like him; she makes it clear that he is indeed an ass.

I once showed an adult friend Pat Hutchins's wordless book *Changes, Changes*, which depicts two wooden dolls and the various objects they build out of blocks; she read it as a funny send-up of the values of the Protestant work ethic. Even though disaster after disaster occurs to the two wooden people who are the main characters of the story, they never indulge in despair, and their smiles imply that they are glad for disasters that create more work for them to do. My friend read *Changes, Changes* as a satire, perhaps because she made the conventional association between cartooning and satire, perhaps because of elements in her own history or character that predisposed her to that conclusion. The book obviously does not have to be seen that way; it might be a charmingly optimistic description of cheerful determination in the face of adversity. The point is, viewers cannot actually determine what these characters are thinking, or what aspects of their past might be causing them to think that way; we even have to guess about the variety of different emotions that might be expressed by the limited repertoire of three different expressions that Hutchins gives them. And, except for the focus provided by the title, there is no way we can know what the illustrator intends us to understand of the meaning or significance of the events she depicts. While the actions of the characters in *Changes, Changes* are clear, their import is highly debatable. Wordless picture books can easily depict actions, not so easily communicate feelings or meanings—and it is that that most distinguishes them from conventional picture books.

Some adults believe that the inadequacies of wordless books are actually their strength; that in leaving some things vague they allow their young viewers to be "creative." Thus, the title page of Barbara Salsberg's wordless *Your Own Story* sums up a common expectation of the genre when it says, "This book contains infinite stories. Waiting within these pages and yourself, is Your Own Story."

Often, however, this sort of creativity comes at the expense of actually paying attention to observable and unchangeable elements of the pictures. When I asked my five-year-old son to tell me the story of *Sir Andrew*, he did so without once mentioning the numerous depictions of Sir Andrew's reflections; so while he accurately described the action, he missed the motivation Winter provides for it. Even though this child of a specialist in children's literature had had far more access to books and pictures than most human beings of his age, his storytelling revealed that his "creativity" was best accounted for by the lack of sophistication of his visual story-making competence.

Unfortunately, we confuse the ignorance of children with imagination far too often. If we encourage children to misuse wordless books in their attempts to find stories in them by ignoring details the pictures actually do show, then these books will indeed be the threat to literacy that some commentators believe them to be. But viewed with an attitude of respect for the communicative powers of visual codes of signification, wordless books can be as powerful a source of education in the attentiveness basic to literacy as are books with words.

Ironically, the book which proudly announces that it contains "infinite stories" turns out to be a prime example of that power; I have shown *Your Own Story* to hundreds of different students of children's literature over a number of years, and the stories they tell are all very much like each other, even down to small details. *Your Own Story* depicts a shapeless yellow creature; to almost everybody who looks at the book, the creature seems to be lonely and to feel alienated from the hostile urban environment until he finds happiness in the company of a blue creature. Then the two of them clearly befriend an angry red creature and calm him down, and the three play in what is obviously perfect harmony until two of them must return to the city, where it seems they will feel less alienated because they each have someone to care for. Unlike the pictures in *Changes, Changes*, those in *Your Own Story* clearly communicate specific emotions and meanings; they can do so because they are filled with conventional codes of visual meaning.

Your Own Story contains speech balloons in which the characters express their feelings by means of various punctuation marks. There are cartoon conventions like action lines, jagged lines to represent explosions, and so on. Furthermore, the characters are drawn so simply that the faces convey the very essence of conventional depictions of various feelings: upturned semicircles for happiness, downturned ones for anger. Beyond that, the book makes use of its own system of color symbolism, so that when the characters feel isolated they each appear against the background of a black circle, and these circles join when two characters come together and then disappear as they feel free together. There are other sorts of symbolism, too, such as a mandala formed by the handshake of two of the shapeless creatures the book depicts.

All these conventional systems of meaning appear here isolated from the representational images that usually contain them. The more representational pictures become, the harder it is to determine the signs they might contain, and therefore the harder it is to understand the stories they might be telling; that is another reason why so many wordless books are cartoons.

Your Own Story has one other quality that makes its story easy to decode: it contains forty-three pictures, a lot more than usual. Given more moments to make connections between, we can make much more definite connections. In fact, Sheila Egoff suggests in *Thursday's Child* that this is why Raymond Briggs's *The Snowman* is superior to most wordless picture books: "it is so tightly controlled in its cartoon strip visual images which resemble animation stills as to almost negate the interjection of the viewer's imagination that the proponents of the wordless picture book so extol" (255).

In fact, *The Snowman* is tightly controlled in every respect. If it stands out from other wordless books, it does so because Briggs has chosen both a subject and a style that allow him to make full use of the potential of this difficult medium. The idea of a snowman coming to life is full of action, and Briggs chooses to show us the snowman and the boy *doing* things, and lots of different ones. We recognize what they are doing because these are familiar actions, the sorts of things we do every day in our own homes. They are funny, because the snowman does not know how to do them. But the soft warmth of the style demands empathy rather than the distance of comedy: we stand back from the snowman but we still like him. He is the ideal candidate for sympathy: he is incompetent not because he is vain or self-satisfied but because he is ignorant and ingenuous. We feel superior to him because he cannot do the things any child can do, things that the boy in the book does well. But because these *are* things any child can do, we feel concern for him. He demands the same response from viewers as Winnie the Pooh does from readers. That he should be capable of flying gracefully through the air after his endearing display of incompetence is an added bonus.

■ ■ ■ ■

CHAPTER SEVEN

———

The Relationships of Pictures and Words

As we respond to picture books, the words of the texts so permeate our experience of the pictures that the two seem to mirror each other. But they do not in fact do so—as becomes obvious as soon as we separate them from each other. I have asked hundreds of different people—both children and adult students of children's literature—to record the stories that occur to them as they experience only the pictures of picture books that do have texts; they always express frustration and arrive at a surprising variety of different stories. While my audience is less frustrated when I perform the reverse procedure and read the texts of picture-book stories without the accompanying pictures, they do often seriously misunderstand the implications of the words they hear. These experiences reveal much about the different ways in which words and pictures contribute to the total effect of a picture-book narrative.

In *The Art of Art for Children's Books,* Diana Klemin asserts that Celestino Piatti's pictures for *The Happy Owls* "cast a powerful illusion of storytelling" (64). That the narrative effect is indeed illusory is made clear in the stories made up by those who view these pictures without hearing the words. As it happens, *The Happy Owls* is an ideal book for this procedure, for the pictures are not on the same page as the words and can easily be separated from them. To avoid the confusion caused by not knowing where the earlier events of a story are leading, I show all the pictures in sequence once through and then ask people to write stories as they see the pictures for a second time. The result is a wide variety of stories: descriptions of an ordinary day in the life of two owls, reports on how two owls distributed important information, attempts to solve a food shortage in a barnyard, disputes about which bird is most beautiful—and not surprisingly, stories about owls whose bafflement or frustration seems to have been transferred from their perplexed storytellers.

But the pictures in *The Happy Owls* are unlike each other both in composition and subject: some focus on a pair of owls, others on groups of other birds, others on forest landscapes; one is a close-up of a sunflower with a human face. Since that lack of consistency may make this book an unfair choice for this experiment, I have also followed the same procedure with a more cohesive series of pictures. Maurice Sendak's pictures for *Mr. Rabbit and the Lovely Present* also appear on separate pages from the text and are enough like each other in style, in subject, and in mood to imply that they might actually be telling a story. And in fact, while the details vary, people do find a series of events in these pictures that are similar to each other—and similar, too, to Charlotte Zolotow's story about a journey through the woods in search of something.

Nevertheless, and not surprisingly, no one ever guesses the fact that the object of the search is a birthday present: the person the present is intended for is prominent in the text but never appears in the pictures. That apparently small detail makes a large difference: without a specific motive for the search, the actions that most people find in these pictures are not really stories at all; they are more like plotless travelogues, in which the rabbit shows the girl a number of unrelated sights merely because they are interesting or beautiful.

That seems a just response to Sendak's pictures: as Barbara Bader quite rightly suggests, the girl and the rabbit "turn up in this dappled painting and that . . . without there being any sense of their going from here to there, without our having any sense, in fact, of where they are or where they're going" (*American Picturebooks* 498). These pictures make the woods look so attractive and suggest so little in the way of danger or even of action that it is logical to assume that their beauty is a key factor in the story.

Interestingly, however, the stories people find in *The Happy Owls* pictures also often focus on the act of seeing and build plots around the owls' viewing of the birds or the forest. In a sense, the actual stories of both *The Happy Owls* and *Mr. Rabbit* are about seeing things; but the owls describe their forest, and the rabbit and girl inspect theirs, for reasons that relate only peripherally to the interest or beauty of appearances. Apparently, the pictures by themselves convey only the general idea of viewing, of looking at interesting or beautiful sights, as perhaps all pictures do. But they provide no suggestion of a focus, no specific idea about *why* one might be looking. Consequently, people asked to find stories in these pictures tend to transform their own interest in looking at the pictures into the interest of the characters within the pictures. Without a context of accompanying words, the visual impact of pictures as sources of sensuous pleasure is more significant than any specific narrative information they might contain.

The extent to which the meaning in pictures depends on exterior contexts is confirmed by the stories that people do and do not find in these two sets of pictures. The stories people do tell tend most often to be versions of the most conventional kinds of children's narratives, descriptions of journeys which end with the statement that home is best or disputes about beauty or talent which end with the realization that we are all beautiful in our own way. That people complete the meaning of these pictures by making use of their prior knowledge of other texts shows that the pictures themselves can imply narrative information only in relationship to a verbal context; if none is actually provided, we tend to find one in our memories. On the other hand, when I show adults Sendak's first picture of the little girl and the huge rabbit, there is always someone who giggles in a knowing way, yet no one has ever made up a sniggly story about a nymphet and a rabbit on the make; the assumption that this is a children's story narrows the range of acceptable interpretations.

Without a text to complete it, furthermore, people tend even to misinterpret the visual information in these pictures in ways that reveal how fragmentary that information is. Some people read gloom and depression into Sendak's moody pictures, and a number of people have interpreted

Piatti's powerful picture of a red sunset over a snow-covered wood as a depiction of a fire. It is particularly revealing that many people create stories about Sendak's pictures in which a house figures prominently, and stories about Piatti's pictures in which a fox figures prominently. While there is a house in one of Sendak's pictures, the text says only that some roofs are red and does not even mention the house, and while there is a fox in one of Piatti's pictures, the text accompanying that picture not only does not mention the fox but actually suggests that the forest in which he appears is a peaceful place. What was simply background for the artist becomes an important fact in need of explanation for those who do not know the specific focus the words provide.

Nevertheless, when I tell people the original stories after the exercise, they are surprised by what they have missed. With the focus offered by the words, it is hard not to see that Piatti's pictures depict changes in season, something viewers probably do not notice at first because they do not expect the time that is supposed to have passed between one picture and the next to be so long; it is usually a matter of minutes or hours, not months. And with the words, it is hard not to notice that Sendak's pictures centrally focus on differences in color, a fact no one even comments on at first. With the words to guide our perception of them, these two sequences of pictures both do create a powerful illusion of storytelling. Words can make pictures into rich narrative resources—but only because they communicate so differently from pictures that they change the meanings of pictures.

For the same reason, also, pictures can change the narrative thrust of words. I hope that the earlier chapters of this book have revealed the variety and subtlety of narrative information that pictures can provide, but in those chapters, of course, I interpreted visual information in the context of the accompanying texts that I was already familiar with, and in consequence I tended to focus on elements that supported the implications of the texts. That pictures actually *change* the meanings of texts in the process of supporting them becomes particularly clear if we perform the reverse experiment of the ones described above and explore the effects on listeners of a story told to them without the accompanying pictures. When I have read the text of Sendak's *Where the Wild Things Are* to adults who have not previously heard it, without showing them the pictures, many feel it to be a terrifying story, too frightening for young children. Without Sendak's *particular* Wild Things to look at, they conjure up wild things out of their own nightmares, and those they find scary indeed. When I then tell them the story accompanied by the pictures, they always change their minds. Sendak's monsters are relatively reassuring, adorable rather than terrifying, and Sendak's Max is much more arrogant and assertive than they had imagined him. In fact, it is the pictures and not the words that tell us there is nothing to worry about, that despite our assumptions about the weakness of children and the violence of monsters, this particular child can take care of himself with these particular monsters. The illustrations in *Wild Things* communicate information that changes the effect and meaning of the story as a whole, just as the words of *The Happy Owls* and *Mr. Rabbit* communicate information that changes the effect and meaning of the story as a whole.

Those changes can occur because words and pictures communicate in ways so different that commentators tend to exaggerate the differences. It has been fashionable in recent years to suggest, on the basis of research into the activity of the human brain, that the two might even require perception by two different organs. The brain consists of two hemispheres joined only by a bundle of interconnecting fibers; studies of patients with lesions in various areas of one half or the other seem to suggest that the two halves are responsible for different kinds of thinking. In general terms, the left hemisphere seems to handle analytical, sequential thinking and thus to control language functioning; the right seems to manage holistic thinking, simultaneous rather than sequential operations, and thus to control visual and spatial capacities.

In a list he calls "The Two Modes of Consciousness: A Tentative Dichotomy," the psychologist Robert Ornstein identifies the qualities of the two hemispheres as two quite different visions of reality; among other things, he suggests that left-hemisphere consciousness is lineal, sequential, causal, focal, explicit, and verbal—typical of Western "rational" thought—and that right-hemisphere consciousness is nonlineal, simultaneous, acausal, diffuse, tacit, and spatial—typical of the "intuitional" thought of so-called primitive societies (83).

In the light of these categories, some commentators have concluded that words communicate in ways that relate to these left-hemisphere activities and that pictures communicate in ways that relate to the right-hemisphere activities. Stories obviously occupy time, pictures space. The stories that words tell are certainly lineal, sequential, causal; a plot is a unified sequence of causes and effects, and it is the order in which events are communicated, and their temporal relationships with each other, that make them into stories. Furthermore, words easily focus our attention. If the shape of a woman's nose is important to the meaning of a story, then the words in the story about her will mention the shape of her nose; looking at a picture of her, we might be so interested by the curtains on the window behind her that we do not even notice the nose. In that way, pictures tend to be diffuse, words explicit. We first experience a picture all at once, a glance taking in the whole image, and theoretically we have no way of determining what in it might have caused what else in it. If we see a woman sitting in front of a window, we do not know if she is smiling because the curtains have been freshly laundered or if she laundered them because she is happy—or if the happy face and the clean curtains have nothing whatsoever to do with each other and that it is actually the nose that we should be paying attention to.

But further consideration reveals that words and pictures are not in fact so totally separable. As the inadequacies of patients with lesions reveal so clearly, the properly working brain requires both its hemispheres. In *The Shattered Mind*, Howard Gardner says, "it is almost unthinkable that our 'normal' minds should not utilize both halves of the brain during waking activity" (376). What research into hemispheric activity actually suggests about picture books is what my experiments in separating words from pictures reveal—not that words and pictures are quite separate from each other but, rather, that placing them into relationship with each other inevitably changes the meaning of both, so that good picture books as a whole are a richer experience than just the simple sum of their parts.

The idea that words are merely lineal and pictures merely spatial is extremely simplistic. We could not read words if we could not interpret the visual symbols that stand for them on paper; reading is itself an act of vision. Furthermore, our understanding of language demands that we find holistic shapes in the sequences of words. In coming to an end, a sentence creates an implication of finality that demands not just our understanding of the words in sequence but also our simultaneous consciousness of everything that has already happened in the sequence so that we can understand the shape of the whole. Stories extend the shaping power of individual sentences. We will not be satisfied with a story until we perceive, consciously or not, that it does indeed contain the organizational patterns that make it a story rather than a "slice of life": most literary criticism is about such patterns, about how writers weave spatial systems of opposition and variation into the lineal structures of a plot, so that stories can shape time and thus conquer time's open-endedness.

Meanwhile, the pictures in a picture book form a sequence—they can contribute to the act of storytelling because they do imply the cause-and-effect relationships of time. And as I suggested in my earlier discussions of how pictures imply meaning, even one picture on its own can organize space in ways that suggest some of the sequential ordering of time and provide some of its focus.

So perception of language requires activity in both hemispheres, and well-wrought words do in fact impose holistic patterns on the lineal; and perception of the visible world also requires activity in both hemispheres, and well-wrought pictures do in fact demand specific lineal interpretations of the visual whole. Describing how we understand words "by partly reversing the linear progress, remembering *simultaneously* what we have read consecutively," and how understanding pictures is "a process *in time*," Joseph Schwarcz rightly concludes, "Following an illustrated text is, then, a complex activity" (*Ways of the Illustrator* 9).

The differences in the activities of the halves of the brain tell us how complex: as we respond to words and pictures which tell us about the same events in different ways, we must integrate two different sorts of information about the same events. We must gather spatial information from both pictures and words; in *Mr. Rabbit,* for instance, the pictures show us the settings, but the words of the text tell us how to see them—the colors that are significant in them. We must also gather temporal information from both words and pictures; in *Mr. Rabbit,* the words imply only the specific time occupied by the words of the conversation—it takes the pictorial depiction of the girl and rabbit in different locations to imply the more extended passage of time in which they move from one part of the forest to another between various parts of the conversation. As in *Mr. Rabbit,* the temporal information in pictures is often different from that offered by words, and the spatial information in words different from that in pictures; we must integrate time and space, and two different versions of time and space, before we can understand the whole.

The whole, then, is more than the sum of its parts. Speaking of cartoons and comic strips, Roland Barthes isolates an effect he calls *relaying:* his description of it could easily apply to picture books also: "Here language . . . and image are in a complementary relation; the words are then fragments of a more general syntagm, as are the images, and the message's unity occurs on a higher level; that of the story" (*Responsibility* 30).

Furthermore, the most successful picture books seem to be those in which the "unity on a higher level" emerges from pictures and texts which are noticeably fragmentary—whose differences from each other are a significant part of the effect and meaning of the whole. In *Problems of Art,* Susanne Langer says that, although the arts are different, "the fact that they are distinct is what enables them to have all sorts of highly specialized, interesting relations to each other" (82). As a highly specialized art form that combines different arts, the picture book is distinguished by the ways in which it takes advantage of such highly specialized relationships. What follows is a discussion of how the relative strengths and weaknesses of words and pictures affect their relationships in picture books.

■ ■ ■ ■

According to William Ivins, it is the "communication of visual information and ideas which, for the last four centuries, has been the primary function of the exactly repeatable pictorial statement" (24). He suggests that, before methods of reproducing pictures were invented, science could not advance, for people could not actually *see* how things worked. In fact, words cannot communicate descriptive information as easily as pictures can. "Common nouns and adjectives, which are the material with which a verbal description is made, are after all only the names of vaguely described classes of things of the most indefinite kind and without precise concrete meanings" (15). A careful artist with words can make them wonderfully evocative, but they merely evoke rather than offer specific visual information, so that a novelist's description of his heroine's face might communicate how we are to respond to her appearance quite exactly, without ever giving us a specific idea of how she looks. And even then, we are forced by the nature of language to follow the writer's logic as he or she guides us through the material; the novelist can make the heroine's nose the most significant aspect of her face by leaving it to the end of the description and thus making it climactic, but that means we "see" the details of her face as a verbal sequence rather than as a visual whole. She has no nose for us at all until we get to the end of the list.

If I try to describe a character's face in words, therefore, I face two problems. First, I have to use words vague in themselves, such as "nose" and "long" and "handsome," in such a way that their relationship to each other can suggest something more or less specific: "handsome long nose"—and I have to assume that those who read my description share my idea about what "long" means and what sort of nose might be considered "handsome." Second, I have to present my information about various features in a sequence to guide my readers through the details of the knowledge I wish to share; the readers must suspend understanding of each of the individual details until the whole list of such details is complete, so that they can see the relationship between "long nose" and descriptions of other features, such as "curly hair"—and the relationship of such specific details to overall impressions, such as "beautiful."

Since words are the separable parts of meaningful sentences, we can understand language only by understanding parts first, then building up to a whole that might in fact be an accurate combination of all the parts. But we see pictures all at once first and only then can begin to notice the potential relationships of their various parts. Our understanding of language starts with details and moves toward wholes; our understanding of pictures starts with wholes and breaks down into details. In terms of the halves of the brain, Jeremy Campbell suggests, "the right side tends to use a 'top-down' strategy, processing information as a whole, perceiving its full meaning rather than approaching it 'bottom-up,' using the parts to construct the whole, which is often more than the sum of its parts" (239–40). We have to approach words bottom-up—one at a time, in the sequence in which they are given us. Consequently, words are best at describing relationships of details, pictures best at giving a sense of the whole. But each can eventually do both, and they can certainly help each other to do both.

Nevertheless, picture-book artists almost always convey information about the ways things look by means of pictures. While that may seem too obvious to be worth saying, the main difficulty facing neophyte writers of texts for picture books is understanding that they must leave such visual information in the hands of their illustrators. A good picture-book text does not tell us that the girl had brown eyes or that the room was gloomy—yet practitioners of literary art use exactly such visual details to establish character, mood, and atmosphere. Writers of picture books must imply character and mood without recourse to such details—and hope that illustrators sensitive to their stories will invent the right visual details to express the appropriate information.

There are two sorts of information that pictures can convey more readily than words: what *type* of object is implied by words and which particular *one* of that type is being referred to. The pictures in alphabet books and in compendia like Richard Scarry's *The Best Word Book Ever* are meant to represent types; if the words on a page say "C is for cat," then the creature depicted on that page is meant to represent cats in general—to show what the word "cat" refers to each time it is used in reference to many different individual creatures of different colors and shapes and sizes. It is by providing us with such visual types that picture books can be informative about the world we live in; they offer us a sort of dictionary of visual ideas, a set of labeled images by which we can identify the objects we actually see. Furthermore, schematic drawings can allow us to understand the workings of things, such as the interior of the human body or the construction of a medieval cathedral.

In the preface to his book about the construction of a medieval cathedral, David Macaulay says, "the cathedral of Chutreaux is imaginary, but the methods of its construction correspond closely to the actual construction of a Gothic cathedral. . . . Although the people of Chutreaux are imaginary, their single-mindedness, their spirit, and their incredible courage are typical of the people of twelfth-, thirteenth-, and fourteenth-century Europe." In order to provide useful information, Macaulay had to normalize—create a "typical" situation rather than the actually untypical circumstances that surrounded the building of each and every actual medieval cathedral. Exactly because they are nothing but typical, because they possess nothing but the characteristics that a number of things share, usefully typical types do not actually exist in the real world. That may be why the illustrations in dictionaries tend to be drawings rather than photographs of specific objects.

Macaulay's solution to that problem is to depict the building of a "typical" cathedral as if it were an actual one; he names specific names, and invents specific dates. In fact, an artist cannot choose but to identify the typical by depicting it as if it were actual; the word "face" carries with it no image of a specific face, but we can convey the idea "face" in a picture only by showing a specific face. The cat depicted beside the words "C is for cat" may be meant to represent all cats; but it would be a bad drawing indeed if it did not in fact look like a possible, actual, unique cat—for it is exactly the way a cat does look that such a picture is attempting to convey.

On the other hand, the drawing would still not be serving its purpose if it had enough distinguishing characteristics to stop it from being typical. A cat with one leg and wearing glasses would not successfully illustrate "C is for cat" for those who did not already know enough about the appearance of cats to realize what was unusual about this one. People who assume (probably incorrectly) that Brian Wildsmith really wanted to convey information in his visually exciting but minimally informative *ABC* might rightly be upset by the fact that his horse has no legs and that his unicorn's most notable feature is its rear end.

The balance required in both capturing the typical and making the typical seem actual is the source of much of the difficulty adults have in coming to terms with picture books. Those who believe that the main purpose of pictures is typical information are upset whenever the objects shown in pictures diverge from ideally normalized types—when Wildsmith in his *ABC* uses some green paint in his depiction of a mouse and they are convinced that mice do not have green fur, or when Sendak's children do not look as blond and pink and ingenuous as conventionally typical children do. In assuming that every picture in a picture book must represent a type, however, we inevitably neglect the other sort of information pictures can convey so well—information about the uniqueness of separate objects; for a picture of a cat can and ideally always does show us not just what cats in general are but also what this particular cat looks like. In her fine discussion of the house style developed in the Golden Books series—the emphasis on caricature, the flattening of space, and so on—Barbara Bader makes an important point: "common to all the foregoing is the intent—to put across an idea or a piece of information rather than to call forth real people, a particular moment. . . . [The difference between these two styles is] generally what is meant, justly or not, by the distinction between illustration-as-communication and illustration-as-art" (*American Picturebooks*

288–89). In order to put across ideas, the Golden Book illustrators, and many others like them, sacrifice details in order to focus on the typical; in assuming that the purpose of pictures in all children's books is to put across ideas, we tend to ignore and misunderstand details. In doing so we miss the unique qualities of the pictures we look at, and that is not only what makes them worthy of consideration as works of art but also an important source of information of a quite different sort.

We look at a picture of a young woman. She is sitting at a window and smiling, and we know a great deal about her—most of it difficult to put into words. Her hair is done in a certain way. She wears a hat that appears to be of some woven or perhaps scalelike material and a dress patterned with leaves and branches and with fur at collar and cuff. She sits in a room that appears to be filled with tapestries; we see into the room from outside, and we also see that outside it is snowing and that the building she sits in appears to be some sort of castle. She holds up a finger. This picture is Nancy Ekholm Burkert's illustration for the words "At a window with a frame of ebony a queen sat and sewed," the opening of *Snow White*. It adds at least six different kinds of information to that provided by the words.

The first is that this is indeed the specific queen the words refer to—the basic relationship between illustration and text, in which the picture confirms the message of the words. The second is that this is a queen, a type of person; and that this is what sewing is. After reading the words and perhaps wondering what a "queen" or "sewing" is, we can look at the picture and see what they look like. So far, the picture merely offers a visual equivalent to the words. But beyond these basic aspects of illustration, the picture adds other information.

Third, and perhaps most important, it communicates what words could never convey, no matter how many of them one used. It communicates in a detailed way what this particular woman looks like and what the world around her looks like. We could make up a verbal list of details that the picture shows, and we could supply them with adjectives for a long time before we would have an exhaustive catalog of all the different information this picture easily provides about how things look. But the length of that catalog would depend on our varying abilities to distinguish specific namable objects, to determine figures by separating them from grounds—it would be a list of separate facts rather than a holistic totality. Even the longest possible such catalog still would not convey all the visual information the picture conveys so effortlessly, and it would have quite a different effect: it would imply visual information rather than specify it.

Fourth, the picture communicates the appearances of objects we do not even have names for—and therefore might not have been able to describe accurately in our catalog. We may not know what a fleur-de-lis is, but we can understand what one looks like simply because there are a number of them on the tapestry behind the woman. We may not know they are called fleurs-de-lis, but that does not prevent us from being able to see them and even admire them. Similarly, we may not know the technical name for the strange hat the woman is wearing, but we can see the hat; and we can guess not just that this woman is wearing a hat but that this is the sort of hat a woman in this situation would be likely to wear. In fact, we might see a similar hat in another picture later on and conclude from the similarity that such hats were once typically worn by a certain sort of woman; we would be able to know that such hats were typical without having a word for them. It would take the technical jargon of a hairdresser to express the exact nature of the woman's upswept locks, and of a seamstress to describe the cut of her dress or the points of her sleeves. But we can understand from the picture what even very exact words could not tell us.

A fifth kind of information: if we bring into play our knowledge of conventions of appearance and gesture, we can guess something about the character of this woman sitting at the window—something that it would take many words to convey. Her clothing and her environment suggest that she is well off. We can guess, from the delicacy of her gesture and the very nature of her activity, that she is a lady. Her gentle features suggest that she is a gentle person, probably a likable one, certainly a quiet one. The picture easily communicates information about personality that writers must work hard at expressing in words.

A more telling example of how pictures readily convey personality can be seen if we compare Burkert's portrait of Snow White, as it appears on the dust jacket of her version of the story, with Snow White as she first appears in Trina Schart Hyman's version. Both girls have a fair complexion and dark hair; a catalog of their features would have to be very specific indeed before it could distinguish between the surprisingly similar shapes of their lips and noses. Yet despite the large degree of similarity, they are clearly two quite different sorts of people. Burkert's Snow White is "pretty," gentle, innocent, well-mannered, like her mother. Hyman's Snow White is a beauty, and something of an ingenuous nymphet; she may not know it herself yet, but she is clearly a sensuous, passionate individual.

But what exactly is it that conveys these important differences? It is hard to say. Part of it is certainly the difference between an attractive girl in front of some precisely drawn leaves and another attractive girl with a malevolent hawk on her wrist in front of trees tossed by tempestuous winds. Part of it is found in the implications of stance and gesture that we usually read without even being conscious that we are aware of them. But it is also something else about the shape of lips and eyes, something literally indefinable, something words could not capture. As Ivins suggests, "When we try to describe a particular object in such a way as to communicate an idea of its personality or unique character to someone who is not actually acquainted with it, all that we can do is to pile up a selected group of . . . class names. . . . But beyond that it is impossible for us to go with words, for the ipseity, the particularity of the object, its this-and-no-otherness, cannot be communicated by the use of class names" (52–53). Interestingly, Gardner's discussion of brain lesions provides support for this idea; Gardner suggests that "unfamiliar shapes tend to be processed by the right hemisphere, whereas shapes capable of verbalization (as well as other linguistic materials) are processed by the left hemisphere" (381). A possible conclusion is that, since language is a codification of what we already know—we would not have learned words to describe experiences we have not encountered yet—the information in pictures that we cannot yet verbalize is the information that is new to us, the information that transcends our preexisting categories or class names. Seen in this way pictures can teach us about unfamiliar visual objects, but only if we use the words of an accompanying text as cognitive maps, schemata to apply to them in order to understand exactly what is new, left over beyond the schemata. We can say "hat" in response to an image of the one on Snow White's mother, then become conscious of how the visual details of the hat in question differ from our idea of a typical hat.

In addition to conveying two quite different Snow Whites by means of the way they depict them, Burkert and Hyman also provide two quite different attitudes toward them—a sixth sort of information. Through the devices of symbol and gesture, of pictorial dynamics, of color and mood and atmosphere that I discussed earlier, Hyman makes Snow White the enticing but ingenuous victim of a lurid romantic melodrama; one must feel sympathy for her. Burkert makes her passive, the sort of girl who always does as she ought and is rightfully admired for her lack of re-belliousness; the admiration demanded implies her triumph from the be-ginning. Similarly, Burkert's picture of Snow White's mother provides a way of thinking about her—an attitude toward her. She depicts her as seen from outside the window as through a frame; the bright, cheerful tapes-tries behind her contrast strongly with the gray walls of the castle and suggest that her place is a warm and comfortable one. But it has no depth; it merely looks like a series of different intricate patterns, a highly deco-rated surface that she herself becomes part of. We can enjoy looking at this pretty woman surrounded by beautiful designs, but we cannot feel much involvement with her. The picture requires us to appreciate the beauty but to keep our distance. Meanwhile, Hyman depicts Snow White's mother from inside the room; we look out with her, rather than at her from with-out. We are asked to empathize, and because we see details of the room— her maid, her religious triptych hanging on the wall, and so on—we know something about the particular interests and lifestyle of the person we are empathizing with.

These artists set out to illustrate the beginning of "Snow White," the idea that a woman sat at a window and sewed. They have each shown one version of what that might have looked like, but they have also shown much else: what *a* queen might look like, what *this* queen might have looked like, where she might have lived and how she might have dressed, what sort of person she might be, and what sort of attitude we might take toward her. While words can convey information about clothing and setting, personality, and the attitudes we should take toward what is being described, pictures do so more readily. We can enjoy looking at this complex portrait of a queen, and even have some sense of the sort of person she is and how we might feel about her, even if we did not comprehend or enjoy the complex language we would need to know in order to understand the amount and kinds of information the pictures so simply show us.

The first sort of information I learned from Burkert's picture of Snow White's mother merely showed what the words say. The second is a generalization that the picture may or may not actually allow, for perhaps all queens did not look like this. But the other four sorts of information imply exactly that—that this queen looks like herself, that she is different from other queens. That amounts to a statement about the uniqueness of this woman at this moment, the particular thing seen at the moment of seeing. To return to the paradox I suggested earlier, pictures provide both information about the world in being typical and information about the specific objects they depict in being unique. But it is uniqueness—in personality, in atmosphere, in attitude—that makes the pictures in picture books so enjoyable. If we allow ourselves to judge them only in terms of their informative typicality, we misrepresent them, and if we encourage children to look at them for such information, we deprive them not only of much pleasure but also of much significant information—information that words are often silent about.

Many picture books—indeed, possibly all of the best ones—do not just reveal that pictures show us more than words can say; they achieve what Barthes called "unity on a higher level" by making the difference between words and pictures a significant source of pleasure. That pleasure is available even in a very simple book like *Goodnight Moon*. Margaret Wise Brown's spare text is little more than a rhythmic catalog of objects, a list of details that encourages those who hear it to look for the objects mentioned in Clement Hurd's pictures. In doing so, however, they learn information the text does not mention. The old lady and the child to whom she says goodnight are both rabbits and not people. The old lady is knitting, and the kittens play with her wool. The "little house" is a playhouse, and it has its own lights; knowledgeable viewers will even realize that the picture on the bedroom wall is actually an illustration from Brown and Hurd's *The Runaway Bunny*. The delight viewers feel in discovering these things with their own eyes rather than with their ears reveals how basic and important is the difference between the information available in words and in pictures.

Anno's hiding of animals in the complex foliage of his *Anno's Animals* is another clever instance of how that delight in searching pictures for details can be evoked, but the difference between this wordless book and the similar picture in Nancy Burkert's *Snow White* of Snow White alone in the forest surrounded by animals hidden in foliage shows how illustrators can use differences between words and picture for more than the simple plea-sure of puzzle solving. Finding Anno's animals is just a game, for no text accompanies these pictures to tell us that they might represent anything more significant. But once we have found Burkert's animals, we must then deal with the fact that the text does not mention them. In fact, they repre-sent a danger to Snow White that she, in her innocence, does not notice either; our perception of them in relation to the words of the text tells us how blind and unprotected innocence may be when threatened by savag-ery. In seeing what she does not see, we come to interpret her situation more specifically than we would have had we not found the animals in the foliage.

That a simple game without words becomes a source of complex narra-tive information when accompanied by them suggests that my analysis of the kinds of information communicated by Burkert's picture of Snow White's mother was incomplete. While pictures can convey these kinds of information, they do so most subtly and most completely in the context of a text that supports and sustains them. A reconsideration makes that clear.

We can learn much about medieval Europe from Burkert's illustrations for Snow White—but only if we *know* already that the details in these pictures are characteristic of medieval Europe. And we could learn that only by being told it in words: by another person or by means of a book like this one that discusses the significance of the pictures in picture books. The pictures themselves can indeed *show* us these details in ways that words could not, but without words to explain that they are doing that, we could not know what the details represent. We need to be told what we are being shown.

Similarly, if we share knowledge of gestures and appearances, we can learn that Snow White's mother was gentle and well-mannered from Burkert's pictures and that Burkert wants us to view her from an objective distance. But unless we *know* the picture represents Snow White's mother, we will not know who it is that is so gentle and well-mannered, and we will not, therefore, have any use for the information. Without a name—that is, a word—to attach to it, the picture communicates nothing of particular interest or value to us. Even if the picture were hung in a gallery as *Portrait of a Woman* rather than as an illustration of Snow White's mother, it would be that context, that set of meaningful words, in which we viewed it and understood it: and if it were, indeed, captioned *Portrait of a Woman*, we would then read it as we have learned to read portraits and look for details that might be evocative of character.

In other words, pictures can communicate much to us, and particularly much of visual significance—but only if words focus them, tell us what it is about them that might be worth paying attention to. In a sense, trying to understand the situation a picture depicts is always an act of imposing language upon it—interpreting visual information in verbal terms; it is not accidental that we speak of "visual literacy," of the "grammar" of pictures, of "reading" pictures. Reading a picture for narrative meaning is a matter of applying our understanding of words—words like mine throughout this book; in applying such words to pictures, we are engaged in the act of turning visual information into verbal, even if we do not actually speak the words aloud. Even wordless books demand our previous knowledge of how stories operate before we can find a story in them, and so do the pictures of *The Happy Owls* and *Mr. Rabbit* divorced from their texts. Walter Ong says, "We have all heard it said that one picture is worth a thousand words. Yet, if this statement is true, why does it have to be a saying? Because a picture is worth a thousand words only under special conditions—which commonly include a context of words in which a picture is set" (7).

That is true for the same reason that pictures can show us more than words can say: in duplicating the surface appearance of objects, a picture inevitably contains more visual information than necessary for the verbal message it accompanies. An artist might want to show us a woman sitting at a window, but in order to do so, the artist *must* show us a particular woman with a particular sort of nose sitting in a particular posture. And the woman must have clothes on, unless the artist is determined to make us respond to her naked body. The characters in novels frequently do not have noses, or elbows, or clothes—or at least, these details are not mentioned—and we are left to assume that they have such features but that those features are simply not important to our understanding of the characters in question. Words can, in this way, focus on what is important, and we can read stories in the faith that, if they are good stories, every detail will be of significance in terms of our understanding of the whole. But because an illustrator has to give every character a nose whether that nose is important or not, or else draw a picture of a person remarkably odd because he has no nose, a picture contains information that might not necessarily be relevant to our understanding of the story as a whole. It takes a context of specific words, or at least a previously established idea of what to look for that was probably first expressed to us in words, to point us toward what is significant and thus lessen the number of words the picture evokes from as many as a thousand down to the few specific words actually found in the text.

In "What Novels Can Do That Films Can't," Seymour Chatman says that "the camera depicts but does not describe" (128). In other words, it shows us objects that ought to interest us, and it might even, by means of switches in camera angles and such, focus our attention on which of those objects ought to attract our attention. But it cannot tell us what it is about these objects that we ought to notice—*why* we should be interested in them. A novelist can say, "The woman was beautiful, despite her shabby clothing." A film—or a picture in a book—can indeed show us a woman in shabby clothing. But we might not share the casting director's conviction that she is beautiful and so miss the point, and we may be more interested in the pony she sits on than in the woman herself and so miss the point altogether. What Chatman suggests of film is true of the pictures in picture books: "The dominant mode is presentational, not assertive. A film doesn't say, 'this is the state of affairs'; it merely shows you that state of affairs" (128).

But in picture books (as, often, in films), the words can focus our attention on pictures in such a way as to make them assertive. Words can provide a cognitive map, a schema that we can apply to inherently unassertive pictures in order to determine the varying significance we might find in their details. Barthes calls this effect of texts in relation to pictures *anchoring:* "Language helps identify purely and simply the elements of the scene and the scene itself. . . . the text *directs* the reader among the various signifieds of the image, causes him to avoid some and to accept others; through an often subtle dispatching, it teleguides him toward a meaning selected in advance" (*Responsibility* 28–29). An obvious example of such "teleguiding" is the caption under a picture in an art gallery—in giving us a name or an idea, it provides us with a pattern to apply to the image before our eyes and thus allows us to see that image in a specific way. We see not just a woman but *Portrait of a Woman;* we see not just a few daubs of red paint but *Composition* or *Angry Evening*—and we look at *Composition* differently from the way we would look at *Angry Evening.*

The texts of picture books often function as anchoring labels in exactly this way. Even the simple sentence "This is a cat" allows us to see the accompanying picture differently from the label "This is my friend, Peter, who is a cat," or the label "Peter was not happy that day." The first merely demands we pick up the general idea of cats, the second asks us to look for something like human personality, and the third requires our attention to a specific emotion. Similarly, Sendak's picture of Zolotow's Mr. Rabbit and little girl relaxing in the woods would look quite different if it were labeled "Have some Madeira, my dear?" That label would change the emotional implications of the visual image—tell us to interpret this visible appearance in terms of different emotions. We cannot see what goes on in the minds of the characters we see in pictures; it takes words to point out the emotional content of visible gestures.

In a slightly less obvious way, the picture in *Wild Things* of Max making mischief by chasing a dog with a fork would be changed drastically if the words accompanying it read, "The dog ran so fast trying to escape the bad boy that she nearly banged her head on the door." With these different words, the same picture is now centrally about the dog and not the boy. Or consider another possibility: "The boy and the dog rushed into the living room to attack the monster; the dog was a little frightened, and looked back to make sure the boy was with her"; now the dog and boy are no longer enemies. Or another: "Max picked up the magic fork and, just as the dog fairy had promised, he began to fly. The dog fairy got out of his way in a hurry."

In these instances, the new words I have provided imply that the same visible gestures might stand for quite different situations. If we then look at the picture and believe that it might indeed be showing us what we have been told, then we have learned something important about the relationships of words and pictures. We would not accept a text that told us that this picture of a boy and a dog showed a goat and a pig running down the stairs; we tend to believe the evidence of our eyes when it comes to appearances. But the fact that we do so easily accept even minimally plausible verbal descriptions that change the meaning of the action suggests how words predominate in our reading of pictorial information about causes and effects and about the passage of time. As I showed earlier, pictures can and do convey these things, just as words can describe faces, but in picture books the texts more significantly specify temporal information, just as the pictures convey the most significant descriptive information.

Some aspects of pictorial meaning are particularly in need of the clarifying presence of texts. A picture cannot by itself tell us that it is a flashback, and without the use of conventions like the cloudy shapes that surround dreams in cartoons, a picture cannot by itself tell us that it represents a character's fantasy. Consequently, when looking at Piatti's *Happy Owls* pictures without the accompanying words, no one guesses that he or she is looking at representations of the visual images the owls are merely talking about. In Arnold Lobel's pictures for Judith Viorst's *I'll Fix Anthony*, similarly, while we see the same characters throughout the book, we see them in two different sorts of reality. At the beginning and end we see what they are actually doing; in the middle they appear inside the young narrator's imagination. But we can only know that the two boys are *not* actually playing bingo on one page but *are* really playing with a toy car on the facing page because of the grammatical relationships provided by the accompanying words. Stephen Roxburgh's suggestion in "A Picture Equals How Many Words" that the first and last pictures in *Outside Over There* are "almost identical images that comprise a sequence depicting an action, in fact, a baby's step" (21) reveals how Sendak takes advantage of the vagueness of the temporal information in pictures: without a text which asserts that the events of the story in between these two pictures occur instantaneously, in the time of a baby's step, we are left only with a sense of something wrong that supports the mystery this book so successfully conveys.

I said earlier that the fact that words do not describe everything that can be seen in a picture creates a game, since we can ourselves notice details that have not been mentioned. That suggests a third important effect of words on pictures. In addition to informing us of the emotional or narrative significance of visible gestures, and specifying cause-and-effect and other grammatical relationships between parts of pictures and series of pictures, words can tell us what matters and what does not. It is the text that tells us that the insignificant-looking bone that we did not even at first notice in *The Amazing Bone* is an important part of the story; on the other hand, it is the text's silence about the fox in Piatti's *The Happy Owls* that tells us not to be concerned about him or to imagine that he has a part in the story—as people believe he has when they do not know Piatti's words. Similar silences inform us that the man in eighteenth-century dress playing a musical instrument inside a cottage in the exact center of one of the pictures in Sendak's *Outside Over There* is not at all significant to the plot and tell us to ignore the goat who appears centrally in some of the pictures in *Rosie's Walk*.

If pictures show us more than words can say, then they can easily confuse us as to what is important about all the things they show. In this sense, the pictures in picture books, like all pictures, are most significantly images to put words around—most interesting, and most communicative, when we have some words to accompany them. The *Mona Lisa* on its own may or may not be an interesting image: it becomes a fascinating one when we look at it with knowledge of even a few of the vast number of words that commentators have woven around it. Even the most abstract of pictures becomes an illustration when its artist provides it with a title, and even a title like *A Canvas All Painted Blue* tells us what to see in what we look at—not night, not melancholy, just the color blue on a canvas. The pictures in picture books are most interesting when the words that accompany them tell us how to understand them.

So far in this chapter, I have suggested two paradoxical truths: first, that words without pictures can be vague and incomplete, incommunicative about important visual information, and second, that pictures without words can be vague and incomplete, lacking the focus, the temporal relationships, and the internal significance so easily communicated by words. In *Ideology and the Image*, Bill Nichols sums up the relative strengths and weaknesses of the two different media when he suggests that language, which is made up of the discrete units of individual words separated by moments of non-sense, is something like the on-off digital code of computers—capable of conveying subtle connections and relationships simply because it misrepresents the continuum of reality by dividing it into discrete parts. But pictorial representation, in which the images do in some way resemble the objects they signify, are an analog code, in which separate meanings are not discrete and tend to shade off into each other. According to Nichols, "The graded quality of analog codes may make them rich in meaning but it also renders them somewhat impoverished in syntactical complexity or semantic precision. By contrast, the discrete units of digital codes may be somewhat impoverished in meaning but capable of much greater complexity or semantic signification. . . . As a consequence of this difference between analog and digital codes we are often in the position of using the complex instrument of language to speak about the rich meaning of art where a proliferation of words can never match the gradations of meaning to which the words allude" (47–48). The words Nichols refers to here are those used in the criticism of art; but in picture books the texts themselves allude to the pictures, and the pictures have been made in response to the texts. The situation has been designed to offer information from both digital and analogical codes at once; the unity of the whole emerges from a subtle interplay of the differing parts. In terms of the geography of the brain, Gardner says, "Since the left hemisphere operates primarily by processing elements in sequence, while the right hemisphere treats elements simultaneously ('in parallel'), activities which exploit both forms are particularly enhanced by interhemispheric collaboration" (376). Reading a picture book is clearly such an activity.

I suggested earlier that the pictures in a sequence act as schemata for each other. When a story is told in words as well as pictures, we first understand both the words and the pictures by means of the schemata we have already established for them—at first, our general expectations about stories and our general understanding about how pictures communicate. Then, the words correct and particularize our understanding of the pictures they accompany, and the pictures provide information that causes us to reinterpret and particularize the meanings of the words. Then all of that information becomes a schema for each new page of words and each new picture as we continue throughout a book.

For instance, if we looked at the first picture in *Where the Wild Things Are* before we hear the text and without knowledge of the images of Wild Things on the title page, we might say that we see a boy, meaning that the figure we see fits our schema of a young human being—and, perhaps because he does not wear a skirt, a young male human being. We might add that he looks angry and upset, his downcurved mouth fitting our schema for unhappiness, and we might be confused by his bushy tail, and conclude, perhaps, that he is not human at all, but half animal. Or we might bring into play our schema of occasions for costumes and assume that it is Halloween. Thus far, our interpretation of the picture depends on our basic models of human behavior.

But if we know the title of the book, the words "Where the Wild Things Are" might change our response—we might assume that this wild-looking child is indeed one of the Wild Things and that, perhaps, equally wild children might appear in later pictures. Or, remembering the images of wild creatures on the title page, we might assume that this child is in the process of being transformed from human to monster. Or we might alternatively bring into play our schema of children's books and toys and assume that it is the stuffed animal on the left who is the main character and that this wild half-human is out to get him. Furthermore, we might also bring into play various of our schema for pictorial conventions: the picture is dark, so it must be a sad story, and so on.

If we now add the words of the text, our perception of the pictures changes—and becomes much more specific. We now know that it is night and therefore not necessarily gloomy. We know that the creature's name is Max and that he is wearing a wolf suit; that means Max is not the dog and that it is indeed a wolf suit, a costume, so that Max is indeed a person, a human being. We know that this person, Max, and not the dog, is the main character. We also know for sure that he is a male, since it is "his" wolf suit. And we are told he is making mischief, which specifies the meaning of his downturned mouth: malevolence, not gloom. Furthermore, we have learned what matters in this picture: that it is not to be about how Max built a tent—not about the specific bad action—but merely an example of the more generalized conception, mischief.

In fact, we read both words and pictures here in relation to each other; rather than make the possible wrong assumptions I have outlined, our simultaneous or almost-simultaneous experience of both words and pictures allows us to use each to correct our understanding of the other. But what might we expect next? According to conventional patterns of human behavior—and, perhaps, of children's stories—we would most likely expect an angry, adult woman to appear in the next picture. But perhaps not; the grammatical incompleteness of the text suggests that there is more of the sentence to come and therefore more mischief to come, most likely a continuation of the same sequence of action we have seen part of already, since that is what we tend to expect in stories. So perhaps we will see Max looking through a large hole in the wall that he has made with his hammer, and his mother's angry face looking through it at him.

In fact, the next picture confirms the grammar's suggestion that there was more to come, but rather than a continuation of the same sequence, we are provided with a quite different action. So the picture tells us that the phrase "of one kind" was indeed meant to be balanced off; its meaning is changed by the words "and another" not because we did not expect those words but because we most likely expected more words than that. But those words on their own set up a sort of repetitive pattern that we might well expect to continue—an extended series of "and anothers" depicting yet more sorts of mischief. The picture changes that expectation by setting up the beginning of a chase that we might well expect to see the end of: the most likely slapstick conclusion to this situation would be a picture of Max barreling into his mother once he gets through the door. The next page thwarts that expectation both by bringing the series to an end and by showing us a quite different sort of scene. Part of the reason this sequence of pictures and words is so interesting is that the words change the meanings of the pictures, and the pictures then change the meanings of the words—sometimes by confirming our expectations and sometimes surprising us by not confirming them.

This process of making assumptions on the basis of our previous knowledge and then correcting them is basic to perception itself. As Ulric Neisser says, "The schemata that accept information and direct the search for more of it are not visual or auditory or tactual, but perceptual. To attend an event means to seek and accept every sort of information about it, regardless of modality, and to integrate all the information as it becomes available. Having heard something, we look to see it, and what we see then determines how we locate and interpret what we hear" (29–30). That last sentence nicely sums up the picture-book experience; picture books elegantly bring into play the basic patterns of perception. Having heard about something in the words, we look to see it, and having seen it, we now interpret what we hear differently. The words change the pictures, and the pictures change the words.

Pictures do that by adding visual information to what we have been told—show us, for instance, that Max is not just making mischief in general but that he is driving a nail into the wall. For that reason many commentators say that the purpose of pictures in picture books is to "extend" the texts, but cognitive theories of perception suggest that extension may be the wrong metaphor. It would be more accurate to say that pictures *limit* the text—and to add that the text also limits the pictures.

Consider some pictures of people suspended above flights of stairs. Without words we might guess that Sendak's Max above the stairs with a fork in his hand and Van Allsburg's Alan above the stairs in Abdul Gasazi's garden are flying or floating, or that Max is a creature that is half human and half animal and that Alan is a girl in jeans, or that both are midgets. But Sendak's words tell us Max is making mischief, and since the text does not refer to them, we discount the less plausible interpretations of the picture, like flying. Even more obviously, Van Allsburg's text tells us that Alan has, indeed, fallen down the stairs. In both cases, the words limit the range of possible responses to the picture.

Now consider the sentence "The boy fell down the stairs" unaccompanied by a picture. It clearly describes an action, but we have no way of understanding the meaning of the action. So we can imagine countless possibilities. The boy tripped. The boy was pushed. The boy was wearing a dress. He was a Norwegian. He was in a wheelchair. And so on. Any picture at all will narrow these possibilities to a very few. A picture of a boy in slacks without a wheelchair will eliminate the possibility of the dress and the wheelchair, and a picture of a boy in a kilt will eliminate the possibility of the Norwegian—and a picture of a boy above a stairway in a garden will demand a quite specific response. Furthermore, the picture might even show us a banana peel that would account for the fall. Furthermore, as I suggested earlier, the quality of the picture itself might inform us of the proper attitude to take toward it; it might be a cartoon that tells us to laugh at the boy, or it might be a broodingly realistic picture that tells us to feel sorry for him. In either case, the picture would limit not only plausible interpretations of the situation but also the range of plausible responses to it.

By limiting each other, words and pictures together take on a meaning that neither possesses without the other—perform the completion of each other that Barthes calls "relaying." The words in *The Garden of Abdul Gasazi* do not in fact tell us that it is a stairway that Alan is falling down; they merely say he slipped and fell. And the picture does not tell us that it is somebody named Alan who is doing the slipping. Each tells us of something the other is incapable of telling or that the other could tell only with difficulty; together, they mean something quite different and a lot more specific than each on its own—in this case, that this is indeed a boy, that his name is Alan, that he has indeed slipped, and that it is indeed a stairway he is falling down.

Because they communicate different kinds of information, and because they work together by limiting each other's meanings, words and pictures necessarily have a combative relationship; their complementarity is a matter of opposites completing each other by virtue of their differences. As a result, the relationships between pictures and texts in picture books tend to be ironic: each speaks about matters on which the other is silent.

■ ■ ■ ■

CHAPTER EIGHT

———

Irony in Picture Books: Subjectivity and Objectivity,
Time and Space

In her discussion in *Problems of Art* of the different ways in which the different arts communicate, Susanne Langer says, "There are no happy marriages in art—only successful rape" (86). Given the differing qualities of words and pictures, the relationships between them in picture books tend to be adversarial: rape rather than marriage. They come together best and most interestingly not when writers and illustrators attempt to have them mirror and duplicate each other but when writers and illustrators use the different qualities of their different arts to communicate different information. When they do that, the texts and illustrations of a book have an ironic relationship to each other: the words tell us what the pictures do not show, and the pictures show us what the words do not tell.

In a discussion of the semiology of film, Christian Metz suggests that films demand from their viewer knowledge of at least five different systems of signification, most of which can also be found in slightly different ways in picture books: culturebound patterns of visual and auditory perception (such as knowing how to understand a perspective drawing), recognition of the objects shown on screen (labeling), knowledge of their cultural significance (such as knowing that black clothing stands for mourning), narrative structures (knowledge of types of stories and how they usually work out), and purely cinematic means of implying significance, such as music and montage. Metz suggests that each complete film, "relying on all these codes, plays them one against the other, eventually arriving at its own individual system, its ultimate (or first?) principle of unification and intelligibility" (100). In other words, filmmakers make use of the differences between various means of communication in the knowledge that each medium they bring into play will finally merely be part of the whole along with all the others; consequently, they deliberately (or sometimes, given the varying narrative capabilities of different media, inevitably) make each incomplete so that it can indeed be part of a whole and so that the meaning will be communicated by the whole and not any specific part of the whole. What the clothing and gesture do not reveal to us, the music or the narrative structure might; and what the clothing and the music communicate separately is different from what they communicate together. So each medium that filmmakers use always communicates different information differently, and all of them express their fullest meaning in terms of the ironies inherent in their differences from each other.

Irony occurs in literature when we know something more and something different from what we are being told. We are aware that the words we are reading are incomplete. Something similar happens when we interpret a picture ironically; we believe we know more and different information from what the picture shows us. For instance, we might say of a photographer's carefully selected view of a rustic cottage, taken for a real estate advertisement, that it is a misrepresentation because he has left out the hamburger stand next door. When words and pictures combine, irony emerges from the way in which the incompleteness of each is revealed by the differing incompleteness of the other. The theoretically "fierce bad rabbit" in Beatrix Potter's book of that name looks soft and cuddly, anything but the evil creature the text refers to. The pictures destroy our confidence in the apparent meaning of the words, and the words destroy our confidence in the apparent implication of the picture. This mutual destruction by words and picture of our confident expectations of what each might mean on its own is characteristic of many picture books, which are like Metz's description of film: "each film is built upon the destruction of its own codes" (102).

An obvious example of the mutual destruction of words by pictures and pictures by words that provides the pleasure of irony is Pat Hutchins's *Rosie's Walk*. The words in this book tell us only that Rosie is a hen, that she went for a rather uninteresting walk across the farmyard, and that she got back in time for dinner. The pictures contradict the text by adding more to our knowledge of the situation. They show us that a fox is following Rosie across the barnyard and attempting to catch her—and that every time he makes a leap for her he gets into slapstick difficulties that prevent him from making the capture. The pictures obviously tell a different and much more specific story than the words do.

Students in children's literature courses often tell me that *Rosie's Walk* would be just as successful without words at all: after all, the words by themselves are so boring, and the pictures in sequence do successfully communicate an interesting series of actions. But while the words are boring, the book would not be as successful without them. In showing more than the words tell us, the pictures not only tell their own story; they also imply an ironic comment on the words. They make the words comic by making them outrageously incomplete, only a half-truth, and by making their incompleteness so obvious. Without the words, the book would tell a funny story about an inadequate fox; but it would not tell an even funnier story about the occasional inadequacy of words to describe everything that matters about a situation. When a friend of mine first read *Rosie's Walk* to his young son, he reported to me that the child was about to tell him there was a fox in these pictures every time he saw it but then each time giggled delightedly and said nothing; he had decided to share an ironic joke by not spilling the beans.

The joke happens only because the words and pictures are so different from each other and so totally contradict each other; their relationship causes us to lose confidence in each on its own. The words are clearly not to be trusted; they do not even mention the most important thing that is happening. But then, how can we trust the pictures if the words ignore so much about them? *Is* the fox really all that important? Is there really any reason for Rosie or the person who speaks the words of the text to be aware of him? Apparently not—for the fox does himself in whether Rosie or the narrator notices him or not, and does so, ironically, because he himself ignores the pond and the rake and such just as much as Rosie and the narrator ignore him. Maybe they are right to ignore him. (And incidentally, notice how the narrator's blindness to events makes him into a character with narrative significance. I would not be postulating any specific narrator at all for these inconsequential words if it were not for the pictures, but the divergence between the words and the pictures forces me to impute complex motivations to the speaker of the words. He is a character exclusive to the text but revealed by the pictures, just as the fox is exclusive to the pictures, while his possible significance as an ironic contrast to the narrator is implied by the text.) The story the words and pictures tell together is subtle and ambiguous—much more (and much more specific) than merely the addition of the words and the pictures to each other.

While not all pictures books are so explicitly and significantly ironic as *Rosie's Walk*, many do make much of differences between words and pictures. One common practice is the tradition of an extended series of pictures to illustrate very simple texts such as nursery rhymes. Randolph Caldecott produced long series of pictures for some very short rhymes; Sendak continues the tradition in his *Hector Protector*, which illustrates a four-line rhyme in a long series of pictures that transforms it into a complex narrative involving a cake, a snake, a lion, some crows, and a Victoria-like Queen and her King. None of these appears in the original rhyme, and at least part of the fun in Sendak's version is our pleasure in his ingenuity—that he could take such simple and apparently nonsensical words and transform them into something so relatively sensible and logical. Without the original words to tell us of this difference, we would not enjoy these pictures so much. In fact, without the contrast of even simpler words, the pictures would themselves seem overly simple and rather uninteresting. Once again, the additional information offered by the pictures changes not only the meaning but the tone and purpose of the text, and vice versa. Both are only minimally interesting on their own; not only is the combination of the two of them far more complex and rewarding than the individual components, but the symbiotic relationship between them makes each of the individual components seem more complex and rewarding.

A more subtle sort of irony occurs when the tone of the words in a picture book does not seem to match the situation the pictures show us. In picture books, where the language is usually simple and the pictures are usually complicated, tonal ironies are often based on a text's matter-of-fact acceptance of what ought to be exciting or alarming. We see a child ruining the walls of the family home and chasing the family dog with a fork for what must be sinister and painful intentions, and we are told only that he is making mischief. No horror, no surprise; at least some of our pleasure here is in the inadequacy of these words to describe the strange situation, which it seems merely to take for granted. Picture books often provide vague verbal labels for complex and detailed visual images, and the difference between the two often provides the words with a tone of laconic acceptance they could not convey without accompanying pictures.

Something a little stranger happens when the picture and the words seem to express different tones or moods. The obvious example is *Mr. Rabbit and the Lovely Present*. The pictures by themselves are dreamy, moody, romantic, bucolic; the words are staccato, pragmatic, a little humorous. On their own, the words are annoyingly repetitive and do not tell much of a story; with the sort of illustrations we might have expected— simple, exuberant cartoons focusing on the primary colors the text focuses on—it would be eminently forgettable. The pictures by themselves are accomplished but rather like each other and in the long run not all that interesting; they are in an impressionistic style that rarely suggests much narrative content, and as the stories that people usually make around these pictures after seeing them apart from the text reveal, they are unenergetic. But the two together are more than the sum of these two disappointing parts. How did these subtle and complex impressionistic figures get involved in this inane conversation about absurdly insignificant details? How did this practical problem of finding a birthday present ever develop in the midst of a pastoral dream? These unanswerable mysteries create a complex mood that makes the book interesting.

But the distance between words and pictures also changes each into something else. The dreaminess of the pictures creates some sense of depth and intimacy in the relationship of the rabbit and the girl that the words on their own do not evoke; the pictures make the words seem warmer. Meanwhile, the words provide a sense of lightness and humor that changes the seriously nostalgic mood of the pictures.

The irony inherent in the different natures of pictures and words is often subtle—easy to experience but hard to notice and comment upon. But while all the ironic relationships between words and pictures are not obvious ones, all the relationships between words and pictures *are* ironic. *Where the Wild Things Are* is often praised for the way in which its pictures mirror and convey the mood of the text, but the reactions of those who hear the words without the pictures make its ironies clear. They imagine nightmarish horrors; Sendak's pictures *prevent* our assuming that the Wild Things are nightmarish. They contradict the implications of the text by suggesting a different interpretation of it, a more specifically cozy one. Meanwhile, the cartoonish style of the pictures and the sheer adorability of Sendak's Wild Things are themselves contradicted by the text, which provides the information that the Wild Things had "terrible" roars and "terrible" claws and "terrible" teeth; perhaps they are not so safely cute after all. Alone the pictures are relatively unalarming; alone the words are relatively scary. Together, they create a delicious ambiguity that makes the book complex and fascinating.

The pictures made by Burkert and Hyman to accompany the text of "Snow White" also have an ironic relationship with their text, simply because almost everybody who looks at them has both heard the story before and seen other pictures of its heroine. Our consciousness of this particular image of Snow White as one among many others—and as a particular, specific evocation of some vague words—causes us to notice not just the way in which the pictures show us what the text tells us but also the particularities of this particular interpretation of that text: the details the words have evoked but do not themselves mean. We inevitably see the pictures, in being thus detailed, as different from the words; and in being conscious of that difference, we may take pleasure in it.

Illustrators certainly do: the difference between Burkert's picture of

Snow White in a forest filled with dangerous animals and a text which makes no mention of these animals forces us to reinvent both the meaning and the tone of a well-known text that we may already be familiar with and to understand it differently in this different context. In telling more than the text, the picture makes the matter-of-fact directness of the text into a deliberately ironic laconicism. In some illustrated versions of fairy tales, the reverse happens: a matter-of-fact description of surprisingly unexpected creatures or actions—"then a wicked dragon appeared" or "he turned into a bear"—ceases to be ironic understatement and becomes merely labeling information when the text becomes a caption for an illustration that makes the surprising graphically obvious. Sensitive illustrators of this sort of text find ways of enriching the wonder rather than dispersing it, in ways that create ironic relationships between text and illustration; Burkert does so by never showing us the face of the witch whose beauty is the central fact of the plot of *Snow White,* and Hyman does so merely by creating an intense mood and implying strongly emotional personalities for the characters that operate in ironic tension with the unemotional text.

Of all the picture books I have focused on in this study, Burton's *The Little House* seems to be most without irony—a book in which picture and text exactly mirror each other. Both spiral through repetitive patterns, and the pictures seem to show us exactly what the words tell us. But do they? In fact, the text without the pictures sounds pretentious; it is devoid of the humor we find in the pictures, which humanize the house and the sun and which have enough of the pleasantness of folk art to undermine the stodgy high-mindedness of endless sentences about years following years. At the same time, the pictures by themselves have a cute "childlikeness" that seems a little vapid, a little uninvolved with real emotion. But something magical happens when we combine that childlike distance and that portentous prose: together, they seem wise rather than sentimental, and emotion-filled rather than distant. Pictures are always different from words, and pictures and words together are always different from either on their own.

Two specific sorts of irony which develop when words and pictures come together in narratives are inevitable, because they are inherent differences between verbal narration and pictorial depiction. The first is the distance between the relative objectivity of pictures and the relative subjectivity of words; the second is the distance between the temporal movement of stories and the fixed timelessness usual in pictures. All picture books are ironic to the extent that they express these qualities.

Words tend always to imply one subjective way of seeing things that might be seen otherwise. The words "The room was cozy and comfortable" evoke and demand complicity in a subjective attitude; even the apparently objective words "This is a room" still assert one specific attitude that should be taken toward the room, an attitude that precludes other possible ones. But the fact that visual images do actually resemble the objects they represent means that they cannot force a subjective attitude toward the objects depicted as directly and as efficiently as verbal imagery does. Visual images cannot directly assert attitudes; they can only imply them by creating images which evoke contexts that suggest the attitudes, and those images might convey unintended attitudes to those who view them in terms of different contexts. Consequently, an artist's attempt to persuade us that a room is cozy and comfortable might backfire if the armchair depicted strikes us as being depressingly dilapidated rather than comfortably broken in—the image of the armchair inevitably conveys the objective existence of the chair more directly than it expresses the subjective attitude to be taken toward it.

Furthermore, representational art can depict understandable objects only by showing them from a distance that will allow us to make sense of what we see—a distance that itself implies objectivity; and we can make sense of these objects only when we keep some distance from them. We cannot actually see a picture if our nose is rubbing against it, and even if we stand back from it, we can make little sense of a picture of an object depicted from a point of view that does not imply some distance; a chair seen from two inches above its surface would look like a pattern, not a chair. Walter J. Ong suggests that all vision is objective: "sight situates the observer outside what he views" (72).

Furthermore, the objectivity of actual visual images is not shared by the visual images implied by words, so that words and pictures together provide two different and possibly contradictory sorts of visual information. Speaking in *The Act of Reading* of the universal disappointment people feel with illustrations of fictional characters and scenes we have first responded to without illustrations, Wolfgang Iser suggests that "objects, unlike meanings, are highly determinate, and it is this determinacy which makes us feel disappointed. . . . Our mental images do not serve to make the character physically visible; their optical poverty is an indication of the fact that they illuminate the character, not as an object, but as a bearer of meaning" (138). Iser believes that, when we respond to verbal descriptions of characters, we understand them not as purely visual information but as a source of potential meaning; that meaning is something we then help to create by interpreting the significance of the visual details provided, and as a result our mental images of characters are as much a part of ourselves, our own distinct habits of thinking and imagining, as they are part of the text which gives us the information that allows us to manufacture them. But a filmed image of a written scene "not only reproduces an existing object, but it also excludes me from a world which I can see but which I have not helped to create" (139). Something similar happens in our response to the pictures in picture books; the pictures enforce a division between subject and object, viewer and picture, quite different from the breaking down of the subject-object division implied and called forth by language on its own.

Of course, some kinds of pictures are more decidedly objective than others. In a film, for instance, the camera might be positioned in a close-up in such a way that we are given the impression that our nose is indeed almost rubbing against the object we see; and the constant variations in point of view common in films tend to diminish the objectivity of the visual experience. If we agree to imagine as we watch a film that our eyes have somehow left our bodies and are free to accompany the camera as it darts in and out of and around the action, we tend to lose our distance; movies draw us in, force us to see and feel as the camera sees and feels.

"Because the movie camera can move and 'see' the way a character in a film would, it allows film makers to use a first-person point of view" (Huss and Silverstein 106).

But as I suggested earlier, picture books make limited use of such variations in point of view, particularly of close-ups. Even books that do indulge in such variations, such as Leaf and Lawson's *Ferdinand*, lack the fluidity, and thus the implied subjectivity and involvement, of the moving film camera. And without fluidity the shifts in *Ferdinand* imply a viewpoint of detached irony more than they create a subjective involvement. Perhaps because shifting viewpoints cannot actually achieve their most useful effect in the limited number of pictures usual in a picture book, most picture books typically show characters from a distance and in settings and imply information about the characters' situations and states of mind through details in those settings rather than through shifts in points of view.

Indeed, picture books are more like theater in their storytelling conventions than they are like films, for picture-book artists most often place us as viewers where we must necessarily be in a seat in a theater: always at the same distance and angle from the actors and seeing always their complete bodies instead of just sometimes their faces, sometimes their torsos, and so on. According to Susan Sontag, "We see what happens on the stage with our own eyes. We see on the screen what the camera sees" (257–58). In picture books, we usually see with our own eyes, and the visual distance automatically translates into an emotional objectivity. We see the characters in illustrations as we see all real people but those with whom we have the most intimate relationships, and we tend to think of them as objects of potential interest and understanding rather than as surrogates for our own subjectively involved selves. They are like figures on stage rather than characters on film—and it is surely not accidental that the traditional behavior of the fans of stage stars is the desire to possess them, whereas the fans of film stars more usually want to be like them; possessiveness implies separation and difference rather than identification. This is not to say that we do not become involved with the characters in picture books. But our involvement is less immediate and thoughtless, more controlled and thoughtful, for we must think about what we see before we can come to feel anything about it—and as I suggested earlier, we may even sometimes actually want to possess what we see.

In a sense, the words of picture books are like a voice-over narration in a film that tells us what to see in the pictures, how to interpret them. But since the pictures themselves tend to the objectivity of the theater, there is an ironic distance between the subjective focus of words and the objective wholeness of pictures; unlike film or theater, picture books can be both objective and subjective at the same time.

In fact, they almost always are. Words can tell us that Snow White's mother pricked her finger and then looked at the snow and the window frame, but a picture that showed us just the pricked finger and a window frame and snow would make no sense to us. All the illustrations I know of this scene also include one other object that makes sense of all the rest: Snow White's mother. And that creates an irony: the words allow us to put ourselves in her place and follow her actions; the pictures demand that we stand back and look at her—observe her actions.

Nearly all pictures books display exactly this irony. The texts of stories tend to be written from the viewpoint of either a clearly definable narrator or of one of the characters involved or of both. Even if we hear nothing of a narrator's or any of the characters' emotions and opinions, we do centrally focus on one or two central protagonists and follow them through the story and thus assume a special involvement with them. In the text of *Peter Rabbit*, for instance, we both hear of Peter's reactions to events, his feeling ill or frightened, and also follow his actions, so that we hear of his encounter with Mr. McGregor in terms of how Mr. McGregor intrudes upon Peter's consciousness; when Peter escapes into the shed, the story remains with Peter alone in the shed rather than with Mr. McGregor out in the garden. But even as the text enforces our involvement with Peter by telling of his interior feelings and implying his subjective point of view on the events that transpire, the accompanying pictures include representations of Peter himself, as seen by somebody outside his consciousness. In these pictures, he is a very rabbitlike rabbit, not a human personality to identify with. There is an interesting tension between distance and involvement, subjectivity and objectivity.

In less carefully worked out picture books, this sort of tension is without narrative significance, merely an annoying or unconsidered limitation of the medium of picture books; but Potter uses the tension to support the ambiguity of the entire story, in which it is unclear whether we are to judge Peter objectively or sympathize with him subjectively. In fact, the tension between subjectivity and objectivity allows the words to change the implications of the pictures and vice versa. When we look at Peter lying under a net, we see only a rabbit under a net; he might be asleep or dead. The text tells us of his despair and forces us to read despair into the picture, and meanwhile, the image of a little rabbit lying under a net gives us the distance to put the deep emotion the text describes in perspective.

More subtly, Potter uses the distance between the subjective text and the objective pictures to focus on the oddity of the fact that she is writing about animals with human habits. The picture on the first page, which gives these rabbits the cute names of house pets, merely shows four unclothed rabbits by a tree, seen as if suddenly caught by a person passing by. But the words insist that this is a fairy tale that happened "Once upon a time" to some characters named, of all silly things, Flopsy, Mopsy, and Cottontail; the picture creates an unresolved ambiguity by suggesting it happened not to fantasy characters but to real-looking rabbits, wild ones of the sort that are not likely to have the names of pets. Then, as we turn the page, we see the rabbits dressed in human clothing, transformed from natural animals into fantasy figures, and looking, from an objective point of view, just as silly as the names Flopsy and Mopsy might imply and just as inconsequential and as divorced from real life; furthermore, they have been separated from the background, so that we must focus in on them as individuals, characters with a history rather than rabbits in a setting natural to rabbits. But the irony continues, for it is at this point that Mrs. Rabbit warns her children about what serious things happen to real rabbits who enter the gardens of human beings. In both cases the objective conclusion we reach by perusing the pictures conflicts interestingly with the viewpoint demanded by the words; not surprisingly, this ambiguous discussion of whether Peter is a civilized child who should obey his mother or a rabbit with a natural taste for carrots, a person who needs some regard for his clothing or an animal who can move easily when he loses his clothing, continues throughout the book.

Sometimes the subjective implications of a text are slight indeed. The text of *Outside Over There*, for instance, has enough of the matter-of-fact tone of a fairy tale to seem to be just as objective about Ida and what happens to her as the pictures are. But not quite, for the narrator insists on his interpretations of the story in a way that the pictures cannot. He tells us not that Ida deserves what she gets when the goblins steal her sister but rather that she is "Poor Ida"; in other words, he asks for an identification with her when the picture of her horrid situation—hugging a baby made of ice because she did not do her job well—might cause us in fact to stand back and feel at some distance from her. Throughout, we merely see Ida as one object in the midst of others, and we see at least one baby in every picture except the sequence in which the ice baby melts; considering pictures alone, this might be the baby's story. It is the words that make Ida the focus of our attention, demand sympathy for her, and tell us that she is the central character.

Something similar happens in *Wild Things*, although perhaps in the opposite direction. The words tend to focus on the insignificance of Max's action at the start—it was just mischief, after all—and on the terribleness of the Wild Things later, but the pictures show us that the mischief was not so easily dismissable as the narrator seems to suggest, that it was itself pretty terrible, and that Max is capable of handling any Wild Things that come along. The pictures remove any excess amount of concern for Max that the words might have implied. We speak of children identifying with the characters they read about. But as soon as we *see* characters like Max— and see, from a distance, that they are individuals, with individual faces different from the face of any given one of their viewers, some of the power of the identification with them that the text on its own would demand is lost. As Iser suggests in his comparison of mental images and actual ones, picture books enforce distance in the mere act of showing us their characters as well as telling us about them.

Nevertheless, the words in picture books demand involvement. Burton's clever depiction of the little house in *The Little House* might be viewed by someone without knowledge of the words with no sense that it is a sentient being—that it has a subjective personality; it is merely a house, with two windows, a door, and a front step. But the text tells us that the house has feelings and observes the world around her and thinks about it; it demands that we think of her as a person, a meaningful entity as well as a visible object. Having heard that she has a subjective point of view and learned what it is, we do two things. Most obviously, we interpret these simple depictions of landscape and cityscape as having the symbolic values the little house herself attaches to them; less obviously, we look at the depiction of the little house itself and see that the windows might be eyes and the door a nose and that the front step might represent a smile. In fact, having noticed that, we might be delighted to go through the book again and notice how the slightly different lines that depict that step change it from a smile in some pictures to a look of dejection in others and then back to a smile again at the end. The subjectivity implied by the text changes the objective implications of the pictures.

A more subtle sort of objectivity develops when a picture informs us that the viewpoint of a character as conveyed by the text and even supported by the picture is nevertheless limited or one-sided. Given their tendency to depict visible circumstances that extend beyond the narrow focus of a text, pictures can offer extra information that suggests the limitations of that narrowness. As William Moebius says, an illustrator can "represent points of view other than those of the main character . . . by depicting tacit witnesses on the fringes or in the foreground or background of the picture" (148). Most often, these witnesses confirm the main character's interpretation of events—as do the sparrows who substantiate the seriousness of Peter Rabbit's plight when they hover around his fallen body as they implore him to exert himself. Sometimes in picture books, however, minor characters who ignore the main action provide the ironic message that what seems monumentally important to the person centrally involved in it often means nothing to objective outsiders. The goat in *Rosie's Walk* provides such a message. His total lack of interest implies not only that Rosie's walk is not as important as the text suggests but also that the fox's traumatic experience is not as important as the pictures suggest; the goat supports the book's central concern with the limitations of subjective experience by being as comically oblivious of his surroundings as are Rosie, the fox, and the voice of the narrator. More subtly, the black cat who accompanies and even frequently mirrors the gestures of Hyman's Queen throughout her *Snow White* signals the subjective solitude of the Queen's moment of defeat by placidly looking away from her through a window at some birds as she herself stares horrifically off into space.

In the books I have been discussing, the ironic relationships of subjectivity and objectivity are relatively subtle and not always readily apparent. But the difference between subjective involvement and objective distance is used in some highly ironic picture books in more obvious and often in remarkably clever ways. These books do actually tell a story from a subjective point of view—that of a first-person narrator. In Ann Jonas's *The Quilt*, for instance, a young girl tells of a strange voyage in search of her stuffed dog, a voyage filled with fearful moments in strange landscapes; the text asks us to share her worry. But the pictures reveal that she has fallen asleep while looking at her new quilt and that the places she visits in search of her dog have been suggested by the varying designs on the blocks of the quilt. Each individual picture is not ironic, in that it merely mirrors the text by showing us objectively what the girl sees or imagines herself seeing subjectively. But since it is representing the girl's point of view, the text leaves out the transition between consciousness and dream, reality and fantasy. As objective outsiders viewing the pictures in sequence, we can *see* the transition. As we look at the sequence of pictures, we see not only the strange landscape but also the girl herself in pictures in which the quilt is gradually changed into the strange landscape, and our objective knowledge of the transformations allows us to regard the pictures with pleasure rather than fear and to think of what we see as dream imagery and objectively compare it with the actual elements of the quilt it is based on. In other words we are both in the dream sharing its strong emotions and outside of it realizing it is just a dream and appreciating its ingenuity.

In Ellen Raskin's *Nothing Ever Happens on My Block*, a young boy himself tells us how nothing happens, while we see from a distance both the boy and the block he speaks of. We clearly do not see it from young Chester's point of view, since his point of view would not include Chester himself as seen from a distance. And seeing from a distance, we understand his words differently from the way he intends them. Chester speaks about how nothing happens while all around him curious, interesting, and even magical things are happening: children are skipping and breaking their legs and playing pranks, lightning is striking and causing a fire, trees are growing, and witches are multiplying. But this child is too involved in himself to notice any of it, and our pleasure in the book is in seeing not just more than he tells us to see but the very opposite of what he insists is there: *everything* is happening on his block.

But we do not merely understand that he is wrong; we feel superior to him. From our objective distance, we not only see that he is wrong but we also see how unhappy he looks. In his unwillingness to notice the world about him, he looks like a very unlikable person, not somebody to sympathize with or feel sorry for. According to Bader, "What Raskin does . . . is to pit visual hijinks against a deadpan text and the effect, by itself, is comic opera" (*American Picturebooks* 538). In fact, the vast gulf between words and pictures here is not just a matter of different interpretations of reality but also of a clear gulf between the subjective and the objective—even, in this case, between self-indulgent egocentricity and the delights of observation of the objective world outside oneself, for the pictures show us that all the exciting things Chester lusts after are in fact right there on his block, if he would only take the time to notice them; as he wishes for "courageous hunters hunting," a policeman hunts a robber, and as he wishes for "ferocious lions and tigers," a cat tries to attract his attention. This book uses the distinctions between objective pictures and subjective words to make a point about the relative value of personal subjectivity and objectivity.

Judith Viorst's *Alexander and the Terrible, Horrible, No-Good, Very Bad Day* is enriched by Ray Cruz's pictures in an opposite way. As Alexander himself tells us of his horrible day, we see him in the center of pictures of the terrible happenings. The result is, we do not have to take his word for anything; we see that it really did happen, just as he said it did. So the pictures, in their objective substantiating of the truth of Alexander's version of his day, allow us to feel more sympathy for him; he is not just self-indulgent, self-pitying; unlike Raskin's objective devastation of Chester Filbert's vision of the world, the objectivity of Cruz's pictures supports Alexander's vision.

Nevertheless, the relationship between words and pictures does remain ironic here; the pictures show us something different from the words—the world with Alexander in it, not the world that Alexander sees. Furthermore, they depict Alexander's day in terms of the comedic implications of cartooning, so that the great agony Alexander himself feels and expresses is qualified and controlled by the pictures, which forces us to laugh at him as well as to sympathize with his plight. In other words, it is once more the objectivity of the pictures that points out the excessive self-pity of the text. While that is a more subtle sort of ironic distance than the kind Raskin creates, it is still ironic: it communicates by forcing us to compare the words with the different information offered by the pictures.

Obviously, a more directly ironic book like *Nothing Ever Happens on My Block* or *Rosie's Walk* depends on that distance—the ironic relationship between the narrator's subjective view of what is happening and our objective understanding of what the pictures show us. But as David Topper suggests in a *ChLA Quarterly* article, *Rosie's Walk* can play its clever game because of an interesting incapability of pictures: since they exist out of time, they cannot express sound, which is created by waves moving through other objects and is therefore possible only in time. Surely Rosie ought to have heard the fox, for he is involved in some particularly noisy shenanigans, and we might say the same of the things that happen in *Nothing Ever Happens on My Block*. But while we can *see* some of the sources of noise, we cannot in fact actually hear them: the splash in *Rosie's Walk* exists on the page for the viewer to observe, but it may be ignored both by the narrator and Rosie because it cannot actually be heard. There is an ironic distance between the temporal sequence of the story and the timeless quality of pictures that can only depict actions stopped—as seen at one specific instant removed from the flux of time.

That sort of ironic relationship between the sequential storytelling of words and the series of stopped moments we see in a sequence of pictures is, I believe, the essence of picture-book storytelling. In his discussion of novels and films, George Bluestone says that the two are basically unlike in that one describes time and can only imply space, while the other depicts space and can only imply time. "The novel renders the illusion of space by going from point to point in time. The film renders time by going from point to point in space" (300). The words of a novel can provide a sequential, that is, temporal, description of the details of a room that will eventually allow us to imagine the room as a whole—to create the mental image that Iser spoke of; a film, meanwhile, consists of a series of still pictures that, seen in sequence, imply the passage of time. Picture books, in containing both words and pictures, combine both of these two sorts or relationships between space and time.

In *Rosie's Walk*, for instance, the words evoke the farmyard for us by telling us the order and nature of Rosie's trip across it: around the pond, then past the mill, and so on. Considered without pictures, the temporal actions described in this text would evoke for us an imaginary conception of a farmyard we would not actually see—a farmyard less objectively visual than meaningful. Meanwhile, the pictures evoke time by showing us how things look in the farmyard at various separate moments. First we see the fox about to leap at Rosie, then we see him fall in the pond; if the words were not there we would have to invent for ourselves a series of actions in time that would join these two timeless evocations of space.

Taken together, obviously, the pictures here show us what the words can only ask us to imagine, and the words can tell us what the pictures can only ask us to imagine.

But in that way they imply different versions of both space and time that have an ironic distance from each other. The words focus on what happens without much interest in where it happens or in what it looks like as it happens: the whole point is what Rosie did in what sequence, not in what she or the farmyard looked like as she did it. The pond and the mill simply signify the route of Rosie's walk. Meanwhile, the pictures show us the pond and the haystack and insist that the way they look from an outsider's point of view matters as much as the fact that Rosie moved past them. And in terms of time, the pictures focus on key events rather than on the fluid connection of one action with the next. They move from high point to high point and ignore the moments in between those high points: the fox about to leap at Rosie, then the fox in the pond, but nothing in between. Furthermore, and like most pictures in picture books, these pictures are cartoons in style, but they are cartoons with their spaces colored in, so that the energy of their line is weakened by the solidity of their shapes. As a result, the time the pictures imply is a series of strong moments with nothing between them, significantly different from the time the story tells us about, and the space the words imply has a different significance from the space the pictures show us. It is this doubleness that allows the irony in *Rosie's Walk:* time as Rosie perceives it and as described by the text is not the temporal sequence we must supply in order to explain the pictures, and the space we actually see is a lot more complicated and contains more significant details of action than the space implied by the verbal description of Rosie's actions.

Most picture books have a similar doubleness of both space and time. In *The Little House,* for instance, the changes of time of day and of season that we notice when we move from one picture to the next do suggest the regular passage of time that the words speak of; but the pictures show us each season only at its central moment of ripeness. In one picture we see the trees in full color then, in the next picture, the landscape buried by the snows of winter—and nothing in between. But the text tells us how the nights get colder and the leaves begin to turn and so on, apparently until we get to the full-fledged autumn we see in the picture. So the pictures in sequence focus on the large transitions—the difference between autumn and winter; the accompanying words operate in a different, more fluid time and focus on the gradual change from one to the other. The words evoke a physical space that has the endless mutability of time itself; the pictures evoke transitions that almost deny the flux of time by ignoring all those smaller, subtler changes and showing two different visions of the same space. They imply that sense of the eternal sameness of the passing seasons that is one of the important messages of the book.

According to Bluestone, novels create space by using time, and films create time by using space. The temporal sequence of the words of a novel implies a setting for the events it describes, a setting we imagine but do not actually see, and the images we see on a screen imply the passing of time from one image to the next one, a time that we do not actually experience passing. Picture books do both, but in ways that seem to contradict each other. As in *Rosie's Walk* and *The Little House*, good picture-book artists take advantage of those apparent contradictions to create the basic involving tensions of their stories. That they do so is such a distinct and important aspect of picture-book art that it deserves a separate chapter of its own.

C H A P T E R   N I N E

———

The Rhythms of Picture-Book Narrative

Reading a novel is a matter of absorbing a sequence of carefully integrated words, an activity so involving that readers often lose consciousness of their actual surroundings as they read. While we respond to both the words we hear and the images we see as we watch a movie or a play, we do both at the same time. But when we read a picture book to ourselves, we must look closely at the words in order to understand them and so we cannot at the same time look at pictures, and while we look at a picture we cannot at the same time be looking at words carefully enough to decode them. Furthermore, the alternation between words and pictures requires constant switches between two different ways of seeing—from a pattern of left-to-right and top-to-bottom scanning to a much less regulated consciousness of holistic form and then back again. These two ways of seeing may require two different kinds of thinking.

In the following discussion of how we put together the information from these two different sources, I make some assumptions about the most likely set of circumstances under which most readers absorb the story in a picture book. Because pictures so successfully attract attention, I suspect that most of us look at the picture (or pictures) on each set of facing pages before we read the words. Even if we do not, our peripheral vision will provide us with a sense of color, density, and style, and therefore of mood, so that we come to the words with at least some sense of how to understand them from the picture. Then, because we know we can use the information provided by a text to better interpret a picture, we most likely will look at the picture more closely again after we have read the text. In many picture books, furthermore, the pictures are on the right-hand side of each two-page spread, the words on the left; consequently, our understanding that time conventionally moves from left to right will cause us to look at the picture once again after reading the text, before we go on to the next page.

As a result, the basic pattern by which most of us look at picture books must be something like this: first picture, then words, then the same picture again, then turn the page, then the next picture, then the words—and so on. For picture books with different pictures on each of two facing pages, the pattern probably doubles: left picture, right picture, left text, left picture, right picture, right text, right picture, turn the page. In books with more than two pictures on each set of facing pages, we most likely treat each pairing of picture and text separately: after a first glance tells us that the visual information as a whole is too complex to be absorbed all at once, we will look at the first picture, then the accompanying text, then the first picture again, then the second picture, and so on.

On their own, pictures and words each first allow a number of different narrative possibilities; together, they make each other more specific. As we move from one to another in a picture book, therefore, the story gradually becomes more specific. But it does so not in terms of the gradual amplification that we usually expect from stories—the gradual unfolding of a plot that eventually makes all things clear—but rather in terms of a contrapuntal arrangement of mutual correction: since words and pictures give us different insights into the same events, we move from one to the other in terms of how the text forces us to go back and reinterpret the pictures and how the reinterpreted picture then forces us to go back and reinterpret the text again—but without ever forgetting that picture and text are separate and different from each other.

I have suggested that the visual spaces depicted in pictures imply time and that the temporal sequences depicted by words imply space. Consequently, the typical pattern of movement from picture to words through a book requires that we move from one densely textured depiction of space to another by means of a specifically described temporal sequence which provides only vague spatial information. Then, as we review and reinterpret the visual space we have already seen and turn the page and see another strongly evoked visual space, we can imagine narrative continuity only by extrapolating it from the connections between two depictions of space. In other words, we move constantly between strong evocations of space that more weakly evoke time to strong evocations of temporal passage that more weakly evoke space.

According to Christian Metz, "codes which deserve to be called rhythmical (other than metaphorically) are manifested in diverse materials of expression which all have the feature of temporality" (222). Both the words and pictures of picture books have temporality—both can imply the passage of time, the words by their very nature and the pictures by their sequence. Consequently, both are capable of having rhythms, and the two together create a third rhythm: the rhythm of picture-book narrative.

As we move through a series of pictures, we have to imagine what happens between the moments of stopped time that we actually see. Most picture books show us only a small number of such moments, even though the events they imply may take place over an extended length of time: the pictures in *Where the Wild Things Are* show only eighteen moments out of a series of events that takes place, at least in theory, over two years and two days; the twenty-one pictures in *The Little House* imply the passage of many decades but actually depict only twenty-one moments. That strong focus puts tremendous emphasis on the moments we do see: they clearly become the most significant moments out of all the possible ones we might have seen, the ones most worthy of our attention. For instance, we may assume that the rabbits went inside the house and got dressed in between the first two pictures in *Peter Rabbit,* but the focus is on the two moments we do actually see and therefore on the sharp contrast between them. Illustrators' choices of specific moments work to create a particular rhythm that is characteristic of pictures in sequence, a series of heavy contrasts between image and no image.

The rhythm of a narrative text is different. In order for words to become

a story, they must be tied together in such a way that they have a beginning, a middle, and an end; in other words, they must reveal how one
moment fits into the next moment, so that the series of moments described
has a satisfying sense of wholeness. Furthermore, we find such series of
interrelated events most satisfying when they create suspense and have a
climax; that is, each one of the events we hear about must seem incomplete
enough to make us want to hear how it might be completed. A well-orga-
nized series of events forces us constantly to ask, And then what happened? What did that lead to? So a forest grew—and then what happened?
So Peter went into the garden—and then what happened? The focus is on
the onward thrust of the whole sequence of interrelated moments as they
accelerate in intensity until they finally reach a climax.

The rhythm of pictures in sequence is regular: one strong beat following
an equally strong beat. The rhythm of verbal narrative is climactic: the
intensifying that unifies the moments by showing how they lead into and
emerge from each other. In picture books these two rhythms collide with
each other. I have suggested that as we look at a picture book, each set of
words is interrupted by at least two pictures. So as well as having the
narrative information available from words, we have the narrative effect of
two pictures in a row. As we move from picture to picture, we move from
isolated significant moment to isolated significant moment; then we have a
series of integrated moments described in words, followed again by a focus
on at least two significant moments depicted visually yet once more.

That obviously causes some frustration. Each segment of text is part of
an intensifying acceleration that ought at least in theory to run through a
book as a whole, but the acceleration is being interrupted by repetitive
strong beats. Meanwhile we have had to drop our focus on the strong beat
in order to absorb a part of the acceleration. Furthermore, our second
glance at a picture before we turn the page makes it less of a strong beat,
for we now see it in light of the information about temporal sequencing
provided by the text. The strong beat interrupts the intensifying of the
acceleration, and the acceleration weakens the regularity of the strong
beat.

If we are reading a story told in words alone, we will have one main question always on our minds: What happened next? In other words, our attention is always pointed toward the future; we want to turn the page and keep reading. But if the page also contains a picture, then the picture stops us. The picture demands our attention; not only that, it says in the very nature of its being, Don't be concerned with what happens next, think about what is happening now, at this moment. Don't worry about what happens after the forest grows in Max's room; think about what it looks like as it grows. Don't worry about whether Mr. McGregor catches Peter; watch Peter as he is falling into a flowerpot. Meanwhile, of course, the words are making their opposite demand: Stop enjoying that picture. Stop looking at it intently—read on, find out what happens next.

Even after we do know what happens next—even after we have read a story once—our pleasure in it will be in its unity, in the way it makes one moment lead naturally and inevitably into the next. Our pleasure in that integration is interrupted by our pleasure in the pictures, and our pleasure in those pictures is interrupted by our need to go on and complete the story. The frustration, then, is in the opposition of these two demands, demands that are inherent in the basic differences between these two different means of communication.

If that frustration is inevitable, then good picture-book artists must know how to deal with it. The best ones do so by taking advantage of it—by reinforcing the opposite demands of words and pictures so that they become a major feature of the stories that picture books tell—a major characteristic of the particular form of unity unique to this genre.

How they do that is clarified by a consideration of the way novelists handle the communication of visual information. The pictures in picture books operate as descriptive passages operate in novels; they interrupt the action so that readers may be informed of the way things and people look. Unsophisticated readers of fiction often take so much pleasure in the ongoing thrust of well-integrated plots that they find description boring and intrusive; many ignore the descriptive passages in the novels they read. Furthermore, they are often right to do so, for many writers are incapable of making such passages an important and inevitable part of the story they are telling. But some writers can in fact do that—and how they do it might suggest how picture-book artists might best integrate pictures with the story their words tell.

Seymour Chatman suggests that, because descriptive passages interrupt the flow of time in which the events of a story take place, they in fact create a second sort of time: the time in which the story is being told, which includes the time it takes readers to absorb those descriptive passages: "what happens in description is that the time line of the story is interrupted and frozen. Events are stopped, though our reading and discourse time continues, and we look at the characters and the setting elements as a *tableau vivant*" ("What Novels Can Do" 123). Our response to the pictures in picture books is similar: we look at the characters and settings as a *tableau vivant*, and the events are stopped even though we continue to absorb the story in sequence. In other words, the time in which picture books communicate a story is different from the time of their events. First we spend time absorbing information from a fixed image that depicts the characters in stopped time, then events take place in the words of the story, and then we continue to move through time as readers and viewers as we absorb the information about the characters in stopped time in the next picture.

Sometimes that is merely frustrating, but sometimes the tension it creates is exciting. The difference, I think, begins with our understanding that the information contained in descriptive passages in novels or in pictures in picture books is not merely information about how things look that allows us to develop images of characters and settings in our heads but that it is, in fact, a significant part of the story—something that we need to know. Furthermore, we must have the conviction that the moment an author or illustrator reveals such information to us is exactly the moment at which we need to know it.

The children's novelist Jill Paton Walsh speaks of the "trajectory" of a novel: "the trajectory of a book is the route chosen by the author through his material. It is the action of a book, considered not as the movement of paraphrasable events in that book but as the movement of the author's exposition and the reader's experience of it" (187–88). In other words, the trajectory occurs in the time of our reading experience, rather than just in the time of the events described; it includes descriptive passages that stop time as well as events that take place in time. "And," says Paton Walsh, "a good trajectory is the optimum, the most emotionally loaded flight path across the subject to the projected end. . . . We are not bored by description and entertained by happenings. Instead, we are bored by any kind of writing in a book either when the author is off trajectory or when through our failings or his we have misunderstood the trajectory we are on" (187–89).

In good picture books, the pictures are always on the trajectory. They must be where they are and show what they show at exactly that moment; even though they stop the action, they must be an integral part of our sense of the story as a whole while we read it. In what follows, I discuss various ways in which the pictures in a picture book—and, for that matter, the words also—can be part of the trajectory.

■ ■ ■ ■

Because pictures are inherently attractive, because they inevitably attract attention to themselves, their mere presence changes the texts they accompany. Their intrusiveness has a strong effect on narrative even apart from their subject or their mood. Pictures in picture books can, in fact must, operate as punctuation: they demand that we pause before we go on to the words on the next page. Not all illustrators or text writers use the pauses created by page breaks and the presence of picture breaks well: consider, for instance, the last two pages of Jan Wahl and Adrienne Adams's *Cabbage Moon,* one of which ends with "and made Jennie the" and the other of which has only the word "watchdog." Here the effect of trying to join together naturally related words by spreading them over two pages is clumsy; the word "the" so needs immediate completion that we have no choice but to hurry over our perusal of the picture. A competent writer of picture-book texts will plan out the text so that the inevitable pauses will have a more positive effect on the rhythm and shape of the words.

Because of the number of pictures in a picture book, their presence provides more breaks in the text than we usually expect in stories. Picture books usually have fewer than a thousand words, and most have fewer than five hundred; this small number of words is spread more or less evenly over many pages. Consequently, each page contains a relatively small a-mount of text, and stories tend to move forward in equal increments. A picture-book text is more like a poem in a regular pattern than like most narrative prose: it is made up of fairly equal segments, all clearly divided from each other in the way that the stanzas of a poem are divided from each other.

For that reason, picture-book prose tends to be choppy. We move from one short segment of prose to another of about the same length; and the time we spend looking at pictures between our experiences of those two segments of prose works divides them from each other. In undistinguished picture books, the sentences themselves are short and repetitive, and the equally repetitive segments of text on each page end with a complete stop and seem isolated from each other. In other words, the mere fact that it is told over a number of pages broken up by pictures forces a picture-book narrative to tend toward the strong rhythmic beat of pictures in sequence. Stories consisting of small segments of separate activity lack the continuity and the suspense we identify with good storytelling.

A good picture-book text not only contains the wider variety of sentences we might expect but also uses the pauses created by the presence of pictures more imaginatively. In *Where the Wild Things Are* a number of the pages contain texts that are grammatical fragments—incomplete until we turn to the next page to complete the sentence. The text on the first page makes no grammatical sense at all: not only does "The night Max wore his wolf suit and made mischief of one kind" not yet make sense but "of one kind" implies the need of something to complete it—the "and another" that we do in fact find on the next page. The text creates dissatisfaction by coming to an end where it does; a sentence must be complete before we can hope to understand it, and this one is not completed until we turn the page. But we cannot turn the page until we have spent some time looking at the picture and determining its relevance to the words. In this way, Sendak creates a tension that increases our interest and involvement in the story: we want to go forward and find out how the sentence will be completed; but we also want to stay where we are and look at the picture. Sendak has both effectively joined together the words on two separate pages—we will not be satisfied until we understand their relationship—and effectively used their separation from each other. The pause between them created by the presence of the picture is now part of the structure of the story, not just an unfortunate aspect of the nature of picture books.

On many of the pages of *The Tale of Peter Rabbit,* the text comes to a complete halt and ends with a period, but just about every time that happens, we are in the midst of an exciting and suspenseful action whose outcome is not clear: we want to turn the page, but we can do so only after we look at the picture; the result is an intensifying of suspense. There are also many pages in which the text completes a particular episode; there is no suspense as to the outcome. For instance, after Peter gets into the garden, "First he ate some lettuces and some French beans; and then he ate some radishes"; we might well assume that this is all we will hear about his eating. But this time, the text ends with a semicolon, so we know there is more, and even though we want to look at the picture, we will feel the need to turn the page and complete the sentence: "And then, feeling rather sick, he went to look for some parsley." Now the sentence comes to a halt; but we are likely to be curious about whether Peter will or will not be sick, so the information presented is incomplete enough to make us want to turn the page again. Throughout the book, in fact, the divisions between the sections of text create suspense either by their subject or their grammar. When Peter gets into difficulty, the page usually ends with a period or an exclamation mark, and when he gets out of it, the page ends with either a semicolon or a comma.

According to Patrick Groff, "The text of the good picture storybook remains a piece of distinguished linguistic art even without pictures. That is, the presence or lack of pictures does not necessarily signal its success, or demise" (300). But the words of such a text written down continuously, as they would be if they were not in a picture book, often seem flat and undistinguished; it is the long pauses between the sections, caused both by their being printed on a number of different pages and by the presence of those pages of pictures that demand attention, that give them their rhythm and also, paradoxically, their fluidity.

The first sentence of *Where the Wild Things Are* is repetitive and graceless if spoken without pause, as its punctuation suggests it should be—the only punctuation is the exclamation mark at the end. But it is impossible to read those words continuously if we come upon them on three different double-page spreads of a picture book, accompanied by three different, interesting pictures. The pause after "one kind" while we look at the picture to see *what* kind it is becomes a rhythmic beat in the sentence, and so does the pause after "and another" that occupies the time in which we look at the picture of the other kind on the next page. In the context of these pictures and the pauses they create, this undistinguished sentence approaches the rhythmic organization of poetry. Even the exceedingly long last sentence of the book seems fluid and graceful when interrupted by the pauses that develop from its being spread over four double-page spreads; these seventy words without a single punctuation mark are divided off by the three major pauses caused by page breaks and the seven minor pauses created by the placement of words on a page.

Lincoln F. Johnson, speaking of film editing, says, "Acceleration and deceleration of the cutting rate modify the pace of a film and the nature of a spectator's experience" (66). That is equally true of a picture book like *Wild Things*. Sendak has put more or fewer words on a page, and bigger or smaller pictures, in terms of a rhythmic intensifying and weakening of attention that supports the overall structure and meaning of the story. First the text is built around strong repetitive patterns: "of one kind / and another," "grew / and grew," and so on. These verbal pairs have the strong beat we expect of pictures in sequence, and each segment is in fact accompanied by a picture that amplifies that strength even more. So the book is built not just on strong repetitive rhythms but on a repeated series of such rhythms: first a series of kinds of mischief, then a series of kinds of growing, then a series of days and weeks and years, then a variety of aspects of a wild rumpus.

But the book moves forward despite the strong repetitiveness of its basic rhythms because Sendak builds accelerations into the basic repeating patterns. The relatively long text of the first page is followed by a very short text that repeats the pattern of the first and that we must hasten past in some excitement, and then by a longer text that comes to a complete stop. A similar long but incomplete beginning, this time describing the forest growing, is found on the next page, and again it is followed by a repetitive short text that we must hasten past and then by a longer text that brings the episode to an end. So while these first two episodes echo each other, they do so by each creating suspense and demanding completeness.

After the last text about the forest growing, furthermore, there is no period. Even though the episode is over we move forward and embark on a movement of repetitive "and" phrases that comes to a complete but brief stop only after another series of repetitive actions that brings Max to the Wild Things. Sendak has once again used the repetitive strong beats found earlier—even amplified them, for there are now six "ands" before the end of the sentence—but he has also created an acceleration through them.

The central sequence describing the encounter between Max and the Wild Things that follows repeats and further intensifies the patterns we now have come to expect by presenting them in a different way; while there are actually long bursts of words at its beginning and end, the middle has no words at all and consists only of the strong beats of three double-page spreads containing nothing but pictures. The words on either side of this sequence of pictures are themselves strongly repetitive; if we see this sequence as moving into and out of the central rumpus, then the beginning and end almost duplicate each other, for both describe the Wild Things in terms of repeated uses of the word "terrible." In this entire sequence, then, the strong beat intensifies, but the whole movement from suspenseful arrival to triumph to releasing rumpus to repose still has the acceleration of a traditional plot, one which is now arriving at its most intense climactic moment. Both the strong beat of repetitions and the acceleration of the plot intensify at the same time and so continue in the same balanced relationship to each other.

While the final long movement, the sentence that spans the last four segments of text, pushes us on until we reach its period, it too is filled with the strong beats of repetitions—both internal repetitions and repetitions of phrases that occurred earlier—and like all the other sentences in the book, it begins with a long burst of words, moves through a series of shorter repetitive phrases, and then ends in a longer, more fluid grouping of words. That shape echoed in each sentence of the book is also an echo of the shape of the book as a whole, which moves from lots of words in a long series to a series of strong beats at its very center as we watch a series of repetitive actions unaccompanied by any words, and then concludes in another long burst of words.

In the subtle rhythmic patterns of this book, Sendak has managed to create the satisfyingly suspenseful forward thrust we expect of stories and still to enforce a repeating pattern that places the emphasis on the similarity of the episodes to each other rather than on their linear interconnectedness and on the exact middle of the story rather than on how it moves toward its end. Meanwhile, the pictures grow in size and then diminish; each one inevitably has a regular strong beat, but as a whole they form the accelerating pattern we expect of narrative. *Wild Things* is both a story in words shaped like a poem that nevertheless remains a satisfying story and a set of pictures shaped like a story that nevertheless has the strong rhythmic beat we expect of such a visual sequence.

Paul Arakelian finds the meaning of the story in these interrelated patterns: "the text and drawings of *Wild Things* contribute to a subtle crescendo of mastery as the boy controls the wild things, and then a decrescendo as he returns to his room. As the size of the drawings increases and then shrinks, all sorts of other developments, such as the metaphors of time and place, the topics of the illustrations, the compounding style of both text and drawing, also expand and contract, drawing us into this ordered, controlled experience. The entire enterprise—text, drawings, printing, story—becomes one metaphor for Max's going and coming" (126). *Where the Wild Things Are* has attracted many commentators and has been interpreted in many different ways; as Arakelian implies, its rich suggestiveness depends on its complex but carefully controlled rhythmic patterns.

The Little House offers a different rhythmic pattern and uses it for a different purpose. Each page of text is complete. Furthermore, the prose in this book lacks the usual matter-of-fact blandness of picture-book prose; it is itself highly patterned, highly rhythmic, and highly repetitive: "Pretty soon there were more of them. . . . Pretty soon along came some surveyors. . . . Pretty soon along came a steamroller." This sort of prose, in insisting on repetitive pattern rather than developmental sequence, reinforces the broken-up quality inevitable in stories told in small, discrete segments. In *The Little House*, in fact, the rhythms of the prose echo the strong beats of the pictures. The result is a deliberate reinforcement of the antinarrative qualities of this story: it is about how things always happen in the same way, about how cycles triumph over developments—about how spring always follows winter and rebirth always follows decay.

One of the reasons that illustrated versions of poems, particularly poems with regular and repeating patterns, are often unsatisfactory is the parallel between repeating verbal patterns and the strong beats of pictures in sequence that Burton uses to advantage in *The Little House*. It is difficult to avoid the numbing effect of repetitive prose accompanied by repetitive pictures that Burton deliberately evokes. Illustrators of poems must work hard to give their pictures the forward-moving energy that is always retarded by the regular beats of the text and by the mere fact of a series of pictures. In an earlier chapter, I spoke of the surprising but not unpleasing lethargy of Arnold Lobel's pictures for Jack Prelutsky's highly regular poems about the circus. In his illustrations of *The Highwayman*, Charles Keeping uses every device that an artist has at hand to give his pictures energy: highly dynamic uses of line, dramatic contrasts between black and white, and so on. As a strongly accented series of highly energetic moments, these pictures admirably balance the contrapuntal effect of the poem itself, a regular and highly repetitive evocation of intensely melodramatic feeling.

The regular rhythms of the poem that makes up the text of Dr. Seuss's *And to Think That I Saw It on Mulberry Street* have the strong beats and obvious patterns we usually expect of pictures in sequence; and as usual in a Dr. Seuss book, the action-filled cartooning does much to break up the regular rhythms inevitable in a pictorial sequence. But as the boy, Marco, adds details to his complex story of what he saw on Mulberry Street, the pictures become more and more complex, more and more filled with detail—but always in terms of the same basic compositional patterns: the elephant is always in the same place on each spread, and so on. So the pictures both build in intensity and maintain their narrative connection with each other, as the words in a story usually do; in each picture we look for new information to add to old, rather than having to start from scratch about what we are seeing each time, as usually happens in picture books. At the same time, the segments of text get shorter and tend to be interrupted by more periods. The result is a curious reversal, in which the text adds the strong regular beat and the pictures provide a surprisingly interconnected narrative intensity. Indeed, many fine picture books create the rich tensions of successful narrative in pictures that strain toward the narrative qualities of text and in texts that strain toward the narrative qualities of pictures: they have repetitive rhythmic texts, and pictures with accelerating intensity.

■ ■ ■ ■

While the mere presence of pictures in a picture book interrupts our perusal of the text, the pause between one segment of text and the next is never empty, so that the presence of pictures in a narrative does more than merely punctuate it. The pictures always depict something and consequently always add more to what we know about the events being described. In a story told in words alone, every action described is of equal significance as part of the whole, but a series of pictures that interrupt a text force us to pay special attention to some particular moments out of the whole action, and that profoundly affects both the meaning and the rhythm of picture-book stories.

In terms of meaning, Edward Hodnett suggests that the most important decision of any illustrator of fiction is that of "which of all the possible moments of choice are the ones that are most significant in terms of contributing to the reader's understanding of the text and of reinforcing the emotional effect sought by the author" (8). Max's mischief would seem different if we actually saw him stick the fork in the dog, instead of being just about to; most viewers would like Max much less. And the magical feeling of *The Garden of Abdul Gasazi* would be destroyed by a picture of Alan at the bottom of the stairs, landing with a thump, rather than floating gracefully above them.

Furthermore, what is not shown can be as important as what is. Beatrix Potter accompanies the information that Peter Rabbit lost one of his shoes not by a picture of him without the shoe but by a picture of the shoe without him. This human artifact looks singularly out of place as a robin inspects it under a cabbage; its incongruity is firmly established, while a picture of Peter with only one shoe would have made him look funny enough to lose some of our sympathy. In the first sequence of *Wild Things*, similarly, while the text describes Max's battle with his mother, the pictures never show her to us. Her presence would seriously disturb the interior, private feeling the entire book emits—in fact the story is not about the fight at all but about Max's part in it and about how he responds to it.

But such differences are fairly obvious; in many picture books, the choices of moments are subtle and highly particularized—not just Alan falling down stairs but Alan caught at a specific moment of his flight that can be made to look like floating; and not just Max without his mother but Max caught at moments when his mischief can convey the meanings I have discussed earlier. In *Peter Rabbit* a picture shows Peter squeezing under the gate, just as the text tells us that he squeezes under the gate. But the one specific moment depicted is actually only part of a whole complex action, and there is some significance in Potter's choice of the specific part. She shows us Peter not all the way into the garden but almost—only his back end is still behind the picket; that allows us easily to guess the completion of the action and thus imagine an action that is not actually depicted.

The picture shows both how the gate holds Peter back and how he pushes his way past it anyway; a second picture that showed Peter either on one side of the gate in trepidation or on the other in triumph would destroy the perfect balance between fear and aggressiveness that makes this picture an ideal component of this perfectly balanced story. It would also create a different rhythm, a different sort of counterpoint between pictures and words. The numbers of pictures that illustrate a particular episode not only directly convey meaning through the choices of moments but indirectly add to meaning by assisting in the creation of rhythm.

In *The Amazing Bone*, we see a group of robbers twice on one page, first at the top of the page waving guns and knives and then at the bottom of the page pointing their weapons menacingly at the heroine, Pearl. While one of these pictures by itself would have established how frightening they are, it takes two to establish two different responses in Pearl—first boldness and then dismay. When we get two pictures of how Max makes mischief in *Wild Things*, we are offered insight into his diabolic inventiveness; just one sort of mischief might merely suggest nastiness, but two different ones imply a wide repertoire—a third would be superfluous. Something similar happens in three pictures of wild rumpusing—a more intense section of the story whose intensity is conveyed by the presence of three pictures rather than just two.

As I suggested earlier, it is the pattern established by these sets of pictures—Max making mischief, the forest growing, the rumpus—that underpins the rhythmic structure of the story as a whole. Much of the fun of *Rosie's Walk* is the fact that the pictures come in pairs. In each pair, the first picture shows the fox about to get himself into physical difficulty, and the second shows the result of the movement forward implied by the first. First, the fox in midair, about to land on a rake; second, the rake hitting the fox in the face. First, the fox about to leap on Rosie; second, the fox in the pond he has not noticed. In choosing these two particular sorts of moments, Hutchins implies an entire sequence of actions; she has selected those moments that best suggest movement forward or the consequences of previous actions. In focusing on the unexpected results of the fox's action, furthermore, these pairs of pictures constantly reveal how the fox is as unconscious of his surroundings as is Rosie herself: she may have no eyes for foxes, but foxes appear to have no eyes for rakes and ponds. These pairs of pictures create mood as well as meaning. Their repetitive rhythm gives the story the detached feeling of a series of jokes rather than the evolving intensity of a plot; we can laugh as our familiarity with the pattern develops because we know the story is going to keep going through variations of the same situation rather than moving forward toward a climax.

Almost every picture in *Peter Rabbit* shows a moment toward the end of the actions implied by the text but not at the very end: Peter almost under the gate, but not quite, Peter about to eat a radish, but not quite. That establishes a rhythmic pattern of relationships between words and pictures. Our first glance informs us of the isolated moment we see in each picture; then, as we read the text, we move backward to what came before that moment, through the moment again as the text describes it, and then beyond it as the text moves beyond it; then we return to that moment again as we peruse the picture a second time. First we see Mrs. Rabbit walking through the woods; then we are told how she got herself ready to walk through the woods, walked through the woods, and bought baked goods, and then we go back and see her walking through the woods again. Since the action shown by the picture comes at some point after the beginning of the action as described by the text, we read the text in some anticipation: when will we come to the moment of that picture? Because the action described by the text always moves beyond the picture, our close look at the picture creates a retardation, a backward movement that builds tension and thus suspense. Since the same sort of pattern recurs on almost every opening of the book, a strong contrapuntal pattern develops.

A similar forward and backward movement is even more obvious in *The*

Garden of Abdul Gasazi, as for instance when Alan falls down the stairs. In the text that action is described in the middle sentence of a long passage that leads Alan from his first entry into the garden, past the fall on the stairs, and into another chase after the dog. Here, the last action described is so frenetic, and its outcome so uncertain, that the movement back to look at the fall in that mysteriously still picture creates a large frustration that adds both to the feeling of mystery and to the sense of oddity about the book as a whole. Van Allsburg uses exactly the same trick on the next two spreads, where we see Alan still in the forest even though the text gets him up to the brick wall of the house, and then Alan staring at the house even though the text has him climbing up its stairs.

The Amazing Bone establishes a different rhythm. Here, most of the pictures show the moment after the entire sequence of actions described in the accompanying text. We see the fox grinning at Pearl, as the last sentence of the text suggests, and then we see him seizing her in an embrace, as the last sentence of the text suggests. Since the moments depicted by the pictures come exactly at the place in the sequence of events that they occur in their physical interruption of the text, the pictures seem more like confirmation of what we know already than like additional information; they therefore do not establish much of a contrapuntal rhythm.

But *The Amazing Bone* tends to focus throughout on the kind of information that comes best through words: the suspenseful intensifying of an interrelated series of events, the emotional responses of characters to those events, and the meaning of the plot as a whole. The simplified cartooning of the pictures makes them provide more information about action than about mood or character or setting, which the text does frequently talk about. Paradoxically, then, these pictures focus on the actions we expect of texts, while the text adds color and mood and meaning to those actions, qualities we usually expect of pictures. The placement of pictures at the exact moment of the plot the text has arrived at confirms the emphasis on plot that the text itself tends to bury in detail, and it forces us past them in order to find out what the text will reveal next.

Interestingly, the only occasions on which that clearly does not happen are toward the end of the book, when the picture of Pearl's embrace by her parents depicts a moment described in the first of two paragraphs of text, and then the picture of Pearl showing her parents the bone depicts a moment described in the first sentence of an extended passage; also, strangely, both these segments of text appear above the pictures, so that there is an insistence on the retardation effect, of our going back as we have not done before. The excitement of the story and our interest in what the text will tell us next are gradually lessening, and we can afford the time it takes to look back at a picture.

In *The Amazing Bone,* the matching of picture breaks with picture content—the text taking us only as far as the picture shows and no farther— creates a focus on plot rather than character; it reinforces our desire to know what happens next rather than asking us to pay attention to, and thus better understand, something that has happened already. In *Peter Rabbit,* the text's movement toward and then away from the moments depicted in the pictures focuses interest on character and meaning rather than on plot; even though we want to know what happens next, we must go back and spend time considering in some detail a moment we have already heard about, usually a moment when Peter experiences discomfort and therefore demands our sympathy. In *Sam, Bangs, and Moonshine,* a significant shift from one of these techniques to the other suggests a shift in focus in the story itself. In the first part of the book, the pictures show events described in early sentences of the accompanying texts; we see Thomas in front of his home even though the text accompanying that picture takes him all the way down the hill to Sam's house. The retardation effect here focuses our attention on the characters and on the implications of Sam's bad habits, the central concern of the plot. But later, when Thomas gets into trouble and we will want to know what happens next, the pictures show the moments reached at the end of each segment of text: this creates a quickening of pace, an excited interest in what happens next rather than a dwelling on its interior meaning. After the excitement dies down a little, the earlier pattern returns, and we are again asked to consider the implications of actions rather than to pay attention to actions themselves.

In forming a plot, a sequence of events that is not yet ended, the text of a story leads us forward. In showing how things look at one moment and asking us to dwell on them, the pictures hold us back. The rhythm of picture-book stories is a continual move forward and then stop, forward and then stop. Artists like Potter and Van Allsburg tend to exaggerate that alternation: forward and then backward a little, then forward some more; artists like Steig do not often actually require a movement back so much as a pause in the present. But our habit of glancing at a picture first provides a strong forward and back movement even in *The Amazing Bone:* first we see where the text will get us, then we go back, read the text and see how we got there, and then we look at where we have arrived again. Some version of that counterpoint provides the basic rhythm of all picture-book narrative and makes this sort of narrative different from the smooth acceleration of stories told in words by themselves.

Earlier I discussed how the interruptions created by the mere presence of pictures created contrapuntal rhythms in the text of *Where the Wild Things Are*. Now I would like to add to that a consideration of how the information actually contained in those pictures, the specific choices of moments depicted, gives the story as a whole, the story told by words and pictures, a contrapuntal effect.

The first picture shows a boy, the text tells us that it is Max and that he is making mischief, and the second picture adds another sort of mischief. Both pictures show a moment in the middle of the action that the text describes rather than before or after that action is complete, and both show a moment that implies a logical completion. Consequently, these pictures drive us forward to complete the action. The third picture, which follows the first period in the text, reinforces a strong pause by illustrating a moment that follows the sequence of events described in the text; it shows Max already in his room after the dispute with his mother. The next five pictures show moments in the middle of the incomplete action described in each of the segments of the text that accompany them; as with the pictures of Max's mischief, looking at them as we read does not force us to go either forward or backward. But the picture accompanying the information that Max comes to where the Wild Things are once again depicts a moment that follows both the text and the period at the end of that text that marks a strong pause; we see Max just as his boat hits the shore. In fact, the choice of moments depicted echoes the shape of the text by itself up to this point; the strong pauses of the text are accompanied by pictures that enforce a distinction by moving the action forward rather than merely echoing the action the text describes.

Not surprisingly, the next sequence repeats that pattern: two pictures show moments in the middle of the actions described by the accompanying texts—the Wild Things being terrifying, Max taming them but not yet having finished the task—and then the next picture focuses on the moment at the end of the first sentence in the accompanying text, when Max is made king. Since that sentence is on the left-hand side of a two-page spread and the rest of the text is on the right-hand side, we have a sort of symmetry here—the picture comes exactly in between the two sentences. Not surprisingly, the same pattern is repeated in the set of words and pictures on the two-page spread that comes immediately after the wild rumpus: we see Max being lonely in his tent, as described on the left-hand page, and before he smells good things to eat, as described on the right-hand page.

In between these balanced moments is the wild rumpus; the pictures show a sequence of moments that comes between the moment described in the words that immediately precede the rumpus and announce its start and the words that immediately follow it and announce its stop. In this way, the entire sequence that begins as Max is made king and ends when he feels lonely mirrors the pattern of its beginning and ending two-page spread. That intricate symmetry reinforces the focus on the centrality of the rumpus, and the symmetry is itself reinforced by the fact that the moments depicted in the last three pictures in the book reverse the pattern established by the first three—as revealed in the following list, in which the numbers represent the consecutive spreads of the story:

1. Middle of text (Max making mischief)
2. Middle of text (Max making mischief)
3. End of text (Max in his room)
16. End of text (Max waving good-bye)
17. Middle of text (Max sailing)
18. Middle of text (Max in his room but seemingly not yet noticing his supper)

As much as any picture book, *Where the Wild Things Are* reveals the peculiarity of picture-book art. A story whose climax is at its middle rather than toward its end and whose plot is a matter of rhythmic counterpoints rather than intensifying suspense is different from what we usually expect of fiction, but it is, in fact, typical of picture-book narrative—and it is that, I suspect, because of the peculiar dual nature of picture books. Finally, we must most admire *Where the Wild Things Are* not because of its intricate symmetries and counterpoints but because Sendak manages to establish those patterns and still to drive the story forward to a satisfying climax by means of them.

There is one provisio to add to this discussion of the counterpoint between pictures and words. When a story is read aloud to an audience, the ironies and rhythms that I have been describing may not be as noticeable as they are when we read a book silently to ourselves. Hearing someone else read a book, we are able to look at each picture during the whole time that the words printed with it are spoken. Furthermore, hearing the words read aloud causes us to focus on them as a whole sequence—to want to know what happens next rather than to be content to pause and look at a picture when, for instance, a sentence has not been completed on a page. It is easy to hold the first page of words in *Wild Things* in our heads as we read the book to ourselves, even though they are not grammatically complete, in order to pause and look at the picture; it is less easy to do that in spoken language, where the pause is actual rather than just imaginary. A reader can imagine a shorter pause than the one he actually indulges in; a listener must experience the actual pause. We tend to join words on different pages together more in reading a story aloud than in reading it to ourselves, and thus we allow an audience to look at the pictures less. Consequently, the various ironies and rhythms inherent in the counterpoint of words and pictures diminish.

Interestingly, however, children who cannot read are rarely content to sit through a consecutive reading of a picture-book text: characteristically they demand that the reader stop and allow perusal of the pictures, and they point out pictorial details and ask questions about them. In doing so, they are not displaying a lack of readerly competence or a short attention span; they are merely and quite rightly doing exactly what every picture book inevitably demands of its most aware readers. In working to absorb information from two different sources in order to understand the way all the information is integrated into a whole story, they recreate the counterpoint inherent in the actual structure of a picture book.

▪ ▪ ▪ ▪

The texts of the books I have been discussing in this chapter were all written with the idea that they would be illustrated; presumably, the illustrators' choices of moments that create various kinds of ironies and counterpoints and that complete a story by balancing two different kinds of information are responses to gaps left in the texts themselves. But illustrated versions of preexisting stories such as fairy tales are a different matter; in effect, illustrators must create the gaps before they can choose how to fill them. The illustrator's freedom to interpret such texts is particularly broad; as Joseph Schwarcz says of such books, "it is in the illustrators' power to shift accents and express opinions by what they draw, how they draw it [and] by what they omit to draw" (*Ways of the Illustrator* 100). For this reason, an exploration of the chosen moments of illustrated versions of fairy tales is particularly revealing and a particularly good way to conclude this discussion; nothing makes the power of pictures to transform the shape and the meaning of a text clearer than a consideration of how a different set of pictures can make exactly the same words into a different story.

As it happens, those stories from the folk tradition that we call fairy tales share one quality that makes them particularly open to illustration: they can remain the same story even while being told in different ways. Everyone knows "Snow White and the Seven Dwarfs"—but everyone knows it in a slightly different way. What everyone knows—the essential story underlying all the different versions—is a series of specific events in a specific order that arrives always at the same conclusion. What differs is the character of the people these events happen to, the reason they happen, and the relative amount of information we are offered about where they take place and about what they mean. The illustrations that accompany fairy tales can add this sort of information just as well as verbal descriptions can. Earlier, I showed how specific choices of costume and setting can make the same sets of events, the stories of Snow White or Cinderella, anything from pseudonostalgic evocations of a nonexistent past to painfully exact documentaries about a specific time and place in history; how other choices can make a character like Snow White herself into an innocent child or a passionate nymphet; and how choices of style can make Snow White's return to life anything from the romantic melodrama of Trina Schart Hyman to the slapstick of Jack Kent.

In *The Illustration of Books,* David Bland says, "The early wood-cutters . . . often chose the decisive moments in the story; and this natural tendency has continued ever since" (164). But given the ability of fairy tales to be told in many different ways, artists illustrating them can settle on different moments to be the decisive ones; and some of the differences I have described depend on such choices. It is the choice of that moment in which Snow White slides out of the coffin amid a shower of breaking glass that defines Kent's version as a comic one. Burkert and Hyman both clearly wish to avoid such comic possibilities, for one shows the moment just before and the other the moment just after the coffin bearers stumble.

Meanwhile, Hyman focuses the story on the anguish of the wicked Queen by depicting her staring out at us from the center of at least six pictures; Burkert shows her only twice, both times with her back to us. Burkert's focus is less on the Queen than on all the characters equally in the context of their world at large; the pictures always surround the characters with interesting and often symbolic objects that make their social interactions and their moral relationships more significant than any of their individual feelings.

As well as choosing different moments to depict, these illustrators create different rhythms by means of the number of illustrations they have made. Of course, that number is defined by the kind of book in question, and an illustrator who has contracted to produce a specific number of pictures may have had no say in what that number was; nevertheless, an illustrator making one illustration for each story in a collection will choose differently from one who has the freedom to fill twenty or more pages of a picture book.

Maurice Sendak's one picture for "Snow White" in *The Juniper Tree* has a vastly different effect from Trina Schart Hyman's twenty-six illustrations for a similar version of the story. Sendak must evoke the whole story by means of this one picture, and he does so by choosing a moment that sums up all its different components; he shows the Queen at a moment of triumph, the mirror behind her displaying an apple with a bite out of it, a perplexed dwarf, and an apparently dead Snow White. At the center of the picture is an owl mysteriously peering in at the window behind Snow White, which frames him like a picture; indeed, the window, the rafters in the dwarfs' ceiling, the mirror, and the white space around the picture itself all pin down the characters and seem to imprison them in fixity. But Hyman's many illustrations have something of the effect of continuity that we expect of a movie—and so do Jack Kent's twenty-eight pictures for a much shorter text. Hyman shows three moments in the short history of the dwarfs' returning to their home and finding Snow White there; the effect is like a film editor's cutting from one shot to another as we move from the dwarfs' faces peering in the door to them surrounding the bed in which Snow White sleeps to Snow White awake in the same bed and staring at them. Kent also offers three pictures of the dwarfs' return, and they are similar enough in their composition that they have a clear relationship to each other: the transition from Snow White in bed surrounded by dwarfs to Snow White sitting on the floor surrounded by dwarfs has the effect of a form cut.

But Burkert does not depict the dwarfs' return at all. Furthermore, none of the scenes she depicts has the same setting: we have one picture of the castle, one of the dwarfs' house, one of the forest, and so on. In fact, her pictures are all unlike one another: one is like a portrait painting, one is a delicate landscape, one evokes the style of medieval illuminations. Reading her version of the tale is less like watching a movie than like walking through an art gallery and seeing the work of a number of different artists.

Furthermore, there are only ten pictures in Burkert's version, including the portrait of Snow White on the cover, the decoration on the title page, and the illuminated letter that begins the text. Of the seven remaining pictures, all but the first are two-page spreads with no words on them; the text appears on the spreads in between those containing pictures. The effect of this isolation of picture from text and of each picture from all the others is different from Hyman's pictures, which are more similar to each other in style and organization and which occupy all of every two-page spread except the small square at the center of one page containing the text. The effect of Kent's version, in which a series of similar pictures and portions of text are arranged on each page, is different again.

Burkert's alternation of spreads of word and image intensifies the contrapuntal relationships of words and pictures. We read a page of text, then must turn the page before we see a picture that illustrates the last moment described by the text. And because each picture is so different from the one preceding it and so filled with attractive details, we must look at the picture in some detail before we turn the page and find out what happens next. In emphasizing the difference between words and pictures so much, Burkert focuses attention on the pictures as pictures: objects to look at from a distance, to admire for their aesthetic beauty, and to understand for their intellectual content; the book as a whole has the objective, uninvolved tone of the words it contains.

Kent's version has some of the effect of comic books: the emphasis is on action, since we see a large number of pictures on each page, and they often depict a series of moments within the same action. Like Hutchins's pairs of pictures of the fox getting into trouble in *Rosie's Walk*, Kent's pictures here come in groups that focus on the comic consequences of actions. Furthermore, in organizing words and pictures so that we move from verbal information to visual vignette and then back again a number of times on the same page, Kent reinforces narrative continuity. Kent's tone is as detached as is Burkert's, but it is a different sort of detachment: not the intellectual overview that allows us to understand the differences between good and evil but the objective distance that allows us to laugh at the pain of others in slapstick comedy.

Hyman's emphasis is on a different sort of continuity—the focus is not on the action but on the dense texture and equally dense moodiness of these dark, rich pictures, which cover most of the available space and which constantly depict characters making melodramatic gestures that reveal great depths of feeling. These pictures are like the musical scores that tie together and add emotional intensity to the various parts of a story being told on screen; the focus is on how the characters respond to events, and reading this version is like being immersed in a seamless and intensifying flow of tempestuous melodrama.

Differing numbers and differing placements of pictures clearly have a profound effect on the rhythm of the story being told. It is worth considering whether or not any one of these three different rhythms of storytelling is more appropriate than the others. Are some ways of illustrating fairy tales more authentic than others?

As it happens, the structure of fairy tales seems to be unlike the plots of other sorts of stories and surprisingly similar to some of the patterns of picture-book narrative I discussed earlier in this chapter. Most stories move through a series of unified, integrated actions, each of which is an inevitable part of the whole; but the mere fact that fairy tales may be told in many different ways implies a different sort of construction. If we investigate what remains the same and what differs in different versions of the same fairy tale, we discover that each of the tellings contains something like a spine: a series of actions that appear in every version and that always appear in the same order but which may be connected to each other in any given version by any number of other events, or any number of descriptions of characters or setting and such. Red Riding Hood must tell the wolf about her grandmother; but after that, she may pick flowers, she may simply walk slowly and enjoy the weather, or she may do nothing at all that is reported to us before we get to the next spinal event: the wolf arriving at grandmother's.

If we explore "authentic" versions of fairy tales, particularly those in the collection of the Grimm brothers, we discover that they tend to place particular emphasis on those central episodes that form the spine of the tale and to describe them in more detail. In the story called "Little Red Cap," we hear a lot about the little girl's conversation with the wolf but only a quick summary of her flower picking. Further attention is drawn to the spinal episodes because so many of them repeat each other; the Queen tries to kill Snow White four times, and Red Riding Hood asks the wolf about a number of his physical characteristics. Furthermore, there often tend to be curious parallels and contrasts that relate even those spinal episodes that are not directly repetitive with each other and that focus our attention on them. In the Grimms' "Little Red Cap," for instance, the central moments are all conversations, and most of them involve somebody theoretically wiser telling Little Red Cap what to do—first her mother, then the wolf, then the wolf disguised.

As we read or hear a fairy tale, these patterns result in a rhythmic intensifying and lessening of interest as we move from central episode to less central episode and then back again; the effect is different from the gradual intensifying toward a climax that we get in other sorts of stories. And for those of us who already know the popular fairy tales we hear—and that surely is most of us at some point early in our childhoods—our pleasure in them must derive from repetition of that rhythmic pattern rather than from the suspense we usually enjoy in story; if we already know the story, there can be no suspense in it for us.

In any case, fairy tales in "authentic" versions tend to proceed with the same sort of pause-action-pause movement of picture books: we hear a lot about one particular episode then move forward through a quick depiction of actions to another moment described in great detail. In theory, then, it would seem that the most logical moments to illustrate in a fairy tale would be the ones that occur along the central spine of the story—those the original tale itself describes in most detail. For instance, it would best mirror the story if we had an illustration of Red Riding Hood talking to the wolf and then one of the wolf frightening Grandmother, but none of the inessential flower picking in between.

In "Snow White," many of those central moments are themselves visual images: descriptions of things seen. The first of them is a descriptive picture of Snow White's mother and of what she sees as she looks out her window, and the second is another descriptive picture of the Queen and what she sees as she looks in her mirror. It is this sort of readily depictable scene that we might expect an illustrator to concentrate on. Furthermore, many of the spinal moments of "Snow White" are not just visual descriptions but descriptions of people looking and of what they look at. Here is a list of them:

1. Snow White's mother looks out the window.
2. The Queen looks in the mirror.
3. Snow White pleads for her life, and the Hunter saves her for her beauty—the way she looks.
4. Snow White sees the dwarfs' house.
5. The dwarfs see Snow White in their house.
6, 7, 8. The Queen tempts Snow White through the window, by getting her to look, first at the laces, then at the comb, then at the apple.
9. The dwarfs see Snow White dead.
10. The dwarfs place Snow White in the glass coffin.

11. The Prince sees Snow White in the coffin.
12. The coffin breaks.
13. Snow White and the Prince marry, and the Queen dies.

Almost all these events involve looking or seeing; a surprising number of them involve windows, mirrors, and other glass objects. This is a story about the differences between looking out beyond oneself and looking in on oneself, about the danger of looking out as opposed to the necessity of it, and about the relationship between the way things look and the way they actually are. Snow White's mother looks out her window and imagines Snow White; Snow White looks out her window and lets in the Queen. The Queen looks not out but at her own image in glass; the Prince frees Snow White by breaking the glass. Snow White wrongly admires the beauty of the poisonous apple; the Prince rightly falls in love with Snow White's appearance, for it mirrors her goodness. We might expect an "authentic" version of "Snow White" to put an emphasis on all those moments of looking and seeing. Such a choice would doubly emphasize the interesting patterns of similarity and contrast we find here—the structural pattern that ties this story together even more than does the related sequence of its events.

Among the twenty-eight pictures in the Kent version, there are depictions of all but the first of those moments, and since the text makes no mention of Snow White's mother, every spinal moment that this version includes is represented. But the effect is unlike that of the Grimm tale, for these depictions of spinal moments are interspersed with other pictures that give equal weight to other parts of the story. We see Snow White as a baby before we see the Queen looking in her mirror; we see Snow White being beautiful and the Queen being angry before we see the Hunter and Snow White in the woods. Furthermore, the pictures tend to come in pairs and in trios: we see Snow White in the coffin, then the Prince looking at her, then the Prince offering to buy the coffin, then the coffin breaking— so that there is a sense of narrative sequence that dilutes the weight of the spinal moments. While the effect is repetitive rather than intensifying, the components of the repetitive pattern are sequences of jokes rather than the sequence of spinal moments described by the Grimms.

Hyman depicts ten of the thirteen moments I have isolated; instead of Snow White pleading for her life, she depicts the Hunter fleeing and leaving Snow White alone, and she does not show the last time the dwarfs discover Snow White dead nor anything of the story after her final awakening. As in Kent, the spinal moments are so interspersed with so many other pictures that their effect is diluted, but paradoxically, the pictures that come between them almost all repeat their central subject: looking and seeing. After the Queen looks in her mirror, we see her looking enviously at Snow White; later we see her looking at the book that tells her how to prepare the poisoned apple. And when Snow White and the dwarfs are not looking at each other, a dog (or is it a tame fox?) looks at her. Furthermore, many pictures depict characters staring out directly at us or else posed so that they seem to be looking out at something in front of the picture plane; the Queen does so in four of the eight pictures in which she appears.

But while the detachment of the original story asks us to divide our attention between the way things look and the way they affect the people who look at them, Hyman focuses always on the people looking and their response to what they see, rather than on the objects seen. This weakens the rhythmic pattern established by the text and the detachment that pattern engenders and replaces it with a relatively unrhythmic but far more intensely involving concentration on feeling. This version is "inauthentic" because it frees the character's emotions from the various patterns that contain them and distance us from them in the original, but it is nevertheless persuasive, a good story in its own right. Furthermore, it makes an excellent picture-book story exactly because the intensity and continuity of the pictures provide such an interesting counterpoint to the distance and repetitive patterning of the text.

Illustrators of "Snow White" often ignore many of the spinal moments in favor of a single-minded concentration on dwarfs. Kent, Svend Otto S., Fritz Wegner, and even Wanda Gag provide a sizable number of pictures with no particular purpose other than to show how adorably cute their dwarfs are. The ultimate example of how this story has become refocused around the charm of little creatures and away from its original interest in passion and retribution is the Walt Disney film version. A picture book of this film published by Golden Press contains so many pictures of Snow White cavorting with both forest animals and dwarfs that there is no space left for a depiction of the Queen's demise or even of "Love's First Kiss," which is significantly featured in both the movie version and in the text of the picture book. Another Golden Press version that claims to represent Disney tells the story from the dwarfs' point of view—it tells us how lonely they are, announces Snow White's arrival—and then ends. The trouble with such stories is less their lack of authenticity than their inadequacy as stories in their own right.

Not surprisingly, a number of cheap editions of "Snow White" I found in a discount bookstore also focused on dwarfs. But in these poorly drawn versions, the pictures tend to illustrate the key spinal moments more often than not—or at least, those which are not threatening, for there are few depictions of the coffin shattering, and none of the Queen's demise. Furthermore, there are usually few other pictures in these books; they do tend to move neatly through the sequence of moments we might expect. If anything, the spinal moments are overemphasized; in the Lady Bird "Read It Yourself" version, the Brimax "Now You Can Read" version, and the Award Classic version, there are entire sequences of pictures that depict three of the central episodes: first, the Queen at her mirror, then Snow White exploring the dwarfs' house, then the dwarfs finding Snow White.

But while all these versions focus on the act of seeing, they distort the emphasis of the original story, and in a direction opposite from Hyman. We are required to be interested in the wonderful things these characters see, not in how the characters respond to them. These are "illustrations" in the most basic sense of the word: their purpose is to show what the objects described by words look like. Because they do little more than that, because they merely amplify the already amplified moments of the text, they do little to change the rhythm of the original story. In merely duplicating what we already have from the words, these pictures do not justify their own existence.

A glance at Susan Jeffers's version of "Snow White" confirms that adherence to the rhythmic shape and focus of the original story may not be the best way to go about illustrating fairy tales. Of the versions of this story I have seen, this one comes closest to duplicating both the rhythm and focus of the original. Jeffers depicts twelve of the key moments—all but the shattering of the coffin—and all the other pictures in the book add to the emphasis in these spinal pictures on looking and seeing. As in Hyman, almost every picture is in some way related to the idea of vision; people look at each other, or at objects, or out of the picture at us. But unlike in Hyman, and also unlike in the cheap versions, these pictures focus both on what is seen and how it affects the person who sees it. As well as seeing the Queen look in the mirror, we ourselves are drawn to look in admiration at the highly intricate pattern of her dress, and as well as looking at Snow White in the forest, we must look at all the interesting animals hidden in the foliage behind her. But despite this adherence to the patterns of the text, this "Snow White" is not one of Jeffers's better books; it lacks a satisfying intensity because in merely duplicating the patterns and focus of the words, its pictures are more or less superfluous.

Paradoxically, Burkert's *Snow White* is more intensely affecting exactly because the detachment and objectivity of these pictures are *not* balanced by involving emotions. Both Jeffers and Burkert show Snow White in the wood surrounded by animals hidden in foliage, but Jeffers's Snow White stares at them in obvious anguish, so that the detachment required by our act of finding all the animals is diluted by the concern we are asked to feel for her—our involvement in her response to the situation. Burkert's Snow White responds differently; she seems to notice none of the animals but an unthreatening deer, and the picture de-emphasizes her terror enough for us to remain detached observers as we look at it.

If Jeffers perfectly balances involvement and detachment in the fashion of the original story, and if Hyman's pictures move the balance in favor of intensity, then Burkert's pictures move the balance in the opposite direction. Like Hyman, she creates a new counterpoint. Burkert's pictures show not a single one of the key moments. Some of them do get close: we do see Snow White's mother at the window but before she has pricked her finger, for there is no drop of blood, and we do see the Prince look at Snow White in the coffin—but not as he first sees her, only after he has begun to carry off the coffin. In fact, all the pictures in this book depict moments between and around the significant episodes of the plot. We see Snow White after she is left alone in the forest. We see her doing housework for the dwarfs after she has found their house but before the Queen has found her. We see Snow White lying dead after being laced and the Queen in her workroom after the episodes of the laces and the comb but before delivering the apple. The final picture shows a moment after the Queen has died but before the Prince and Snow White are married. Considered separately from the text, these pictures actually tell an entirely different story from the text: they depict a series of ordinary moments in the life of people in the past instead of an exciting sequence of events.

Furthermore, these pictures display no exciting action and none of the intense emotion we find in Hyman. Snow White's mother sits. Snow White calls the dwarfs to dinner or lies dead. Only the Queen seems to move with any speed, and she always does it with her back to us, so that we regard her action with emotional distance. In reading this book, we move from the fast thrusts forward of the text to lengthy pauses as we respond to pictures of people in repose that are detailed in a way that demands objective analysis, and then back to quick action again; the effect is strong dramatic tension. In fact, it is the interesting contrast between the very objective, detached, distant pictures and the fast action of the plot that makes the detachment acceptable, and it is the detachment that makes this a convincing story of dispassionate justice.

The Hyman and Burkert versions are the most successful picture books of this group, and not just because they happen to contain the most complex and satisfying pictures; they also both have the contrapuntal narrative rhythms that we expect both of good fairy tales and of good picture books. Hyman and Burkert have created authentic picture-book stories by distorting rather than duplicating the intentions of the original text. The directions of their distortions create highly distinct stories with clearly defined styles, so that they have both done what all good storytellers do: they have told their own personal versions of familiar tales well enough to make them convincing. Such versions may well be the only "authentic" fairy tales.

Authentic or not, the moments these illustrators choose to depict and the rhythms that result from the combination of those moments with the words of a text are the qualities that most significantly give rise to the individual flavor and meaning of their versions. They are also the features that most specifically make use of the distinguishing characteristics of picture books as a medium of narrative communication. All kinds of pictures can convey visual information and create moods; all illustrations can amplify the meaning of a text. But it is the unique rhythm of pictures and words working together that distinguishes picture books from all other forms of both visual and verbal art.

■ ■ ■ ■

CHAPTER TEN

———

The Unguarded Face

As I have discussed the various ways in which pictures contribute to the narrative effect of picture books, I have operated on what may be an unwarranted assumption. Like most North American adults who deal with children, I have simply taken it for granted that pictures do indeed deserve a place in the literature we provide for children. Yet there may be good reasons for questioning that assumption, and there are a number of people who do, on two grounds: first, pictures are counterproductive in the teaching of reading, and second, pictures can limit the imagination of children.

As I said in the first chapter, research does support the conclusion that pictures can sometimes distract young readers from the task of reading, and anyone who watches children struggle with their early readers and pays attention to the sources of their problems will have cause to question the usefulness of the pictures in them. In theory, these pictures allow children to figure out what the words represent; they see the image of a dog, identify it as a dog, and then can use the information to decode the word "dog" in the accompanying text. As I have shown, however, pictures are so vague in their communication of this sort of linguistic information that they tend to confuse children more than to help them: a child who guessed that the image represented either just an animal in general or specifically a Shetland sheepdog would not find the picture useful in decoding the actual word on the page. More significantly, even a child who did guess that the image represented a dog could easily use that information as a replacement for reading and appear to understand a book by interpreting its pictures instead of actually attempting to decode the letters and read the word. Children who seem able to read the texts in books with pictures often flounder when confronted with the same texts without the pictures.

So there appears to be a valid argument against the educational value of pictures; not only may they be counterproductive to the goal of teaching reading but their very attractiveness, the usual justification for including them in children's books, may merely draw attention away from the texts that the pictures are meant to illuminate. This does not mean, however, that the interpretation of pictures should not play a part in the reading process, only that it should not replace that process altogether. In fact, pictures are counterproductive only for those who have not been made conscious of how to use them; and as well as suggesting the distracting quality of pictures, the research that Evelyn Goldsmith discusses in *Research into Illustration* reveals that those who know how to use pictures often find them helpful in the processes of decoding and comprehension.

The second charge made against pictures is that, in showing us the appearances and circumstances of the characters in stories, pictures may in some significant way limit the imagination of young readers. It is true, of course, that the mere presence of a picture in a storybook can prevent us from perceiving how we might have imagined the story for ourselves. But it is only as true as the fact that any specific new experience limits our ability to imagine alternatives. Visiting a city for the first time prevents us from continuing to imagine fantasy versions of what that city might be like. Similarly, even reading the words of a story without pictures limits our creativity by forcing us to visualize specific events rather than the random ones we might happen to think of without having read the story.

Obviously, then, the limitation of imagination provided by pictures is not necessarily negative and may actually be enriching; pictures offer viewers more, and more specific, information to consider and to base further and more complex imaginings upon. Moreover, as I have suggested throughout this book, it is exactly by being rich sources of specific and complex narrative information that pictures play their special part in the unique communicative power of picture-book narrative; while most picture-book texts deprived of their accompanying illustration are indeed vague enough to allow readers a great degree of creativity, that is surely a weakness and not a strength.

But there still may be a case that can be made against illustrated versions of traditional materials, such as the books based on fairy tales that I discussed in the last chapter. These books provide pictures where no pictures are actually needed, for despite (or even because of) their ability to be told in many different ways, these stories have been told successfully for centuries without pictures. As Brian Alderson says in *Looking at Picture Books*, "traditional tales are essentially an oral art-form. They were told before ever they were printed and they carry within themselves all the illustration that they need" (37).

What Alderson says is true; as an oral art form, fairy tales do indeed convey all the visual imagery they require. But it is not a logical objection to illustrated versions of fairy tales, for as tales printed in books, they are no longer merely an oral art form, a form which has quite different qualities and offers a quite different experience: they have become literature and must be judged as we judge literature.

As Walter J. Ong's discussion of orality reveals, an oral story focuses our attention on different sorts of information and in different ways from a written text; a good story read aloud by someone else may not be a particularly good one read silently to oneself. In terms of conventional ideas about literature, in fact, fairy tales are not good fiction: they lack the detailed visual description, the richly textured "reality" we tend to demand as a quality of good written narrative. Paradoxically, however, the very deficiencies of oral tales as literature make the written texts of fairy tales surprisingly similar to the texts written especially for picture books; they focus on action, they are sparse in physical detail, and they move from highly detailed moment to highly detailed moment by means of quickly described action. Consequently, the addition of pictures is a logical move; it transforms a successful oral text into a successful written one without actually changing the text itself.

Furthermore, pictures have the useful effect of normalizing fairy tales—making them more like the other kinds of fiction that adults are familiar with and that young readers are in the process of learning to comprehend. It is in containing both texts and pictures, in offering both sequential and descriptive narrative information, that picture books relate most significantly to other kinds of fiction; so fairy tales accompanied by pictures merely share the qualities of all picture-book narrative. A child who read no illustrated versions of fairy tales would be no less and no more deprived than a child who heard no oral tales unaccompanied by pictures, for each offers a different but enjoyable sort of narrative experience; but a child who neither heard tales read aloud nor saw illustrated versions of them, a child whose only experience of these stories was the silent reading of unillustrated texts of them, would be deprived of two important kinds of pleasure.

MacCann and Richard have a different objection to the detailed visual information in illustrated versions of fairy tales that relates more immediately to the idea that pictures might stifle imagination: "Illustrating individual folk tales gives them a literal dimension that must be viewed as a mixed blessing, even when the pictures are very good. Illustrations, by definition, depict content, and this is sometimes a problem in tales containing supernatural elements (trolls, elves, witches and so on) and highly symbolic heroes and heroines. When outlined solely by the listener's imagination, characters of this sort retain more of their mysterious or ideal quality" (*The Child's First Books* 104). Mysterious indeed, but not necessarily interesting. I referred earlier to Iser's discussion of our dissatisfaction with filmed versions of stories we already know; but Iser pointed to the uninterpreted, objective quality of photographic images as the source of this disappointment, and the images drawn by illustrators are in fact interpretations, filled with potential meaning and anything but uninteresting. This comment by MacCann and Richard denies the value of the ability of skilled and imaginative artists to make us see what we could never have imagined for ourselves; the story of Snow White as outlined by the imaginations of most ordinary human beings is not necessarily more ideal than Trina Hyman's *Snow White*, only more vague and, I believe, less interesting.

But while most adults would agree that watching a Shakespeare play allows most of us to think more, feel more, and imagine more of interest than watching a bare stage, we do tend to believe that children need barer stages, that the products of other and richer imaginations can indeed stifle the tender imaginings of youngsters. This conviction seems to be related to the Wordsworthian notion that children carry a wonderful wisdom with them into this world, an ability to see more than adults do. Their "innocent" imaginings offer them insight into a world different from and better than the reality that adults come to share, a world more ideal and more mysteriously incomprehensible; giving them too much information about our limited adult ways of viewing our reality or imagining our fantasies will corrupt and spoil that insight.

In recent years, there has been much concern about the supposed "disappearance" of childhood; and there is much to be concerned about in the fact that children become conscious of their sexuality younger, give up "childish" activities like fairy tales younger, express a sophisticated cynicism about the way of the world earlier. In other words, they have become less innocent. But to believe that it is dangerous and wrong to offer children insight into the complex possibilities of the world they live in because it is wrong to encourage them to ape the supposedly sophisticated attitudes of supposedly mature adults is to confuse two different things. Knowledge of the world does not inevitably lead to a cynical attitude toward it; truly thoughtful adults are rarely the most cynical ones. Furthermore, the supposedly mature adults who express those cynical attitudes may themselves be accused of indulging in childish behavior; distrust of imaginative fantasy and cynical pessimism are not necessarily signs of mature wisdom, and the childish attitudes of contemporary adults that contemporary children so frequently ape—egocentricity, thoughtlessness of others, disregard of the consequences of actions, and so on—may merely be the untampered-with attitudes of their own childhood, the attitudes of people with no actual knowledge of the complex and demanding world as it is. It may actually be maturity that is disappearing and not childhood at all.

If we wish to prevent that disappearance, then we must work to make children wise and thoughtful. It may well be true, as developmental psychologists insist, that children think differently from the way adults do, but no one has disproved that they may do so only because they have been offered so little access to adult thought patterns, because no one has tried to teach them more—because they are merely inexperienced. In any case, we must not use our utopian faith in their innocence as a reason to keep them ignorant. We will be farther ahead if we treat children not as different sorts of beings incapable of mature thought but as beginners at mature thought who need and are able to acquire experience of it.

Complex and highly detailed pictures like those in the versions of "Snow White" by Burkert and Hyman can play an important part in the acquiring of such experience. Rather than leaving the disturbingly strange or symbolically ideal undepicted, they give it faces: and in putting real faces to our fantasies, they show us how those fantasies are inseparable from the real world—real and serious. Having seen disturbingly actual dragons and witches such as the ones Hyman presents in her version of Howard Pyle's *King Stork*, we can no longer dismiss dragons and witches as endearing fantasies, the imagining of which is merely a pastime; the literal picture forces us to confront the actual horror, the potential for savage destruction that dragons and witches represent. Similarly, Hyman's very real depictions of Snow White and the Queen tell us that these idealized figures are just people after all, that their idealized innocence and intense evil are not so wildly fantastic as to be dismissable; these very human faces force us to confront the implications of these characters in terms of our acquaintances and of ourselves, in a way that our own vaguely mysterious imaginings never could. Such pictures tell us much about what it is to be human, how hard it is and how rich an experience it is, and in doing so, they force us to understand how the fairy tales they accompany themselves provide such insights. These illustrated versions may indeed allow less mystery than unillustrated ones, but that is merely because they demand more insight, because they force us to read the texts they illustrate more deeply and more subtly. In Iser's terms, they arouse mental images richer than the ones most of us might imagine from words alone.

In fact, the relationship of words and pictures as it is found in all good picture books may be of particular significance in the education of children into mature human beings. The basic, distinguishing peculiarity of picture-book storytelling is that it tells of the same events by means of two quite different media and therefore in two quite different ways. In doing so, it mirrors the process by which human beings come to know their world, better than does any other imaginative experience.

As I suggested earlier, cognitive psychologists believe that we understand new experiences by using old experiences as a pattern or schema; in determining what we know already about something new to us, we may focus our attention on what is new—and so learn more than we did before. This is like what Piaget calls "assimilation"—the use of old learning in the process of new learning. Information theorists postulate a relationship in messages between what we already know and can depend on and what we might learn in terms of "redundancy"; that aspect of a message which always remains the same. If we recognize the redundancies, the patterns or conventions, then we may focus on and have a context for understanding what is new. According to Jeremy Campbell, "This means that some sameness is mixed in with change. Change is the essence of information. A message source must be free to vary its messages, to send different sequences of symbols. There is no point in sending the same sequence over and over again. But redundancy insures that a pattern of probabilities remains constant across all the messages. That is something the receiver can depend on. A measure of consistency is introduced into a system which, by its very nature, needs to be partly inconsistent, to surprise us with the unexpected" (201).

That last word, "unexpected," is particularly interesting. Expectation and surprise have the same relationship as redundancy and change, schema and experience. Not surprisingly, literary critics who concern themselves with how readers respond to and come to understand literature speak much of "expectations." Louise M. Rosenblatt says that as one reads, "one evolves certain expectations about the diction, the subject, the ideas, the kind of text that will be forthcoming. Each sentence, each phrase, each word, will signal certain possibilities and exclude others, thus limiting the arc of expectations" (54). And Iser says, "throughout the reading process there is a continual interplay between modified expectations and transformed memories" (83).

In picture books, the pictures act as schema for the words and vice versa. We have the usual pattern of expectation giving rise to information, but with a significant difference: the information comes from two decidedly different sources. As a result, we constantly experience sudden switches of focus on the same information, from visual to verbal, from causal to spatial, and so on, and in doing so, we derive far more knowledge from far less information than we could from words by themselves or from pictures by themselves. As I have suggested, Hyman's *Snow White* as a whole is more complex, more detailed, more specific, and more informative than either the story told by the Grimm brothers or Hyman's pictures unaccompanied by the words of that story, and the complex information that arises our of the relationship of that less informative text and those less informative pictures is easy to absorb. In other words, the combination of words and pictures is an ideal way to learn a lot in a relatively painless way.

That can happen best, of course, to those for whom the redundancies of both text and picture are known: "information theory teaches that without structure, without a code, a system is useless. It is perfectly free, but the freedom is indistinguishable from noise" (Campbell 263). The conclusion is obvious: without knowledge of the patterns and conventions, first of stories told in words, then of the narrative impact of pictures, and finally of how words and pictures tell stories together, children will have a freedom that is indistinguishable from the anarchy of noise. In being able to imagine everything, they will imagine nothing communicable—they will be locked inside the prison of their own consciousnesses. Teaching children an awareness of the conventions is freeing; it lets them partake in the communication that human beings may have with each other across the chasms that put distance between us.

A consciousness of what stories are, of what art is, offers an even greater freedom—the freedom that comes at the end of innocence, when one knows that what one takes for granted is not all there is but merely a set of expectations that can, indeed, be delightfully or sometimes even horribly thwarted. According to Edmund Leach, "It is noticeable that the things which are commonly recognized as 'works of art' have nearly always been created quite explicitly for exhibition in taboo contexts on ritual occasions and in ritual places. Art suggests ideas which at those times and in those places must not be suggested. Put in another way, a work of art corresponds to our expectations, but it goes a little beyond into what is forbidden and unexpected" (227). In doing so, of course, it expands our consciousness—makes us see more and forces us to become conscious of the limitations of what we prefer to believe. Susanne Langer puts it another way: "the arts we live with—our picture books and stories and the music we hear—actually form our emotive experience" (71–72). Herbert Read similarly suggests that art, in offering us the unexpected, increases the range of what we might expect: "what we call art, and too cursorily treat as an ornament of civilization, is really a vital activity, an energy of the senses that must continually convert the dead rain of matter into the radiant images of life" (*Icon and Idea* 140).

Good picture books, then, offer us what all good art offers us: greater consciousness—the opportunity, in other words, to be more human. That means to be less innocent, more wise. It also means both to feel more objectively and to think with more involvement. How those two apparently paradoxical qualities come together in art is brilliantly suggested by P. S. Rushforth's description, in his novel *Kindergarten*, of a picture in a fictional picture book: an illustration made by a character in the novel for the tale of "Hansel and Gretel":

> The little boy, and the younger girl, stood hand in hand at the edge of an immense dark forest, towering high above them, dressed in the fashion of the 1930s, the little girl with an elaborately-woven shawl

around her shoulders. They filled most of the picture, standing in the center of the scene. The girl was looking in front of her, into the forest, and seemed frightened. The boy was looking over his shoulder, back the way he had come, looking straight into the face of anyone looking at the picture. The details were as intensely-observed as in a Victorian genre-painting, and the boy's open, unguarded face could be studied in a detailed way that one could only give to a face in a painting or a photograph, or the face of someone who was loved, and who returned that love. (8)

The unguarded face, freely observed—and observed not in uncomprehending possessiveness but with the informed observation that teaches us the subtlety and individuality, and thus the value, of what we see. That joining together of the objective detachment of art and the vulnerability of love say more about what picture-book art offers children than I could say in many pages: it is objective awareness based on deep understanding that allows us first to know the world and then to love the world we know.

. . . .

WORKS CONSULTED

Alderson, Brian. *Looking at Picture Books, 1973.* Catalog for an exhibition by the National Book League. Oxford, 1973.

————, comp. *Catalogue for an Exhibition of Pictures by Maurice Sendak at the Ashmolean Museum, Oxford, December 16 to February 29, 1975–6.* London: The Bodley Head, 1975.

Aldrich, Virgil C. "Pictures and Persons—An Analogy." *Review of Metaphysics* 28 (1975): 599–610.

Alpers, Svetlana. *The Art of Describing: Dutch Art in the Seventeenth Century.* Chicago: University of Chicago Press, 1983.

Andrew, J. Dudley. *The Master Film Theories: An Introduction.* New York: Oxford University Press, 1976.

Applebee, Arthur N. *The Child's Concept of Story: Ages Two to Seven.* Chicago: University of Chicago Press, 1978.

Arakelian, Paul. "Text and Illustration: A Stylistic Analysis of Books by Sendak and Mayer." *ChLA Quarterly* 10.3 (Fall 1985): 122–27.

Ardizzone, Edward. "Creation of a Picture Book." Egoff, Stubbs, and Ashley 289–98.

Arnheim, Rudolf. *Art and Visual Perception: A Psychology of the Creative Eye.* The New Version. Berkeley: University of California Press, 1974.

————. "Dynamics and Invariants." John Fisher 166–84.

————. "The Images of Pictures and Words." *Word & Image* 2.4 (1986): 306–10.

————. *Visual Thinking.* Berkeley: University of California Press, 1969.

Bader, Barbara. *American Picturebooks from Noah's Ark to the Beast Within.* New York: Macmillan, 1976.

————. "A Second Look: *Millions of Cats.*" *Horn Book* 55.5 (October 1978): 536–40.

Baker, Steve. "The Hell of Connotation." *Word & Image* 1.2 (April–June 1985): 164–75.

Bancroft-Hunt, Norman. *People of the Totem: The Indians of the Pacific Northwest.* New York: Putnam's, 1979.

Barr, Charles. "Cinemascope: Before and After." Mast and Cohen 120–46.

Barron, Pamela Petrick, and Jennifer Q. Burley, eds. *Jump over the Moon: Selected Professional Readings*. New York: Holt, Rinehart and Winston, 1984.

Barthes, Roland. *Camera Lucida*. Trans. Richard Howard. New York: Hill and Wang-Farrar, Straus and Giroux, 1981.

_____. *Elements of Semiology*. Trans. Annette Lavers and Colin Smith. New York: Hill and Wang-Farrar, Straus and Giroux, 1968.

_____. *Mythologies*. Trans. Annette Lavers. London: Paladin Books-Granada, 1973.

_____. *The Responsibility of Forms: Critical Essays on Music, Art, and Representation*. Trans. Richard Howard. New York: Hill and Wang-Farrar, Straus and Giroux, 1985.

_____. *S/Z*. Trans. Richard Miller. New York: Hill and Wang-Farrar, Straus and Giroux, 1974.

_____. *Writing Degree Zero*. Trans. Annette Lavers and Colin Smith. London: Jonathan Cape, 1967.

Barufaldi, James P., and Maureen A. Dietz. "Effects of Solid Objects and Two-dimensional Representations of the Objects on Visual Observation and Comparison among Urban Children." *Journal of Research in Science Teaching* 12.2 (1975): 127–32.

Bator, Robert, ed. *Signposts to Criticism of Children's Literature*. Chicago: American Library Association, 1983.

Bazin, André. "What Is Cinema?" Mast and Cohen 22–26, 90–102.

Beardsley, Monroe C. "The Role of Psychological Explanation in Aesthetics." John Fisher 185–212.

Bechtel, Louise Seaman. "The Art of Illustrating Books for the Younger Readers." Haviland, *Children and Literature* 173–76.

Bennet, John G. "Depiction and Convention." *Monist* 58.2 (April 1974): 255–69.

Benson, Ciaràn. "Art and Language in Middle Childhood: A Question of Translation." *Word & Image* 2.2 (April–June 1986): 123–40.

Berger, John. *About Looking*. New York: Pantheon, 1980.

_____. *Ways of Seeing*. London: British Broadcasting Corporation; Harmondsworth: Penguin, 1972.

Berridge, Celia. "Illustrators, Books, and Children: An Illustrator's Viewpoint." Barron and Burley 175–82.

_____. "Taking a Good Look at Picture Books." *Signal* 36 (September 1981): 152–58.

Bettelheim, Bruno, and Karen Zelan. *On Learning to Read: The Child's Fascination with Meaning*. New York: Vintage–Random House, 1982.

Blakemore, Colin. "The Baffled Brain." Gregory and Gombrich 8–47.

Bland, David. *A History of Book Illustration*. London: Faber and Faber, 1958.

_____. *The Illustration of Books*. 3d ed. London: Faber and Faber, 1962.

Bloomer, Carolyn. *Principles of Visual Perception*. New York: Van Nostrand Reinhold, 1976.

Bluestone, George. "Limits of the Novel and the Film." Mast and Cohen 291–301.

Boas, Franz. *Primitive Art*. 1927. New York: Dover, 1955.

Bodmer, George R. "Ruth Kraus and Maurice Sendak's Early Illustration." *ChLA Quarterly* 11.4 (Winter 1986–87): 180–83.

Bottigheimer, Ruth B. "Iconographic Continuity in Illustrations of 'The Goosegirl.'" *Children's Literature* 13 (1985): 49–71.

Brooks, Peter, ed. *The Child's Part*. Boston: Beacon Press, 1969.

Brothwell, Don, ed. *Beyond Aesthetics: Investigations into the Nature of Visual Art*. London: Thames and Hudson, 1976.

Brown, Marcia. "My Goals as an Illustrator." *Horn Book* 43 (1967): 305–16.

Bryson, Norman. *Vision and Painting: The Logic of the Gaze*. New Haven: Yale University Press, 1983.

Burkert, Nancy Ekholm. "A Second Look: *Lion*." *Horn Book* 56.6 (December 1980): 671–76.

Buswell, Guy Thomas. *How People Look at Pictures: A Study of Perception in Art*. Chicago: University of Chicago Press, 1935.

Butor, Michel. "The Book as Object." *Inventory: Essays by Michel Butor*. Ed. Richard Howard. London: Jonathan Cape, 1970. 39–56.

Butterworth, George, ed. *The Child's Representation of the World*. New York: Plenum, 1977.

Cahn, Annabelle Simon. "Leo Lionni, Illustrator and Philosopher." *Children's Literature* 2 (1973): 123–29.

Cameron, Eleanor. "Wanda Gag: Myself and Many Me's." *The Green and Burning Tree: On the Writing and Enjoyment of Children's Books*. Boston: Atlantic Monthly Press–Little, Brown, 1969.

Campbell, Jeremy. *Grammatical Man: Information, Entropy, Language, and Life*. New York: Simon and Schuster, 1982.

Canham, Stephen. "What Manner of Beast? Illustrations of 'Beauty and the Beast.'" *Image and Maker*. Ed. Peter Neumeyer 13–25. La Jolla, CA: Green Tiger, 1984.

Capps, Walter Holden, ed. *Seeing with a Native Eye: Essays on Native American Religion*. New York: Forum Books-Harper and Row, 1976.

Cartarette, Edward C., and Morton P. Friedman. *Handbook of Perception 10: Perceptual Ecology*. New York: Academic Press, 1978.

Cass, Joan E. *Literature and the Young Child*. London: Longmans, 1967.

Cech, Jon. "Remembering Caldecott: *The Three Jovial Huntsmen* and the Art of the Picture Book." *Lion and the Unicorn* 7/8 (1983–84): 110–19.

Chappell, Warren. "Bench Marks for Illustrators of Children's Books." Field 73–77.

———. "Illustrations Today in Children's Books." Fryatt 86–91.

Chatman, Seymour. *Story and Discourse: Narrative Structure in Fiction and Film*. Ithaca, NY: Cornell University Press, 1978.

———. "What Novels Can Do That Films Can't." *Critical Inquiry* 7.1 (Autumn 1980): 121–40.

Child, Irvin L. "Aesthetic Theories." Cartarette and Friedman 111–31.

Cianciolo, Patricia. *Illustrations in Children's Books*. 2d ed. Dubuque, IA: Wm. C. Brown, 1976.

———. "Use Wordless Picture Books to Teach Reading, Visual Literacy and to Study Literature." *Top of the News*, April 1973: 226–34.

_____, ed. *Picture Books for Children*. Chicago: American Library Association, 1973.

Cleaver, Elizabeth. "Idea to Image: The Journey of a Picture Book." *Lion and the Unicorn* 7/8 (1983–84): 156–70.

_____. "The Visual Artist and the Creative Process in Picture Books." *Canadian Children's Literature* 4 (1976): 71–79.

Cochran-Smith, Marilyn. "The Art of Nancy Ekholm Burkert." *ChLA Quarterly* 4.3 (Fall 1979): 1, 8–10.

Colby, Jean Poindexter. *Writing, Illustrating, and Editing Children's Books*. New York: Hastings House, 1967.

Collier, Graham. *Form, Space, and Vision: Discovering Design through Drawing*. Englewood Cliffs, NJ: Prentice-Hall, 1963.

Comenius, Joannes Amos. "The Great Didactic." *John Amos Comenius on Education*. New York: Teachers College Press, 1967. 65–114.

_____. *Orbis Sensualium Pictus: Facsimile of the Third London Edition, 1672*. Intro. James Bowen. Sydney: Sydney University Press, 1967.

Cook, Elizabeth. *The Ordinary and the Fabulous: An Introduction to Myths, Legends, and Fairy Tales*. 2d ed. Cambridge: Cambridge University Press, 1976.

Cooney, Barbara. "An Illustrator's Viewpoint." Field 82–86.

_____. "The Spirit Place." *ChLA Quarterly* 9.4 (Winter 1984): 152–53.

Cott, Jonathan. *Pipers at the Gates of Dawn: The Wisdom of Children's Literature*. New York: Random House, 1983.

Crago, Hugh. "Who Does Snow White Look At?" *Signal* 45 (September 1984): 129–45.

Crago, Maureen. "'Snow White': One Child's Response in a Natural Setting." *Signal* 31 (January 1980): 42–56.

Culler, Jonathan. *The Pursuit of Signs*. Ithaca, NY: Cornell University Press, 1981.

_____. *Structuralist Poetics*. Ithaca, NY: Cornell University Press, 1975.

DeLuca, Geraldine. "Art, Illusion, and Children's Picture Books." *ChLA Quarterly* 9.1 (Spring 1984): 21–23.

_____. "Exploring the Levels of Childhood: The Allegorical Sensibility of Maurice Sendak." *Children's Literature* 12 (1984): 3–24.

Denburg, Susan Dalfen. "The Interaction of Picture and Print in Reading Instruction (Abstracted Report)." *Reading Research Quarterly* 12.2 (1976–77): 176–89.

Deregowski, Jan B. "Illusion and Culture." Gregory and Gombrich, *Illusion in Nature and Art* 161–89.

Derrida, Jacques. *Of Grammatology*. Trans. Gayatri Chakravorty Spivak. Baltimore: Johns Hopkins University Press, 1976.

Dockstader, Frederick J. "The Role of the Individual Indian Artist." Forge 113–25.

Dooley, Patricia. "The Art of Peter Spier." *ChLA Quarterly* 4.4 (Winter 1980): 1, 30–31.

_____. "'First Books': From Schlock to Sophistication." May, *Children and Their Literature* 112.

_____. "Gerald McDermott." *ChLA Newsletter* 3.4 (Winter 1979): 1–5.

_____. "Porcelain, Pigtails, Pagodas: Images of China in 19th and 20th Century Illustrated

Editions of 'The Nightingale.'" *Proceedings of the Sixth Annual Conference of the ChLA, University of Toronto, 1979.* Ed. Margaret P. Esmonde and Priscilla A. Ord. Villanova, PA: Villanova University, 1980. 94–105.

————. "Romance and Realism: Pyle's Book Illustrations for Children." *ChLA Quarterly* 8.2 (Summer 1983): 17–19.

Doonan, Jane. "The Object Lesson: Picturebooks of Anthony Browne." *Word & Image* 2.2 (April–June 1986): 159–72.

————. "*Outside Over There:* A Journey in Style." *Signal* 50 (May 1986): 92–103; 51 (September 1986): 172–87.

————. "Talking Pictures: A New Look at Hansel and Gretel." *Signal* 42 (September 1983): 123–31.

————. "Two Artists Telling Tales: Chihiro Iwasaki and Lisbeth Zwerger." *Signal* 44 (May 1984): 93–102.

Dozier, Edward P. *The Pueblo Indians of North America.* New York: Holt, Rinehart and Winston, 1970.

Dressel, Janice Hartwick. "Abstraction in Illustration: Is It Appropriate for Children?" *Children's Literature in Education* 15.2 (Summer 1984): 103–12.

Druce, Robert. "Orbis Pictus Redivivus." *Word & Image* 1.1 (January–March 1985): 109–29.

Duncan, H. F., N. Gourlay, and Wm. Hudson. *A Study of Pictorial Perception among Bantu and White Primary School Children in South Africa.* Human Sciences Research Council Publication Series, 31. Johannesburg: Witwatersrand University Press, 1973.

Durand, Marion. "One Hundred Years of Illustration in French Children's Books." Brooks 85–96.

Duvoisin, Roger. "Children's Book Illustration: The Pleasures and the Problems." Haviland, *Children and Literature* 177–87.

Eagleton, Terry. *Literary Theory: An Introduction.* Minneapolis: University of Minnesota Press, 1983.

Edgerton, Samuel Y., Jr. "The American Super-hero Comic Strip: *True* Descendant of Italian Renaissance Art." *ChLA Quarterly* 9.1 (Spring 1984): 30–33.

Egoff, Sheila. *The Republic of Childhood: A Critical Guide to Canadian Children's Literature in English.* 2d ed. Toronto: Oxford University Press, 1975.

————. *Thursday's Child: Trends and Patterns in Contemporary Children's Literature.* Chicago: American Library Association, 1981. 247–74.

Egoff, Sheila, G. T. Stubbs, and L. F. Ashley. *Only Connect: Readings on Children's Literature.* 2d ed. New York: Oxford University Press, 1980.

Ehrlich, Bettina. "Story and Picture in Children's Books." Field 86–93.

Feaver, William. *When We Were Young: Two Centuries of Children's Book Illustration.* London: Thames and Hudson, 1977.

Feldman, Edmund Burke. *Varieties of Visual Experience: Art as Image and Idea.* 2d ed. Englewood Cliffs, NJ: Prentice-Hall; New York: Abrams, 1972.

Field, Eleanor Whitney, ed. *Horn Book Reflections on Children's Books and Reading.* Boston: Horn Book, 1969.

Fish, Stanley. *Is There a Text in This Class? The Authority of Interpretive Communities.* Cambridge, MA: Harvard University Press, 1980.

Fisher, John, ed. *Perceiving Artworks.* Philosophical Monographs. Philadelphia: Temple University Press, 1980.

Fisher, Margery. *Intent upon Reading: A Critical Appraisal of Modern Fiction for Children.* 2d ed. Leicester: Brockhampton Press, 1964.

———. *Who's Who in Children's Books.* London: Weidenfield and Nicolson, 1975.

Forge, Anthony, ed. *Primitive Art and Society.* New York: Oxford University Press, 1973.

Freeman, G. Laverne, and Ruth Sunderlin Freeman. *The Child and His Picture Book.* Watkins Glen, NY: Century House, 1967.

Freeman, Norm H. *Strategies of Representation in Young Children: Analysis of Spatial Skills and Drawing Processes.* New York: Academic Press, 1980.

Fryatt, Norma R., ed. *A Horn Book Sampler.* Boston: Horn Book, 1959.

Fuller, Peter. *Seeing Berger: A Revaluation.* 2d ed. London: Writers and Readers, 1981.

Gaffron, Mercedes. "Right and Left in Pictures." *Art Quarterly* 13 (1950): 312–31.

Gannon, Susan. "Rudolf Arnheim's 'Psychology of the Creative Eye' and the Criticism of Illustrated Books for Children." *ChLA Quarterly* 9.1 (Spring 1984): 15–18.

Gardner, Howard. *The Shattered Mind: The Person after Brain Damage.* New York: Vintage-Random House, 1976.

Garfield, Viola E., and Paul S. Wingert. *The Tsimshian Indians and Their Arts.* Seattle: University of Washington Press, 1966.

Geertz, Clifford. "Art as a Cultural System." *Modern Language Notes* 91 (1976): 1473–99.

Gibson, J. J. "Foreword: A Preparatory Essay on the Perception of Surfaces versus the Perception of Marking on a Surface." *The Perception of Pictures.* Ed. Margaret A. Hagen. New York: Academic Press, 1980. 1. xi–xiv.

Gilpatrick, Naomi. "Power of Picture Books to Change Child's Self-Image." White 179–84.

Glazer, Joan I. *Literature for Young Children.* Columbus, OH: Charles E. Merrill, 1981.

Glazer, Joan I., and Gurney Williams III. *Introduction to Children's Literature.* New York: McGraw-Hill, 1979.

Godfrey, Vesey. "Of the Visible Appearances of Objects." John Fisher 42–58.

Goldsmith, Evelyn. "Learning from Illustrations: Factors in the Design of Illustrated Educational Books for Middle School Children." *Word & Image* 2.2 (April–June 1986): 111–21.

———. *Research into Illustration: An Approach and a Review.* Cambridge: Cambridge University Press, 1984.

Gombrich, E. H. *Art and Illusion: A Study in the Psychology of Pictorial Representation.* Bollingen Series 35.5. 2d ed. New York: Pantheon, 1961.

———. "Illusion and Art." Gregory and Gombrich 192–243.

———. "Image and Word in Twentieth-century Art." *Word & Image* 1.3 (July–September 1985): 213–41.

———. "Standards of Truth: The Arrested Image and the Moving Eye." *Critical Inquiry* (Winter 1980): 237–73.

————. *The Story of Art.* 12th ed. London: Phaidon Press, 1972.

————. "Style." *International Encyclopedia of the Social Sciences.* New York, 1968.

————. "The Visual Image." *Scientific American* 227 (September 1972): 82–94.

Gombrich, E. H., Julian Hochberg, and Max Black. *Art, Perception, and Reality.* Baltimore: Johns Hopkins University Press, 1972.

Goodman, Nelson. *Languages of Art: An Approach to a Theory of Symbols.* Indianapolis: Bobbs-Merrill, 1968.

————. *Ways of Worldmaking.* Indianapolis: Hackett, 1978.

Grady, Michael P., and Emily A. Luecke. *Education and the Brain.* Bloomington, IN: Phi Delta Kappa Educational Foundation, 1978.

Greene, Graham. "Beatrix Potter." Egoff, Stubbs, and Ashley 258–65.

Gregory, R. L. "The Confounded Eye." Gregory and Gombrich 48–95.

————. *The Intelligent Eye.* New York: McGraw-Hill, 1970.

Gregory, R. L., and E. H. Gombrich, eds. *Illusion in Nature and Art.* London: Duckworth, 1973.

Groff, Patrick. "Children's Literature versus Wordless 'Books.'" *Top of the News,* April 1974: 294–303.

Grotjahn, Martin. "Ferdinand the Bull." White 30–36.

Haberlant, Wolfgang. *The Art of North America.* New York: Greystone Press, 1968.

Hagen, Margaret A. "Representational Art and the Problem of What to Depict." John Fisher 107–30.

Haley, Gail E. "Everyman Jack and the Green Man." *Proceedings of the Ninth Annual Conference of the ChLA, University of Florida, 1982.* Ed. Priscilla A. Ord. New Rochelle, NY: Iona College, 1983. 1–19.

Haviland, Virginia, ed. *Children and Literature: Views and Reviews.* Glenview, IL: Scott, Foresman, 1973.

————. *The Openhearted Audience: Ten Authors Talk about Writing for Children.* Washington: Library of Congress, 1980.

Hearn, Michael Patrick. "A Second Look: Peter Rabbit Redux." *Horn Book* 53.5 (October 1977): 563–66.

Hearne, Betsy, and Marilyn Kaye, eds. *Celebrating Children's Books: Essays on Children's Literature in Honor of Zena Sutherland.* New York: Lothrop, Lee and Shepard, 1981.

Hibben, Frank C. *Kiva Art of the Anasazi at Pottery Mound.* Las Vegas: KG Publications, 1975.

Hochberg, Julian. "Art and Perception." Cartarette and Friedman 225–58.

Hochberg, Julian, and Virginia Brooks. "Pictorial Recognition as an Unlearned Ability: A Study of One Child's Performance." *American Journal of Psychology* 75 (1962): 624–28.

Hodnett, Edward. *Image and Text: Studies in the Illustration of English Literature.* London: Scolar Press, 1982.

Hollindale, Peter. *Choosing Books for Children.* London: Paul Elek, 1974.

Holm, Bill. *Northwest Coast Indian Art: An Analysis of Form.* Seattle: University of Washington Press, 1965.

Hughes, Felicity. "Children's Literature: Theory and Practice." *ELH* 45 (1978): 542–52.

Hurlimann, Bettina. "Illustration and the Emotional World of the Child." *Bookbird*, September 15, 1969: 57–61.

Huss, Roy, and Norman Silverstein. *The Film Experience: Elements of Motion Picture Art.* New York: Delta Books–Dell, 1968.

Iser, Wolfgang. *The Act of Reading: A Theory of Aesthetic Response.* Baltimore: Johns Hopkins University Press, 1978.

Ivins, William M., Jr. *Prints and Visual Communication.* 1953. Reprint. New York: Da Capo Press, 1969.

Jahoda, G., et al. "Pictorial Recognition as an Unlearned Ability: A Replication with Children from Pictorially Deprived Environments." Butterworth 203–13.

James, Philip. *English Book Illustration 1800–1900.* London: King Penguin, 1947.

Johnson, Lincoln F. *Film: Space, Time, Light, and Sound.* New York: Holt, Rinehart and Winston, 1974.

Kamenetsky, Christa. "Arthur Rackham and the Romantic Tradition: The Question of Polarity and Ambiguity." *Children's Literature* 6 (1977): 115–29.

Keeping, Charles. "My Work as a Children's Illustrator." *ChLA Quarterly* 8.4 (Winter 1983): 14–19.

Kennedy, John M. "Depiction Considered as a Representational System." John Fisher 131–65.

————. *A Psychology of Picture Perception: Images and Information.* San Francisco: Jossey-Bass, 1974.

Kepes, Gyorgy. *The Language of Vision.* 1944. Chicago: Paul Theobald, 1969.

Kiefer, Barbara Z. "The Child and the Picture Book: Creating Live Circuits." *ChLA Quarterly* 11.2 (Summer 1986): 63–68.

Kimmel, Eric. "Children's Literature without Children." *Children's Literature in Education* 13.1 (1982): 38–43.

Kingman, Lee. "Virginia Lee Burton's Sense of Design." *Horn Book* 46 (1970): 449–60, 596–602.

————, ed. *The Illustrator's Notebook.* Boston: Horn Book, 1978.

Kingman, Lee, Joanna Foster, and Ruth Giles Lontoff, eds. *Illustrators of Children's Books 1957–1966.* Boston: Horn Book, 1968.

Kingman, Lee, Grace Allen Hogarth, and Harriet Quimby, eds. *Illustrators of Children's Books 1967–1976.* Boston: Horn Book, 1978.

Klemin, Diana. *The Art of Art for Children's Books: A Contemporary Survey.* New York: Clarkson N. Potter, 1966.

Kristeva, Julia. *Desire in Language: A Semiotic Approach to Literature and Art.* Ed. Leon S. Roudiez. Trans. Thomas Gora, Alice Jardine, and Leon S. Roudiez. New York: Columbia University Press, 1980.

Lacy, Lyn Ellen. *Art and Design in Children's Picture Books.* Chicago: American Library Association, 1986.

Lamb, Charles. "On the Genius and Character of Hogarth." *The Portable Charles Lamb*. Ed. John Mason Brown. New York: Viking, 1949. 448–73.

Landes, Sonia. "Picture Books as Literature." *ChLA Quarterly* 10.2 (Summer 1985): 51–54.

Lane, Margaret. *The Tale of Beatrix Potter*. Rev. ed. London: Frederick Warne, 1968.

Lanes, Selma G. *The Art of Maurice Sendak*. New York: Abrams, 1980.

———. *Down the Rabbit Hole: Adventures and Misadventures in the Realm of Children's Literature*. New York: Atheneum, 1976.

Langer, Susanne K. *Problems of Art: Ten Philosophical Lectures*. New York: Scribner's, 1957.

Larkin, David. *The Fantastic Kingdom*. New York: Ballantine, 1974.

Lawson, Robert. "The Genius of Arthur Rackham." Fryatt 55–59.

Leach, Edmund. "Levels of Communication and Problems of Taboo in the Appreciation of Primitive Art." Forge 221–34.

Lent, Blair. "There's Much More to the Picture than Meets the Eye." Bator 156–61.

Levy, Bernard I. "Research into the Psychological Meaning of Color." *American Journal of Art Therapy* 19.4 (July 1980): 87–91.

Lionni, Leo. "Before Images." *Horn Book* 60.6 (November–December 1984): 727–34.

Lister, Raymond. *Victorian Narrative Paintings*. New York: Clarkson N. Potter, 1966.

Lobel, Arnold. "A Good Picture Book Should . . ." Hearne and Kaye 73–80.

Lorraine, Walter. "An Interview with Maurice Sendak." Egoff, Stubbs, and Ashley 326–36.

Lukens, Rebecca J. *A Critical Handbook of Children's Literature*. 2d ed. Glenview, IL: Scott, Foresman, 1982.

Luthi, Max. *Once upon a Time: On the Nature of Fairy Tales*. Trans. Lee Chadeayne and Paul Gottwald. Bloomington: Indiana University Press, 1976.

Macaulay, David. "How to Create a Successful Children's Nonfiction Picture Book." Hearne and Kaye 97–107.

MacCann, Donnarae, and Olga Richard. *The Child's First Books: A Critical Study of Pictures and Texts*. New York: H. W. Wilson, 1973.

———. Review of Selma Lanes, *The Art of Maurice Sendak*. *ChLA Quarterly* 6.4 (Winter 1981–82): 11–17.

MacDonald, Ruth K. "Why This Is Still 1893: *The Tale of Peter Rabbit* and Beatrix Potter's Manipulation of Time into Timelessness." *ChLA Quarterly* 10.4 (Winter 1986): 185–87.

McGavran, James Holt, Jr. "'The Children Sport upon the Shore': Romantic Vision in Two Twentieth Century Picture Books." *ChLA Quarterly* 11.4 (Winter 1986–87): 170–75.

McGillis, Roderick. "Criticism in the Woods: Fairy Tales as Poetry." Nodelman and May 53–58.

McLuhan, Marshall. *The Gutenberg Galaxy: The Making of Typographic Man*. Toronto: University of Toronto Press, 1962.

Mahoney, Bertha E., Louise Payson Latimer, and Beulah Formsbee, eds. *Illustrators of Children's Books, 1744–1945*. Boston: Horn Book, 1947.

Malraux, André. *The Voices of Silence*. Trans. Stuart Gilbert. Garden City, NY: Doubleday, 1953.

Marantz, Kenneth. "The Picture Book as Art Object: A Call for Balanced Reviewing." Bator 152–56.

Marcus, Leonard. "The Artist's Eye: The Picture Books of Mitsumasa Anno." *Lion and the Unicorn* 7/8 (1983–84): 34–46.

———. "Picture Book Animals: How Natural a History?" *Lion and the Unicorn* 7/8 (1983–84): 127–39.

Margolis, Joseph. "Art as Language." *The Monist* 58.2 (April 1974): 175–86.

———. "Prospects for a Science of Aesthetic Perception." John Fisher 213–39.

Martin, Wallace. *Recent Theories of Narrative*. Ithaca, NY: Cornell University Press, 1986.

Massey, Irving. "Words and Images: Harmony and Dissonance." *Georgia Review* 34 (1980): 375–95.

Mast, Gerald, and Marshall Cohen, eds. *Film Theory and Criticism: Introductory Readings*. New York: Oxford University Press, 1974.

Matthias, Margaret, and Graciela Italiano. "Louder than a Thousand Words." Bator 161–65.

May, Jill P. "Illustration as Interpretation: Trina Hyman's Folk Tales." *ChLA Quarterly* 10.3 (Fall 1985): 127–31.

———. "Illustrations in Children's Books." *ChLA Quarterly* 6.4 (Winter 1981–82): 17–21.

———, ed. *Children and Their Literature: A Readings Book*. West Lafayette, IN: ChLA Publications, 1983.

Meigs, Cornelia, et al. *A Critical History of Children's Literature*. New York: Macmillan, 1953.

Metz, Christian. *Language and Cinema*. Trans. Donna Jean Umiker-Sebeok. The Hague: Mouton, 1974.

Mirel, Barbara. "Tradition and the Individual Retelling." *ChLA Quarterly* 9.2 (Summer 1984): 63–66.

Moebius, William. "Introduction to Picturebook Codes." *Word & Image* 2.2 (April–June 1986): 141–58.

Mordoh, Alice Morrison. "Folklife in the Work of Mitsumasa Anno." *ChLA Quarterly* 10.3 (Fall 1985): 104–108.

Moustakis, Christina. "A Plea for Heads: Illustrating Violence in Fairy Tales." *ChLA Quarterly* 7.2 (Summer 1982): 26–30.

Neisser, Ulric. *Cognition and Reality: Principles and Implications of Cognitive Psychology*. San Francisco: W. H. Freeman, 1976.

Neumeyer, Peter. "A Structural Approach to the Study of Literature for Children." *Elementary English* 44.8 (December 1967): 883–87.

Nichols, Bill. *Ideology and the Image: Social Representation in the Cinema and Other Media*. Bloomington: Indiana University Press, 1981.

Nodelman, Perry. "Expectations: Titles, Stories, Pictures." *ChLA Quarterly* 10.1 (Spring 1985): 9–13.

———. "How Picture Books Work." *Image and Maker*. La Jolla, CA: Green Tiger Press, 1984. 1–12.

———. "Non-Native Primitive Art: Elizabeth Cleaver's Indian Legends." *Canadian Children's Literature* 31/32 (1983): 69–79.

————. "Of Nakedness and Children's Picture Books." *ChLA Quarterly* 9.1 (Spring 1984): 25–29.

Nodelman, Perry, and Jill P. May, eds. *Festschrift: A Ten Year Retrospective*. West Lafayette, IN: ChLA Publications, 1983.

Norton, Donna E. *Through the Eyes of a Child: An Introduction to Children's Literature*. Columbus, OH: Charles E. Merrill, 1983.

Ong, Walter J. *Orality and Literacy: The Technologizing of the Word*. London: Methuen, 1982.

Ornstein, Robert E. *The Psychology of Consciousness*. 1972. New York: Penguin, 1975.

Ortiz, Alfonso, ed. *New Perspectives on the Pueblos*. Albuquerque: University of New Mexico Press, 1972.

Osborne, Harold. *The Art of Appreciation*. New York: Oxford University Press, 1970.

Paton Walsh, Jill. "The Lords of Time." Haviland, *The Openhearted Audience* 177–98.

Patterson, Nancy-Lou. *Canadian Native Art: Arts and Crafts of Canadian Indians and Eskimos*. New York: Collier-Macmillan International, 1973.

Penrose, Roland. "In Praise of Illusion." Gregory and Gombrich 244–84.

Pepper, Stephen C. *Principles of Art Appreciation*. New York: Harcourt Brace, 1949. Reprint. Westport, CT: Greenwood Press, 1970.

Peppin, Brigid. *Fantasy: Book Illustration 1860–1920*. London: Studio Vista, 1975.

Pfleiger, Pat. "Fables into Picture Books." *ChLA Quarterly* 9.2 (Summer 1984): 73–75, 80.

Piaget, Jean. *The Language and Thought of the Child*. Trans. Marjorie and Ruth Gabain. 3d ed. London: Routledge and Kegan Paul, 1959.

————. *Six Psychological Studies*. Trans. Anita Tenzer. New York: Random House, 1967.

————. *Structuralism*. Trans. and ed. Chaninah Maschler. New York: Basic Books, 1970.

Pick, Anne D., and Herbert L. Pick, Jr. "Culture and Perception." Cartarette and Friedman 19–39.

Piehl, Kathy. "Noah as Survivor: A Study of Picture Books." *Children's Literature in Education* 13.2 (1982): 80–86.

Pike, Donald G. *Anasazi: Ancient People of the Rock*. Palo Alto, CA: American West Publishing, 1974.

Pissard, Annie. "Long Live Babar!" Trans. Jules Gelernt. *Lion and the Unicorn* 7/8 (1983–84): 70–77.

Pitz, Henry C. "The Art of Illustration." Field 78–81.

————. *The Brandywine Tradition*. Boston: Houghton Mifflin, 1969.

————. *Illustrating Children's Books: History, Technique, Production*. New York: Watson-Guptill, 1963.

Potter, Joyce Elizabeth. "Beautiful for Situation: Bible Literature and Art in Modern Books for Children." *ChLA Quarterly* 11.4 (Winter 1986–87): 186–92.

Pritchard, David. "Daddy, Talk! Thoughts on Reading Early Picture Books." *Lion and the Unicorn* 7/8 (1983–84): 64–69.

Propp, Vladimir. *Morphology of the Folktale*. 2d ed. Trans. Laurence Scott. Rev. Louis A. Wagner. Austin: University of Texas Press, 1968.

Protherough, Robert. "How Children Judge Stories." *Children's Literature in Education* 14.1 (Spring 1983): 3–13.

Rahn, Suzanne. "*Tailpiece:* The Tale of Two Bad Mice." *Children's Literature* 12 (1984): 78–91.

Read, Herbert. *Icon and Idea: The Function of Art in the Development of Human Consciousness.* New York: Schocken, 1965.

——. *The Origins of Form in Art.* New York: Horizon Press, 1965.

Reed, Michael D. "The Female Oedipal Complex in Maurice Sendak's *Outside Over There.*" *ChLA Quarterly* 11.4 (Winter 1986–87): 176–80.

Richard, Olga. "The Visual Language of the Picture Book." Barron and Burley 157–66.

Richardson, Robert. *Literature and Film.* Bloomington: Indiana University Press, 1969.

Roberts, Ellen M. *The Children's Picture Book: How to Write It, How to Sell It.* Cincinnati: Writer's Digest Books, 1981.

Rose, Jacqueline. *The Case of Peter Pan; or, The Impossibility of Children's Fiction.* London: Macmillan, 1984.

Rosenblatt, Louise M. *The Reader, the Text, the Poem: The Transactional Theory of the Literary Work.* Carbondale: Southern Illinois University Press; London: Feffer and Simons, 1978.

Roskill, Mark. "On the Recognition and Identification of Objects in Paintings." *Critical Inquiry* 3.1 (Summer 1977): 677–708.

Ross, Stephanie. "Caricature." *Monist* 58.2 (April 1974): 285-93.

Roxburgh, Stephen. "Anno's Counting Book: A Semiological Analysis." *ChLA Quarterly* 7.3 (Fall 1982): 48–52.

——. "A Picture Equals How Many Words?: Narrative Theory and Picture Books for Children." *Lion and the Unicorn* 7/8 (1983–84): 20–33.

Rushforth, P. S. *Kindergarten.* London: Abacus-Sphere, 1981.

Ruskin, John. *The Art Criticism of John Ruskin.* Ed. Robert L. Herbert. Garden City, NY: Anchor Books-Doubleday, 1964.

Sale, Roger. *Fairy Tales and After: From Snow White to E. B. White.* Cambridge, MA: Harvard University Press, 1978.

Samuels, S. Jay. "Attentional Process in Reading: The Effect of Pictures on the Acquisition of Reading Responses." *Journal of Educational Psychology* 58.6 (1967): 337–42.

Schapiro, Meyer. "Style." *Aesthetics Today.* Ed. Morris Philipson. New York: New American Library, 1974. 81–113.

Schwarcz, Joseph H. "The Textless Contemporary Picture Book: A Minor Art Form." *Phaedrus* 9 (1982): 45–50.

——. *Ways of the Illustrator: Visual Communication in Children's Literature.* Chicago: American Library Association, 1982.

Segal, Elizabeth. "Picture Books and Princesses: The Feminist Contribution." *Proceedings of the Eighth Annual Conference of the ChLA, University of Minnesota, 1981.* Ed. Priscilla A. Ord. New Rochelle, NY: Iona College, 1982. 77–83.

Segall, Marshall H., Donald T. Campbell, and Melville J. Herskovits. *The Influence of Culture on Visual Perception*. Indianapolis: Bobbs-Merrill, 1966.

Selden, Rebecca, and Sarah Smedman. "The Art of the Contemporary Picture Book." *Proceedings of the Seventh Annual Conference of the ChLA, Baylor University, 1980*. Ed. Priscilla A. Ord. New Rochelle, NY: Iona College, 1982. 153–65.

Sendak, Maurice. "Mother Goose's Garnishings." Haviland, *Children and Literature* 188–95.

———. "Picture Book Genesis: A Conversation with Maurice Sendak." *Proceedings of the Fifth Annual ChLA Conference, Harvard University, 1978*. Ed. Margaret P. Esmonde and Priscilla A. Ord. Villanova, PA: Villanova University, 1979. 29–40.

Sendak, Maurice, with Virginia Haviland. "Questions to an Artist Who Is Also an Author." Haviland, *The Openhearted Audience* 25–46.

Shavit, Zohar. *Poetics of Children's Literature*. Athens: University of Georgia Press, 1985.

Sloan, Glenna Davis. *The Child as Critic: Teaching Literature in the Elementary School*. New York: Teachers College Press, 1975.

Smerdon, Gerald. "Children's Preferences in Illustration." *Children's Literature in Education* 20 (Spring 1976): 17–31.

Smith, Jane Adam. *Children's Illustrated Books*. London: Collins, 1948.

Smith, Lillian H. *The Unreluctant Years: A Critical Approach to Children's Literature*. 1953. New York: Penguin Books, 1976.

Sontag, Susan. "Film and Theatre." Mast and Cohen 249–69.

Sparshott, F. E. "Basic Film Aesthetics." Mast and Cohen 209–32.

Steig, Michael. "Reading *Outside over There*." *Children's Literature* 13 (1985): 139–53.

Stewig, John Warren. "Assessing Visual Elements Preferred in Pictures by Young Children." *Reading Improvement*, Summer 1975: 94–97.

———. *Children and Literature*. Chicago: Rand McNally College Publishing, 1980.

Stierle, Karlheinz. "The Reading of Fictional Texts." Sulieman and Crosman 83–105.

Stott, Jon C. "Architectural Structures and Social Values in the Non-Fiction of David Macauley." *ChLA Quarterly* 8.1 (Spring 1983): 15–17.

———. "Joseph Campbell on the Second Mesa: Structure and Meaning in *Arrow to the Sun*." *ChLA Quarterly* 11.3 (Fall 1986): 132–34.

Suddon, Alan. "Walter Crane, Dress, and Children's Illustration." *Canadian Children's Literature* 4 (1976): 80–87.

Sulieman, Susan R., and Inge Crosman, eds. *The Reader in the Text: Essays on Audience and Interpretation*. Princeton: Princeton University Press, 1980.

Sutherland, Zena, and Betsy Hearne. "In Search of the Perfect Picture Book Definition." Barron and Burley 12–14.

Sutherland, Zena, Dianne L. Monson, and May Hill Arbuthnot. *Children and Books*. 6th ed. Glenview, IL: Scott, Foresman, 1981.

Taylor, Joshua C. *Learning to Look: A Handbook for the Visual Arts*. Chicago: University of Chicago Press, 1957.

Taylor, Mary Agnes. "In Defense of the Wild Things." *Horn Book* 46 (1970): 642–46.

Tedlock, Dennis. "Pueblo Literature: Style and Verisimilitude." Ortiz 219–42.

Tedlock, Dennis, and Barbara Tedlock, eds. *Teachings from the American Earth: Indian Religion and Philosophy*. New York: Liveright, 1975.

Thomas, Jane Resh. "The Infernal City: The Arcadian Lament in Children's Picture Books." *Horn Book* 55.1 (February 1978): 24–31.

Todorov, Tzetvan. "Reading as Construction." Sulieman and Crosman 67–82.

Tompkins, Jane P. *Reader Response Criticism: From Formalism to Post-Structuralism*. Baltimore: Johns Hopkins University Press, 1980.

Topper, David R. "Gombrich on What a Picture Is Not." *Canadian Review of Art Education Research* 6/7 (1980–81): 62–67.

———. "On Some Burdens Carried by Pictures." *ChLA Quarterly* 9.1 (Spring 1984): 23–25.

———. "Reflections on the Mirror in Manet's 'Bar': Perception and Media in Rudolf Arnheim's Psychology of Art." *Canadian Review of Art Education Research* 6/7 (1980–81): 46–50.

Townsend, John Rowe. *Written for Children*. Rev. ed. London: Kestrel, 1974.

Usrey, Malcolm. "Mother Goose without Tears: Fantasy and Realism in Mother Goose Illustrations since 1865." *Proceedings of the Seventh Annual Conference of the ChLA, Baylor University, 1980*. Ed. Priscilla A. Ord. New Rochelle, NY: Iona College, 1982. 166–74.

Vandergrift, Kay. *Child and Story: The Literary Connection*. New York: Neal-Schuman, 1980.

Viguers, Ruth Hill, Marcia Dalphin, and Bertha Mahoney Miller, eds. *Illustrators of Children's Books, 1946–1956*. Boston: Horn Book, 1958.

Waller, Jennifer R. "Maurice Sendak and the Blakean Vision of Childhood." *Children's Literature* 6 (1977): 130–40.

Walsh, Jill Paton. See Paton Walsh, Jill.

Ward, John L., and Marian Nitti Fox. "A Look at Some Outstanding Illustrated Books for Children." *ChLA Quarterly* 9.1 (Spring 1984): 19–21.

Wartofsky, Marx W. "Art History and Perception." John Fisher 23–41.

Weissberg, Gabriel P. *The Realist Tradition: French Painting and Drawing, 1830–1900*. Cleveland: Cleveland Museum of Art; Bloomington: Indiana University Press, 1980.

Wexner, Lois B. "The Degree to Which Colors (Hues) Are Associated with Mood Tones." *Journal of Applied Psychology* 36.6 (1954): 432–35.

Whalen-Levitt, Peggy. "Making Picture Books Real: Reflections on a Child's-Eye View." *ChLA Quarterly* 6.4 (Winter 1981–82): 21–25.

———. "Picture Play in Children's Books: A Celebration of Visual Awareness." Barron and Burley 167–74.

White, Mary Lou, ed. *Children's Literature: Criticism and Response*. Columbus, OH: Charles E. Merrill, 1976.

Whorf, Benjamin Lee. "An American Indian Model of the Universe." Tedlock and Tedlock 121–38.

Willsher, Valerie. "Books for the Under-Twos." *Signal* 38 (May 1982): 103–12.

Wright, Benjamin, and Lee Rainwater. "The Meaning of Color." *Journal of General Psychology* 67 (1962): 89–99.

Yolen, Jane. "The Eye and the Ear." *ChLA Quarterly* 6.4 (Winter 1981–82): 8–9.

Zipes, Jack. "A Second Gaze at Little Red Riding Hood's Trials and Tribulations." *Lion and the Unicorn* 7/8 (1983–84): 78–109.

■■■■

CHILDREN'S BOOKS
DISCUSSED

————

(These books are listed in alphabetical order by the name of the illustrators or, if no illustrator is credited in the book, by the title; if not otherwise specified, the illustrator also wrote the text.)

Adams, Adrienne. *Cabbage Moon*. By Jan Wahl. New York: Holt, Rinehart and Winston, 1965.

Anno, Mitsumasa. *Anno's Animals*. New York: Philomel, 1979.

————. *Anno's Britain*. New York: Philomel, 1982.

————. *Anno's Journey*. Cleveland: William Collins and World, 1978.

————. *Anno's Medieval World*. New York: Philomel, 1980.

————. *Anno's USA*. New York: Philomel, 1983.

Baby's Things. New York: Platt and Munk, n.d.

Bang, Molly. *The Grey Lady and the Strawberry Snatcher*. New York: Four Winds Press, 1980.

Baskin, Leonard. *Hosie's Alphabet*. By Hosea, Tobias, and Lisa Baskin. New York: Viking, 1972.

Bayley, Nicola. *Nicola Bayley's Book of Nursery Rhymes*. London: Jonathan Cape, 1975.

Briggs, Raymond. *Fungus the Bogeyman*. London: Hamish Hamilton, 1977.

————. *The Snowman*. London: Hamish Hamilton, 1978.

Brodsky, Beverly. *The Story of Job*. New York: George Braziller, 1986.

Brown, Marcia. *Cinderella*. New York: Scribner's, 1954.

Burkert, Nancy Ekholm. *The Nightingale*. By Hans Christian Andersen. New York: Harper and Row, 1965.

————. *Snow White and the Seven Dwarfs*. By the Brothers Grimm. Trans. Randall Jarrell. New York: Farrar, Straus and Giroux, 1972.

Burningham, John. *The Baby*. London: Jonathan Cape, 1974.

Burton, Virginia Lee. *The Little House*. Boston: Houghton Mifflin, 1942.

Caldecott, Randolph. "The Farmer's Boy." *The Randolph Caldecott Picture Book*. London: Frederick Warne, 1976.

Chernayeff, Ivan. *Sun Moon Star*. By Kurt Vonnegut. New York: Harper and Row, 1980.

Cleaver, Elizabeth. *How Summer Came to Canada*. Retold by William Toye. Toronto: Oxford University Press, 1969.

———. *The Mountain Goats of Temlaham*. Retold by William Toye. Toronto: Oxford University Press, 1969.

Cooney, Barbara. *Demeter and Persephone*. New York: Doubleday, 1972.

Crews, Donald. *Freight Train*. New York: Greenwillow, 1978.

Cruz, Ray. *Alexander, Who Used to Be Rich Last Sunday*. By Judith Viorst. New York: Atheneum, 1978.

———. *Alexander and the Terrible, Horrible, No-Good, Very Bad Day*. By Judith Viorst. New York: Atheneum, 1972.

De Brunhoff, Jean. *The Story of Babar*. Trans. Merle S. Haas. New York: Random House, 1933.

Dillon, Leo and Diane. *Who's in Rabbit's House?* By Verna Aardema. New York: Dial, 1977.

———. *Why Mosquitoes Buzz in People's Ears*. By Verna Aardema. New York: Dial, 1975.

Duvoisin, Roger. *Petunia*. New York: Knopf, 1950.

Emberley, Ed. *Drummer Hoff*. Englewood Cliffs, NJ: Prentice-Hall, 1967.

Ets, Marie Hall. *Elephant in a Well*. New York: Viking, 1972.

A First Book Open and Say. Cambridge: Brimax Books, 1978.

Friere, Carlos. *No Clothes*. By Daniel Wood. Toronto: Annick Press, 1982.

Furchgott, Terry. *Phoebe and the Hot Water Bottles*. By Terry Furchgott and Linda Dawson. London: André Deutsch, 1977.

Gag, Wanda. *Millions of Cats*. New York: Coward, McCann, 1928.

———. *Snow White and the Seven Dwarfs*. New York: Coward, McCann, 1938.

Goodall, John S. *The Surprise Picnic*. New York: Atheneum, 1977.

Haley, Gail E. *The Green Man*. New York: Scribner's, 1979.

———. *A Story, a Story*. New York: Atheneum, 1970.

Hoban, Lillian. *Bread and Jam for Frances*. By Russell Hoban. New York: Scholastic, 1964.

How Do We Help? All About Animals Series. Rev. ed. Cambridge: Brimax Books, 1983.

Hughes, Shirley. *Lucy and Tom's Christmas*. London: Victor Gollancz, 1981.

Hurd, Clement. *Goodnight Moon*. By Margaret Wise Brown. New York: Harper, 1947.

———. *The Runaway Bunny*. By Margaret Wise Brown. Rev. ed. New York: Harper and Row, 1972.

Hutchins, Pat. *Changes, Changes*. New York: Macmillan, 1971.

———. *Goodnight, Owl*. New York: Macmillan, 1972.

———. *Rosie's Walk*. New York: Macmillan, 1968.

Hyman, Trina Schart. *King Stork*. By Howard Pyle. Boston: Little, Brown, 1973.

———. *Sleeping Beauty*. Boston: Little, Brown, 1977.

———. *Snow White*. By the Brothers Grimm. Trans. Paul Heins. Boston: Atlantic Monthly Press-Little, Brown, 1974.

Jeffers, Susan. *Hansel and Gretel*. By the Brothers Grimm. New York: Dial, 1980.

———. *Snow White and the Seven Dwarfs*. Retold by Freya Littledale. New York: Four Winds Press, 1980.

———. *Three Jovial Huntsmen*. New York: Bradbury Press, 1973.

_____. *Wild Robin*. New York: Dutton, 1976.

Jonas, Ann. *The Quilt*. New York: Greenwillow, 1984.

Keats, Ezra Jack. *Apt. 3*. New York: Macmillan, 1971.

_____. *The Snowy Day*. New York: Viking, 1962.

Keeping, Charles. *The God beneath the Sea*. By Leon Garfield and Edward Blishen. London: Longmans, 1970.

_____. *The Golden Shadow*. By Leon Garfield and Edward Blishen. London: Longmans, 1973.

_____. *The Highwayman*. By Alfred Noyes. Oxford: Oxford University Press, 1981.

_____. *Intercity*. Oxford: Oxford University Press, 1977.

_____. *Through the Window*. London: Oxford University Press, 1970.

Kent, Jack. "Snow White and the Seven Dwarfs." *The Happy Ever After Book*. New York: Random House, 1976.

Kerman, Dani. *A Journey to the Land of Words*. By Abba Kovner. Tel Aviv: Sifriat Poalim, 1981.

Khalsa, Dayal Kaur. *Welcome, Twins*. Pittsburgh: Tundra Books, 1984.

Kincaid, Eric. *Now You Can Read . . . Snow White and the Seven Dwarfs*. Adapted by Lucy Kincaid. Cambridge: Brimax Books, n.d.

Krahn, Fernando. *The Mystery of the Giant Footprints*. New York: Dutton, 1977.

Lawson, Robert. *The Story of Ferdinand*. By Munro Leaf. New York: Viking, 1936.

Le Cain, Errol. *Beauty and the Beast*. Retold by Rosemary Harris. New York: Doubleday, 1979.

_____. *Cinderella*. By Charles Perrault. London: Faber and Faber, 1972.

_____. *The Twelve Dancing Princesses*. By the Brothers Grimm. London: Faber and Faber, 1978.

Lent, Blair. *The Funny Little Woman*. By Arlene Mosel. New York: Dutton, 1977.

_____. *Tikki Tikki Tembo*. By Arlene Mosel. New York: Holt, Rinehart and Winston, 1968.

Lionni, Leo. *Swimmy*. New York: Pantheon, 1963.

Lobel, Arnold. *Circus*. By Jack Prelutsky. New York: Macmillan, 1974.

_____. *Frog and Toad Are Friends*. New York: Harper and Row, 1970.

_____. *I'll Fix Anthony*. By Judith Viorst. New York: Harper and Row, 1969.

Macaulay, David. *Cathedral*. Boston: Houghton Mifflin, 1973.

_____. *Unbuilding*. Boston: Houghton Mifflin, 1980.

McCloskey, Robert. *Make Way for Ducklings*. New York: Viking, 1941.

McDermott, Gerald. *Arrow to the Sun*. New York: Viking, 1974.

Mayer, Mercer. *A Boy, a Dog, and a Frog*. New York: Dial, 1967.

Mikolaycak, Charles. *The Changing Maze*. By Zilpha Keatley Snyder. New York: Macmillan, 1985.

Montresor, Beni. *Cinderella*. New York: Knopf, 1965.

Ness, Evaline. *Sam, Bangs, and Moonshine*. New York: Holt, Rinehart and Winston, 1966.

Piatti, Celestino. *The Happy Owls*. New York: Atheneum, 1964.

Potter, Beatrix. *The Story of a Fierce Bad Rabbit.* London: Frederick Warne, n.d.

————. *The Tale of Peter Rabbit.* London: Frederick Warne, 1903.

Raskin, Ellen. *Nothing Ever Happens on My Block.* New York: Atheneum, 1966.

Rayner, Mary. *Mr. and Mrs. Pig's Evening Out.* London: Macmillan, 1976.

Rey, H. A. *Curious George.* Boston: Houghton Mifflin, 1941.

Rojankovsky, Feodor. *Frog Went A-Courtin'.* Retold by John Langstaff. New York: Harcourt Brace, 1955.

S., Svend Otto. *Snow White and the Seven Dwarfs.* London: Pelham, 1975.

Salsberg, Barbara. *Your Own Story.* Toronto: Annick Press, 1977.

Scarry, Richard. *The Best Word Book Ever.* Rev. ed. New York: Golden Press, 1980.

————. *Cars and Trucks and Things That Go.* New York: Golden Press, 1974.

————. *Early Words.* New York: Random House, 1976.

Sendak, Maurice. *Fly by Night.* By Randall Jarrell. New York: Farrar, Straus and Giroux, 1976.

————. *Hector Protector and As I Went over the Water.* New York: Harper and Row, 1965.

————. *Higglety Pigglety Pop! or, There Must Be More to Life.* New York: Harper and Row, 1967.

————. *In the Night Kitchen.* New York: Harper and Row, 1970.

————. *The Light Princess.* By George MacDonald. New York: Farrar, Straus and Giroux, 1969.

————. *Mr. Rabbit and the Lovely Present.* By Charlotte Zolotow. New York: Harper and Row, 1962.

————. *Nutshell Library.* New York: Harper and Row, 1962.

————. *Outside Over There.* New York: Harper and Row, 1981.

————. "Snow White and the Seven Dwarfs." *The Juniper Tree and Other Tales from Grimm.* Trans. Randall Jarrell and Lore Segal. New York: Farrar, Straus and Giroux, 1973.

————. *Where the Wild Things Are.* New York: Harper and Row, 1963.

Seuss, Dr. *And to Think That I Saw It on Mulberry Street.* New York: Vanguard, 1937.

————. *Horton Hatches the Egg.* New York: Random House, 1940.

————. *How the Grinch Stole Christmas.* New York: Random House, 1957.

Shecter, Ben. *Hester the Jester.* New York: Harper and Row, 1977.

Shepherd, Ernest. *The House at Pooh Corner.* By A. A. Milne. New York: Dutton, 1928.

————. *Winnie the Pooh.* By A. A. Milne. New York: Dutton, 1926.

Spier, Peter. *Noah's Ark.* Garden City, NY: Doubleday, 1977.

————. *Oh! Were They Ever Happy!* Garden City, NY: Doubleday, 1978.

Steig, William. *The Amazing Bone.* New York: Farrar, Straus and Giroux, 1976.

————. *Amos and Boris.* New York: Farrar, Straus and Giroux, 1971.

————. *Sylvester and the Magic Pebble.* New York: Simon and Schuster, 1969.

Steptoe, John. *Stevie.* New York: Harper and Row, 1969.

Tait, Douglas. *Once More upon a Totem.* By Christie Harris. New York: Atheneum, 1973.

Tenniel, John. *Alice's Adventures in Wonderland.* By Lewis Carroll. 1865.

————. *Through the Looking Glass.* By Lewis Carroll. 1871.

Ungerer, Tomi. *Snail, Where Are You?* New York: Harper and Row, 1962.

Van Allsburg, Chris. *The Garden of Abdul Gasazi.* Boston: Houghton Mifflin, 1979.

———. *Jumanji.* Boston: Houghton Mifflin, 1981.

———. *The Polar Express.* Boston: Houghton Mifflin, 1985.

———. *Wreck of the Zephyr.* Boston: Houghton Mifflin, 1983.

Walt Disney Presents Snow White and the Seven Dwarfs. Racine, Wisc.: Whitman Publishing, 1967.

Walt Disney Studio. *Walt Disney's Snow White and the Seven Dwarfs.* Adapted by Grant Campbell. Racine, Wisc.: Golden Press-Western Publishing, 1952.

Wegner, Fritz. *Snow White and the Seven Dwarfs.* London: Bodley Head, 1973.

Wells, Rosemary. *Max's First Word.* New York: Dial, 1979.

Wiese, Kurt. *The Story about Ping.* By Marjorie Flack. New York: Viking, 1933.

Wildsmith, Brian. *ABC.* London: Oxford University Press, 1962.

———. *The Circus.* Oxford: Oxford University Press, 1970.

Williams, Garth. *Charlotte's Web.* By E. B. White. New York: Harper, 1952.

Winter, Paula. *Sir Andrew.* New York: Crown, 1980.

Young, Ed. *The Girl Who Loved the Wind.* By Jane Yolen. New York: Crowell, 1972.

INDEX

CPSIA information can be obtained at www.ICGtesting.com
Printed in the USA
BVOW07s1934020913

329986BV00001B/100/A